John Donne

0826 486 24X 0 036 59

Bee Wise as serpents
but inosent as Dovs.
LXXX.
SERMONS
PREACHED BY THAT LEAR-
NED AND REVEREND DIVINE
IOHN DONNE Dr IN DIVINITIE
LATE DEANE OF Ye CATHEDRALL
CHVRCH OF St PAVLES
LONDON.
M Merian Iun

John Donne

Man of Flesh and Spirit

David L. Edwards

CONTINUUM
London and New York

Continuum
The Tower Building
11 York Road
London SE1 7NX

370 Lexington Avenue
New York
NY 10017-6503

First published 2001

British Library Cataloguing-in-Publication Data
A catalogue record for this book is available from the British Library.

ISBN 0 8264 51551

Designed and typeset by Ben Cracknell Studios
Printed and bound in Great Britain by Biddles Ltd, Guildford and King's Lynn

Contents

Preface *vii*
Illustrations *xi*
Dates *xii*

Donne's Life

1 The questions *3*
2 At the dore *34*
3 Winter-seeming *63*
4 Thou hast done *98*

About Donne

5 Thou hast not done *137*
6 Deare honestie *158*

Donne Speaks

7 Let my body raigne *193*
8 Batter my heart *224*
9 Admyring her *244*
10 The Trumpet *299*

Further reading *351*
Index of Writings *359*
General Index *363*

Preface

I have tried to write a book which will interest and persuade a variety of readers because nowadays Donne's public is both large and varied. He is best known as a poet of love, never describing physical beauty in detail but brilliantly able to re-create a man's experience of love's emotions and realities. And he is much else – a poet of the spiritual journey who is so human that he is able to speak to others who find the journey uncomfortable, and in the last quarter of his life a great preacher who can soar into word-music or condense a mysterious area of theology into an epigram. But he is always a wit and although he sparkles he has aroused much disagreement about what he means. What lies behind the clever talk? Is he ever serious? If he is, what is he serious about? In my first chapter I face these questions, which even an enthusiast should not avoid.

When so many books have already been written about Donne, very probably I have no need to mention that his name is best pronounced 'Dun', but certainly I need to explain why I hope that my book will fill a gap. This is not a detailed study of a limited part of the subject, written for other specialists, but I have spent a lot of time reading Donne and much of the vast Donnean literature. After thinking, I have then attempted to make a credible portrait of the man in Chapters 2, 3 and 4. I have offered some fresh suggestions about what seems probable in the story of his life but most of the facts which can be known were assembled in R. C. Bald's solidly factual biography (1970) and I gladly acknowledge my debt to that standard work. I have included two chapters (5 and 6) indicating where I venture to disagree with books about him which seem to be excessively favourable or hostile, or exaggerated in some other way, and I have given references for my quotations from the books by John Carey and Paul Oliver of which I am especially critical, so that readers may check to see whether my criticisms are fair. A lot depends on the interpretation of Donne's work which is offered in the last section of the book, so there I have quoted extensively from the poems and the sermons. My longest chapters are about the relationships which I believe meant most to him – with his wife and his God. I hope I may be forgiven for entering into controversy with scholars who do not share this belief but to me there is nothing very odd in thinking that this very human man was very confused over a long period, very erotic, very much married, and in his latter years very devout.

I give references by volume and page to my quotations from the sermons in their modern edition. Their length (in ten volumes) is one reason why they have often been neglected as evidence about the character of the man, but when dealing with Dr Donne the preacher I may have an advantage over commentators who have concentrated on the poems to the exclusion of the sermons: I have myself been a preacher. I believe that this is the first book about Donne ever to have been written by a man who has preached often in London, as he did. Of course I am prejudiced in favour of giving a preacher a fair hearing, but this approach may be welcomed by readers as a change from the attitude taken in some attempts to get hold of Donne from a position entirely different from his. Any prejudice on my part does not amount to a claim that he was always admirable and my sympathy with Donne does not include a pretence that he always said what I agree with. If any reader is interested in my own opinions I have tried to present them in other books but here, I hope, Donne speaks for himself.

Since I have found my own time with Donne fascinating, my ambition is to reach readers who are not specialists. When rejecting some of the suggestions made by previous writers I always try to say, positively but not elaborately, how I see things (for what that is worth) and in its details I have tried to make the material accessible without difficulty. I have tried to make all my quotations from Donne immediately understandable by a silent reader and I have found that this policy has to involve changing some of the punctuation to modern usage, especially in the sermons. It seems that the rash of commas in the original printing was designed to help the reader to read the writing out aloud and I hope that no one in the twenty-first century is going to preach exactly what Donne said. Commas may, however, be especially useful in the poems since the metre can be half-hidden or deliberately broken, and here I have been more strictly conservative although I do not have the space or the expertise with which to discuss the metrical patterns. I have made other small changes in addition to details which have become standard in modern editions: 'then' becomes 'than' when appropriate and in order to avoid making Donne seem hysterical I have not kept the italics except when he is quoting a passage from the Bible.

I claim to have a precedent for such attempts to help a reader, because when Donne's poems, letters and sermons were printed after his death the editor or the typesetter often used his own judgement about details. For example, Donne wrote his letters with so many abbreviations that if they were to be printed for the public's attention they had to be virtually rewritten. But I have not modernized either the spelling or the capitalization, because I believe that the reader will want my quotations to be as authentic as is possible if the whole of this book is to be readable. A capital letter which to us seems to be oddly placed can be a trouble-free sign that a word is to be slightly stressed, and spelling which is strange to us can remind us that many things must remain mysterious in Donne and his age: the evidence is limited and so is our power to penetrate the past.

As was my happy experience when working on earlier books in my retirement from official duties, I am very thankful for the encouragement of my publisher, for the rich resources of the Cambridge University Library, for the secretarial skills of Khadidjah Mattar, for the eagle eye of Fiona McKenzie, and for the loving support of my wife Sybil.

David L. Edwards

Winchester

Easter 2000

Illustrations

(*Frontispiece*) The first edition of *Eighty Sermons* (1640)
1. The London Donne knew
2. Donne in 1591
3. Donne in 1616
4. Donne in 1620
5. Donne asks for a book while under arrest
6. Donne's receipt for a legacy authorized by Egerton
7. Preaching at Paul's Cross in Donne's time
8. An engraving of Donne in his shroud used as a frontispiece for *Death's Duell*, 1632
9. Donne's effigy

Dates

1572	Born into Roman Catholic family in London
1584–89	Under tutors in Oxford and Cambridge
1589–91	Travels in France, Italy and Spain
1591–96	Studies law and writes poetry
1593	Death of brother Henry; becomes Anglican (?)
1596–97	Volunteer in naval expeditions
1597	Secretary to Sir Thomas Egerton
1601	*Metempsychosis* and marriage
1602–05	In Pyrford, unemployed
1603	Accession of James I
1605–06	Travels with Sir Walter Chute
1606–11	In Mitcham with London lodgings
1607	Refuses parish
1608	*Biathanatos* discusses suicide
1609	'Holy Sonnets'; near despair
1610	*Pseudo-Martyr* defends allegiance
1611	*Ignatius his Conclave* attacks Jesuits
1611–12	'Anniversaries' and travel with Drurys
1614	Last hopes of secular employment
1615	Ordination in Church of England
1616	Reader in Divinity, Lincoln's Inn

1617	Death of wife Anne
1619–20	Chaplain to Viscount Doncaster's embassy
1621	Dean of St Paul's
1623–24	Severe illness, writes *Devotions*
1624	Vicar of St Dunstan-in-the-West
1625	Accession of Charles I
1627	Depression returns, writes 'Nocturnall' (?)
1630–31	Last illness and *Death's Duell*
1631	Dies on 31 March
1633	First edition of poems
1635	Second edition
1640	First volume of sermons; Walton's *Life*

To Sybil

Love, all alike, no season knows, nor clyme,
Nor houres, dayes, moneths, which are the rags of time.

John Donne

PART ONE

Donne's Life

1 The questions

Oh, to vex me, contraryes meet in one
Holy Sonnets *XIX*

In much of his poetry John Donne is brilliant, with a voice which is very much his own. Here he is not really interested either in nature or in society; he does not celebrate either beauty or greatness; he is fascinated by his own emotions. About them he writes with what Coleridge called 'wonder-exciting vigour, intenseness and peculiarity of thought'. But a part of being so self-centred is that he needs to tell others how he feels and although he destroys much of what he writes, and has no wish to see even the best of his work in print, he shows or sends some of his poems to a small circle of friends or patrons. For many years some of the most important remained in private collections while other poems which he had not written were attributed to him, but the surviving and available poems, a mixture of the brilliant and the disappointing, were printed after his death, without any arrangement by date. Now they are accessible all over the English-speaking world, so that if we wish we can all be told what the poem says. And what is that?

Often we can feel close to him for although he is extraordinarily fluent and agile with words these words often express feelings which are no more noble than our own. And he is normal in that his feelings and thoughts are not in different compartments. What he wrote about a blushing girl has become famous:

One whose cleare body was so pure, and thin,
  Because it neede disguise no thought within.
'Twas but a through-light scarfe . . .
  . . . her pure and eloquent blood
Spoke in her cheekes, and so distinckly wrought
That one might almost say, her body thought . . .

But for him the unity of body and thought was not confined to innocent young virgins. He is sexual, and poems which express deep and troubled thought can be given a climax which is explicitly sexual. In other poems he displays himself to us as a man being sexually active in bed or melancholic after rejection, wearing nothing except his body to enclose what he calls the 'naked thinking heart'. 'Full nakedness!' he writes. 'All joyes are due to thee.' So we meet him as an intellectual who is also a man of flesh and blood, passionate rather than calmly wise, up and down in his moods, knowing ecstasy and also knowing grim depression. He has a brain and it never stops working but it is what he calls a 'feeling braine'.

Thus a poem by Donne carries with it a ticket of admission to a world of feelings and thoughts which does not seem entirely strange to us: he is an individual using his own voice but across the centuries we can often recognize what he is talking about. Recently, however, the distance between us and a man who died in 1631 has seemed a deterrent to many readers, in one way at least. His union of feelings and thoughts can make him seem close but his union of sensuality with intense religion can make him seem as distant as a star whose light comes from a remote century. Here is a man who is thoroughly human, and energetically masculine, as well as being highly intelligent – yet he cannot stop talking about religion when he is supposed to be talking about sex, any more than he can stop talking about sex when we expect him to be pious. And he is as passionate about religion as he is, or has been, about his other enthusiasm.

Many readers have found it hard to imagine why or how the Donne of the erotic poetry became first a self-torturing penitent and then an ardent churchman. Should we accept – even if only for the time being, in order to understand – his own interpretation of his life, which was that it was a journey into the God taught by Christianity? Or should we find that explanation false, dishonest or repulsive? Should we study the 'holy sonnets', other 'divine' poems and the sermons, even if it is only in order to enjoy the eloquence or to see how a great poet could feel and think about religion? Or should we pay very little or no attention to him when he is on his knees or in the pulpit – as has often been the practice, even in scholarly books about Donne? Or should we do what he hoped hearers or readers would do, thinking for ourselves about the message he delivers? What are we to make of this man who is clearly not a saint or a mystic, not even a very good man – who is one of us – but who preaches with an urgency more to be expected when a man is inviting a woman into bed?

He preaches that we too stand on the brink of eternity, 'naked before God, without that apparell which he made for us, without all righteousness, and without that apparell which we made for ourselves; not a fig-leaf, not an excuse to cover us' (1:265). He told the doomed Charles I and his courtiers that when they had had the time of their lives they would be in eternity, where 'all the powerful Kings, and all the beautifull Queenes of this world, were but a bed of flowers, some gathered at six, some at seven, some at eight, all in one Morning' (7:138). And we can find ourselves moved by this strange preacher. He has not reached his position by a short or smooth path. Before ordination to the priesthood he has lived most of his life and it has been a life far from any monastery. He has experienced the passions of 'pride and lust' – his words – and much disappointment, much confusion, some acute shame and some despair. And he is emphatic that during his rebellious pilgrimage he has experienced God. That is what he communicates with all the power he can command. Joan Webber, whose *Contrary Music* was a useful book about his prose style in 1963, concluded that 'Donne, as a writer, was only good at one thing, though that one thing was very intense and valuable. He was good at communicating his own experience . . .' No earlier English poet or preacher had been so eloquently intimate before Donne drew on his own experience to speak about those basic and inexhaustible human interests which are indicated by the two three-letter words, sex and God.

So the poet Donne, and Donne the preacher, can seem to be sincere as he experiences and as he communicates. But is he? Are they? Since he was gradually rediscovered in the nineteenth century, and began to be studied as a major figure in the twentieth, confusion has been added to the subject of Donne. A flood of commentary and controversy seems to have drowned the common belief of his contemporaries that he was simply a very masculine lover of women or simply a very devout lover of God, talking about truths which he had found by experiencing them. In 1619, in a letter to a friend which has often been used as a key to his life, he himself contrasted the 'Jack Donne' of the earlier years, brilliant but unhappy, with the 'Dr Donne' who now preached. But how were the two connected? Indeed, what was the truth about either Donne? Or will this great self-exhibitionist always be an enigma if we look closely?

The riddle has been stated in a number of ways, some more historical, others more literary.

There can be questions about how Jack Donne actually behaved while a bachelor. Was he as promiscuous as his poetry suggests? Or did a little casual sex supply raw material for the manufacture of a lot of crafted poetry? Looking back in 1625, he told Sir Robert Ker that 'I did best when I had least truth for my subjects'. Did he then remember with pride his poetic performances as a ventriloquist, able to create many women and many male selves by his skill with voices? Or did he mean that he had done best when he had for his subjects not ideas but people, usually a woman and himself? The phrase which he used to Ker has often been quoted by commentators who have not considered its context. It came in a letter enclosing a poem written at Ker's request in honour of a dead friend of his whom the poet had met only casually. The poem was about the ideas of body and soul, sin and heaven, not about the friend (least of all about the rumour that he had been poisoned). Its grand subjects contained, he wrote, 'so much truth as defeats all Poetry'. So was Donne acknowledging that his best poetry had made things up – or was he reflecting that it had been 'best' when it had dealt with manageable subjects like a man and a woman, not with eternal mysteries (for him, the topic of sermons)? And what did he think had been his 'best' work? He did not say.

If he had many relationships with women in real life, did he always despise and exploit them with a 'masculine perswasive force' which could be cruel because entirely selfish? Or was he in reality as vulnerable and as easily hurt as they were? Or is it impossible to say, because most of the early poetry about unconfined sex was written in order to entertain other men with little or no foundation other than fantasy? Did his anxious courtship and sensational marriage inspire all, or any, of those poems of longing, ecstasy and delight? In 'The Canonization' he wrote some of his most famous words: 'We'll build in sonnets pretty roomes'. Did he refer to a real woman by the 'we' – or to the construction of an artefact by the 'build'? Did he seduce Anne More because he thought she was a rich girl, or did he throw away his career because he loved her with his whole heart? How did he behave after marriage – still as a 'libertine' lusting after many women when he wrote poems or when he prowled around in real life, or was he a family man now that he had settled down? What did he mean when he based his long poems called 'Anniversaries' on the idea that a girl's death had ruined the world? Or when he wrote in a shorter and more heartfelt poem that his wife's death had 'ruin'd mee'? Was he, after all, a bit of a feminist? In her study of *Feminine Engendered Faith* (1992) Maureen Sabine claimed that the Virgin Mary was very close to the centre of his religion and that the half-hidden theme of his 'Anniversaries' was a lament for the psychologically disastrous results of the Protestant destruction of the cult which had been vitally important for English Christians over a thousand years, devotion to Mary. Evidence to support that idea is lacking but Donne did write that he had been led to seek God by a woman, his wife Anne. No English poet before him had been so frank and vivid in the celebration of sexual freedom, but was he also, as has been suggested by Anthony Low, the first English poet who celebrated marriage as a delighted and glorious commitment, in a 'reinvention of love'?

How was it possible for him to combine in the 1590s the writing of frankly and brutally erotic 'elegies' with the writing of loftily censorious 'satyres' rebuking other people's vices? (In his time an 'elegie' was a poem written in elegiac couplets, imitating Latin authors such as Ovid, and was not necessarily serious. A 'satyre' was a harsh attack on vice, imitating other Latin authors such as Juvenal, and was not intended to be comic.) Was the erotic poetry itself a warning against vice, by showing that every sexual relationship outside marriage is bound to end in tears – so that Jack Donne was a preacher long before he entered a pulpit? Why were the 55 poems which were grouped together when printed as 'Songs and Sonets' so mixed both in poetic form and in emotional tone? (Any short poem could called a 'sonet', a word which means 'little sound', although Donne did write sonnets in the form which became standard, in fourteen lines each of ten syllables and with a rhyme in one of a few patterns.) Was the long poem about the transmission of evil in the history of fallen humanity

(*Metempsychosis*) written in bitter disillusionment – or in high spirits? Why was it abandoned? And why was much of the later poetry so polite about the good and the great? Was this deferential poet himself a good man, glad to praise the virtues he admired in others? Or was he writing for money? Or while being less corrupt than some others were in the time of the Tudors and Stuarts, did he need to flatter patrons like everyone else who had talent rather than wealth?

Was Dr Donne the preacher a hypocrite, or at least a poseur? Was he in the pulpit only because he had been so disappointed in his long search for a job in the royal court, in the civil service or in diplomacy? If this was not the only reason why he accepted the king's advice that he should become a preacher, the experience of many years of unemployment while a layman was certainly a factor in his decision: so how important was it? When he reached – or was dragged to – his pulpit, did he preach what the king commanded? Or did he become absorbed by his discovery of a power to deceive and bully the ignorant and the gullible, as he had deceived and bullied women in his youth? If he tried to communicate a sincerely believed religious message, what was it? Did he incline to the Catholicism of his parents or to the Calvinism of many of his fellow Protestants? Or was he one of the pioneers in the Anglican 'middle way' between those positions? Was he surprisingly liberal, tolerant and generously comprehensive? Or did he preach a religion which looked back to the Middle Ages and forward only to the fundamentalism which survives like a museum in the twenty-first century? Or was his religion tortured, almost as if he anticipated the *angst* of the twentieth century in the poems of guilt, doubt and near-despair which W. H. Auden persuaded Benjamin Britten to set to troubled music?

Did religion really mean as much to Donne as he said it did after the time of his marriage, and even more emphatically after his ordination? In his history of English poetry, *Lives of the Poets* (1998),

Michael Schmidt observed that Donne developed a 'talent for sermons' and was willing 'to give sermons on themes and occasions where political interests claimed the right to use him'. But we are told that he 'dealt too with diplomatic correspondence (a form of secular work more to his taste)'. This dismissive verdict on the preaching was delivered although many more than a million words of the sermons have survived. All of them are full of references to the Bible and the Fathers of the Church, and of religious emotion, whereas the whole of the correspondence which may be termed diplomatic (although it was almost certainly about church life and religious controversy in continental Europe) has disappeared. What is interesting is that Schmidt, who has an attractive enthusiasm for a wide variety of poets, feels under no obligation to acknowledge any integrity in Donne the preacher. Even the love poetry may, he thinks, have no 'actual subject', and to him it seems obvious that the actual subject of the sermons is not what Donne says it is.

Has the religion which he preached any right to be heard in our time? In a contribution to a book of essays in 1990 entitled *Soliciting Interpretation*, Professor Stanley Fish put the question sharply. He argued that 'the God Donne imagines' is remarkably like Donne, 'a jealous and overbearing master who brooks no rivals and will go to any lengths (even to the extent of depriving Donne of his wife) in order to secure his rights'. In the erotic poetry about men conquering women Fish saw 'sado-masochism elevated to a principle and glorified . . . in the name of a power that is (supposedly) divine' and in the religious poetry he saw only further self-glorification by the 'self-aggrandizing' poet. 'There is', Fish said, 'no reason to believe that the turn to God is anything but one more instance of feigned devotion' since in reality 'it is the poem's verbal felicity and nothing else that is doing either the assuring (which thus is no more than whistling in the dark) or the assuming' and 'he is no more assured of what he assumes than anyone else'. So Fish concluded that 'Donne is sick and his poetry is sick'.

When Donne preached, was his religion crumbling in his mind like the stonework of the Gothic cathedral around him? Certainly his mind could be changed by new ideas through books. It seems that as a young man he was excited by the poetry and philosophy of the Italian Renaissance. It can also be suggested that when he meditated in his religious poetry he used not direct experience or observation but 'emblem books' which reproduced images recommended for contemplation. We know that during his years as a preacher much of his theology was derived from books. Some were medieval and provided neatly arranged quotations from the Fathers of the Church in an even earlier period, and some were books by the Fathers themselves, but it can be suggested that this traditional faith was deeply troubled by what he learned from books of the sixteenth and seventeenth centuries about astronomy, for example. That was the 'new Philosophy' which 'cals all in doubt' according to his famous reference to the new science in his 'Anniversaries': the earth is no longer stable or central, it moves around the sun. Deep down, was his religion no longer stable and no longer central to life? Was he as full of doubt as are many of his modern or post-modern readers? Dante had thought that God's love moved the sun around the earth. If that was not true, did Donne suspect that God was not real?

Many other questions can be asked about John Donne. He wrote a poem imagining his name engraved on a window, a 'ragged bony name', and he saw that these bones lacked 'the Muscle, Sinew, and Veine' which could make them live. Coleridge was right about his fluency and power in self-expression but in the final analysis his poems, his letters and his sermons can all seem like that skeleton, so that we ask: here are the words, clever no doubt, but after all these fireworks where is the man?

Although Ben Jonson thought Donne 'the first poet in the World, in some things', he also believed that 'Done himself for not being understood would perish'. Another remark, that Donne deserved to be hanged for neglecting 'accent', showed that part of the complaint was about an apparent neglect of metre, which would puzzle readers who expected the conventions of poetry to be observed in a way easy to understand at first sight. But mainly Jonson complained about the difficulty of grasping the sense of many passages: when using his own 'plain' style he proved that he did not overestimate other people's intelligence. Clever wit could seem to be the chief feature of Donne's poetry, and it could be praised – but it could also seem too clever.

After Donne's death a tribute was paid by a minor poet who was a disciple, Thomas Carew:

> The Muses' garden with Pedantique weedes
> O'rspred, was purg'd by thee; The lazie seeds
> Of servile imitation throwne away;
> And fresh invention planted . . .
> Since to the awe of thy imperious wit
> Our stubborne language bends . . .
>
> *Here lies a King, that rul'd as hee thought fit*
> *The universall Monarchy of Wit . . .*

And there Carew left it. But he was a courtier of King Charles I and inevitably readers who do not want to be mere courtiers singing the praises of John Donne as the monarch of wit have exercised their own wits. In the modern age 'new' critics have pointed out that a poem by him can be as artificial as any garden and that it is often a waste of time to look for the earth beneath the flowers and the weeds, although it may be useful to search for sources in Latin, Italian, Spanish or other literature. The only productive approach, we are told, is to concentrate on the writing in its intricate density, on its strategic arrangement of images and feelings, and on its defiantly personal choice of grammar, syntax and metre, since the poet's life outside his mind at that moment is hidden from us. The poem should be enjoyed as what the poet has created, as his 'invention' – for it cannot be more than that.

That 'new' criticism advocated by T. S. Eliot for a time was vigorous in the middle of the twentieth century but – as tends to happen in intellectual history – its emphasis was to seem too narrow while not being entirely wrong. Later critics have insisted that while literature is indeed an artefact created by authors the reader still has a right to think about its substance as well as its form. That analysis has produced a biographical approach to Eliot's own poetry, reducing his status. And these critics (would 'newer' be the right term?) have often been very critical of the substance of Donne's work. They have maintained that the language of a poem constructs what may appear to be a timeless reality but what is in fact the product of the writer's own psychology, gender or position in society – and so we are encouraged to be suspicious. And of course we are advised to be even more suspicious when a poet becomes a preacher.

This most recent approach, which may be called deconstructive or post-structuralist or post-modern, and which owes much to the theories about 'culture' taught by thinkers such as Althusser, Foucault and Raymond Williams, has great advantages in that it invites a reading which is even closer than anything thought necessary when the study of 'great literature' was more deferential. Valuable issues have been raised by connecting a poet such as Donne with psychoanalysis (what emotional wounds suffered in the past were bleeding as he wrote?) or feminism (why did he treat women like that?) or sociology (what ideology was he defending, and with how much conviction?). There are, however, difficulties in this deconstructive criticism, because in its attempt to answer the questions it raises it can construct speculations which are not based very firmly on the evidence now available.

It is difficult enough to psychoanalyse the living but the problems are larger when the passions have been dead for a long time, leaving behind evidence which is no more than what Donne saw on the seashore at low tide – 'embroider'd works upon the sand'. Some critics write as if the waves had created solid and large sandcastles still available for them to examine. It is difficult enough to get to the bottom of relationships between living people but our curiosity may have to remain unsatisfied if we try to probe too deeply into the lives of the dead. For example, we now speak freely about someone's need to acknowledge a 'homosexual' nature – but no one called himself or herself a 'homosexual' before late in the nineteenth century and this was not merely a matter of not using the word: it was believed that everyone was by nature heterosexual but was capable of perversity. We now think that a 'suicide' should arouse compassion – but that word was not used within Donne's lifetime about an action which was treated as a deadly sin and a terrible crime. We now think that a woman should not allow herself to be exploited outside or inside marriage – but in Donne's time men and women were taught inequality from childhood. We now despise people who flatter dictators – but in that age courtiers were thought to be honouring monarchs anointed by God. And it is difficult enough to know what really motivates the living without trying to reach certainty about the real preoccupations of the dead. When Donne was marrying a woman or writing a religious poem or preaching a sermon he was also a man who was ambitious for money and power, but critics who have asserted that he was always driven by careerism make a suggestion which goes beyond what we can know about him or about what we normally expect from lovers or worshippers or intellectuals when at their own kinds of work. We cannot be certain that a book or article offering a sour interpretation of Donne's motives was written mainly because the author wanted promotion or reputation in the academic world; it therefore seems fair to give the benefit of the doubt to the commentators – and, at least in some instances, to Donne.

Because they have tended to treat his poems and sermons as elaborate codes which need to be deciphered if we are to be shown what Donne was really thinking, some recent critics have left the impression that reading him is hard work which is best left to those who are exceptionally clever and exceptionally suspicious.

When Andrew Mousley edited contemporary critical essays on *John Donne* (1999), he summed up the conclusions of his contributors: 'we might say that a typical Donne text is at once that densely populated place where diverse ideas, feelings and cultural references meet, clash, and interchange; and at the same time a distinctive verbal construct, driven by its own idiosyncratic logic'. And in his study of *John Donne, Coterie Poet* (1986) Arthur Marotti thought that even for the poet's first readers, who might have been expected to belong to his world of thought, the metaphors in his poems were 'multivalent, ambiguous, and fundamentally *resistant* to interpretation'. Agreeing with this verdict in the volume edited by Mousley, Richard Halpern has written of Donne's intention to generate 'a fog of obscurity'. But as he reflected on many years spent in the compilation of bibliographies of criticism of Donne, John Roberts issued a warning that critics could be more difficult to understand than Donne himself. 'In many cases', he wrote in the inaugural number of the *John Donne Journal* (1982), 'Donne has been so successfully returned to his niche in the seventeenth century that many readers are content to leave him there. In other instances, Donne has been explained in such complicated terms that even highly educated readers feel intimidated and put off.' Roberts regarded this as paradoxical, since 'his poems were intended to communicate his particularly brilliant sense of reality' – as were his sermons.

So uncertainties and difficulties piled up in the twentieth century's debate about Donne. Ought we now to say out loud that he was a wit who entertained his contemporaries but has very little to say to us? A case can be made for that dismissive conclusion. His poems are not only varied in mood: even a short poem can have an end which contradicts the beginning. We may hope to hear his real voice in his letters but these, too, are often literary exercises – especially his letters in verse, a sixth of all his surviving poems, where the compliments are often ridiculously extravagant. His religious poems seem to open his heart and his sermons seem to be the answers to his own religious questions, but when what he says is an echo of orthodoxy we may wonder whether he really means it. He always seems to be passionate, but how seriously should we take him as a feeler? He always seems to be arguing, but is he a serious thinker?

Was Rupert Brooke right to say that 'when passion shook him, and his being ached for utterance to relieve the stress, expression came through the intellect'? The reply can be made that Brooke was too enthusiastic because he was looking for an alternative to most of the poetry of his time, including his own poetry. Was T. S. Eliot right to say that 'a thought to Donne was an experience; it modified his sensibility'? Eliot himself became worried because that widely quoted and accepted phrase of his did not correspond to the reality of Donne, which included much that was not wholly real. He published a second opinion, which was that a thought could attract Donne because it could fit into a poem or sermon. The 'sensuous apprehension of thought' which had previously seemed to involve the whole self like the experience of smelling a rose now appeared to be a literary craftsman's more detached enjoyment of an idea, 'almost as if it were something he could touch or stroke'. What Eliot now found in Donne was not 'thinking' at all but 'a vast jumble of incoherent erudition on which he drew for purely poetic effects'. And A. E. Housman, who cultivated simplicity as a poet and felt that the beauty of nature was the only reliable consolation for the tragedy of life, more briefly dismissed Donne as 'intellectually frivolous'.

The concentration by some twentieth-century critics on the artificiality of Donne was a return to what had been said by earlier critics.

In 1693 John Dryden could anticipate the harsher condemnations of wit that were to come in the Age of Reason: 'if we are not so great wits as Donne, yet certainly we are better poets'. His complaint about an over-clever poet was that he 'perplexes the minds of the fair sex with nice speculations of philosophy, when he should engage their hearts, and entertain them with the softness of love'. He seems to have been under the impression that Donne wrote for a readership of genteel young ladies who wanted poets to offer flowery compliments and perhaps a few soft kisses – but Donne wrote about raw sex, either for the enjoyment of other lusty young bachelors or in celebration of his own promiscuity, courtship and marriage.

Dryden was on safer ground when he was the first to use the term 'metaphysical' about Donne's poetry. The Greek word *metaphysika* was originally used simply in order to group together the books which Aristotle wrote apart from those on physical subjects, but later it was applied to any philosophy which attempted to rise above physical reality into speculative abstract or over-subtle thought. Dryden complained that poets such as Donne were too fanciful and his criticism of this style was developed by others who thought that (like everyone else with a claim to be civilized) poets ought to be realistic and reasonable. In the eighteenth century an attack by David Hume, normally a calm and urbane philosopher, was more savage: as he saw Donne, the wit was 'totally suffocated and buried by the harshest and most uncouth expression that is any-where to be met with'.

A more famous rebuke was delivered by Samuel Johnson when in 1779 he gave 'some account' of 'a race of writers that may be termed the metaphysical poets'. 'Their thoughts', he declared, 'are often new, but seldom natural; they are not devious, but neither are they just.' In particular he objected to the frequency of a 'conceit', which he defined. 'The most heterogeneous ideas are yoked by violence together; nature and art are ransacked for illustrations, comparisons and allusions; their learning instructs, and their subtilty surprises; but the reader, . . . though he sometimes admires, is seldom pleased' – because the reader is not shown 'truth' by these ingeniously artificial 'conceits'. 'To shew their learning', said the great Dr Johnson, 'was their whole endeavour.' He was not entirely hostile to these 'metaphysical' poets: 'to write on their plan it was at least necessary to read and think'. But his verdict was that they 'fail to give delight by their desire of exciting admiration'. He complained that 'their courtship is devoid of fondness, and their lamentation of sorrow'. And this verdict has been thought to apply to Donne, although Johnson was writing mainly about Abraham Cowley, a later poet.

In 1713 Alexander Pope admired Donne but thought it necessary to translate him into 'correct' verse if a more polished age was to give him a hearing. In 1733 Donne's poetry could be called by Lewis Theobald a 'continued Heap of Riddles'. A century later the young Henry Alford made an attempt to persuade the public to buy and admire reprinted sermons by Donne, but the six volumes did not sell; down-to-earth Englishmen, if they noticed, were indignant to see that the preacher's arguments too often depended not on facts but on conceits. When tributes were paid to Donne in the nineteenth century, it was often as if nuggets of gold had been found in the bed of a remote river. Thomas Campbell included four pieces in his *Specimens* of English poetry in 1819, but he reproduced only two of them completely and he added this comment: 'His ruggedness and whim are almost proverbially known, yet there is a beauty of thought which at intervals arises from his chaotic imagination, like Venus smiling on the waters.' A *Cyclopaedia of English Literature* in 1844 acknowledged that 'there is much real poetry, and that of a high order' – but only 'amid much rubbish'. Robert Browning often praised Donne's poetry, particularly when it was conversational, but did not imitate it: he wanted to achieve something more lifelike. Anthologists might include isolated specimens of Donne's poetry, and in 1872 A. B. Grosart collected most of it in a new edition, but it was presented with apologies for its 'faults' and when editing the most influential of all the anthologies, his *Golden Treasury* of English poetry in 1861, Francis Palgrave thought it wisest to omit Donne altogether.

Yet the most eloquent of Donne's critics was Donne – and he would certainly have agreed that he was complicated and that his style in poetry or prose reflected this personal complexity. On his own testimony he should not be interpreted in any oversimple fashion and the acceptance of his own realistic self-assessment must be our starting point as we try to understand him as he really was: not praising or condemning, but understanding. There were different periods in his life, and within any period, perhaps within any day, there were different moods. He often watched himself, and he saw not a simple character but a whole little world, divided by a civil war:

> I am a little world made cunningly
> Of Elements, and an Angelike spright,
> But black sinne hath betraid to endless night
> My world's both parts, and (oh) both parts must die.

He hoped that the spirit in him linked him with God's angels. But he knew that the elements in his body, which the Creator had made cunningly, could drag body and soul down to endless night.

And he knew that his mind was a battlefield between the forces of light and the powers of 'lust and envie'. He could occupy the high moral ground but soon find himself rolling in the mud of sex or trying to climb in the world by flattery of the rich. He could pray and preach with a burning intensity but soon find his mind wandering. He could, he said, 'neglect God and his Angels for the noise of a Flie, for the ratling of a Coach, for the whining of a dore . . . A memory of yesterday's pleasures, a fear of tomorrow's dangers, a straw under my knee, a noise in mine eare, an any thing, a nothing, a fancy . . . troubles me in my prayer' (7:264–5). While in the pulpit he could be 'at home in my Library' asking whether some other commentator had not interpreted the Bible better – or he could be wondering 'what is likely you will say to one another, when I have done' (3:110).

The medical authorities of his age, repeating the second-century Galen, had taught him that a character or a mood was caused when a 'humour' overflowed. There were four of these humours in any human body: blood, phlegm, black and yellow bile. They made a person sanguine or phlegmatic, choleric or melancholy. But Donne found other humours in himself, one heating him with lust, another icing him with shame:

> Oh, to vex me, contraryes meet in one:
> Inconstancy unnaturally hath begott
> A constant habit; that when I would not
> I change in vowes, and in devotione.
> As humorous is my contritione
> As my prophane Love, and as soon forgott . . .

There was, he claimed, truth in his mind: once he wrote about his 'minde's white truth'. In this poem he declared

> Those are my best days, when I shake with feare.

But he was honest with himself and confessed that he had other days:

> As ridlingly distempered, cold and hott . . .
> I durst not view heaven yesterday; and to day
> In prayers and flattering speeches I court God:
> To morrow I quake with true feare of his rod.

That poem seems to have been written when Donne had been for some time a priest and a preacher and if this was the case we can see why there is an unusual intensity in its ashamed selfexamination: he is not the assured Christian whom the public sees. Even in his private 'devotione' or his penitential 'contritione' his piety comes and goes like a fever. And yet we should notice both his honesty and his humility: he does not admire himself when he prays and he dares not 'view heaven' like a tourist. He quakes with fear as he remembers that God is just, and he is at his 'best' when begging for mercy. In a letter he told a friend that short prayers are best 'for long prayers have more of the man, as ambition of eloquence and a complacencie in the work, and more of the Devil . . .'

Such was Donne as he saw himself when he thought he was standing and trembling in the presence of his Judge. If we want to discover the truth about such a man, we must not try to cover his personality by one small and neat label. Behind all the clever words, and behind the varying moods which the words express, there is a man whom we can meet and he is a living man with what belongs to humanity (including us): the complications, the limitations, the strengths. He is a man not of words only but also of flesh and spirit. Such a man is not simple – but perhaps he is understandable.

We can profitably begin the task of understanding the real, complex, not always admirable Donne by comparing him with a few of his contemporaries. At least the comparison will bring out what he was not. If we compare him with George Herbert, also a great poet and also a man who became an Anglican priest after many troubled years, we can see why Donne is never likely to be treated by the public as a saint, whatever may be claimed by some of his fans: he lacked simplicity, he lacked serenity, he was not sufficiently willing to forget himself in the love of God and neighbour, he was too like George Herbert's brother Edward. If we compare him with two other great poets of his generation, Jonson and Shakespeare, we can see how he was more limited in his interests and therefore why he is more restricted in his appeal: he was always so interested in himself, and often also so interested in God in relation to himself, that he was never content simply to write about other people with a care to describe their independent reality.

In their boyhoods both John Donne and George Herbert were greatly influenced by a widowed mother, but while Donne inherited great complications from the fervent Roman Catholicism of the family into which he was born, Herbert's mother was (as Donne declared eloquently when preaching at her memorial service) an Anglican saint. Both received a good education, but while Donne had to learn from tutors, Herbert went to a famous school and became a Fellow of Trinity College, Cambridge. Both men had ambitions for a profitable career in the service of the Crown and both were frustrated, but Herbert's financial worries were comparatively mild and his efforts to get a job comparatively relaxed. Both had the feelings of a young man and Herbert wrote that 'my stuffe is flesh, not brasse', but only Donne had reasons to feel any great guilt. (Herbert's confessions were that as a boy 'I had my way' amid 'milk and sweetnesses', that he sought and enjoyed 'academick praise' for his elegance as the university's official orator, and that he hoped to get a position with 'Honour' by 'the quick returns of courtesie and wit' in his contacts with the king and the court.) Both resisted ordination to the priesthood but Herbert found that his resistance, called by him 'fierce and wilde', could be silenced quite easily:

> Methought I heard one calling, 'Childe',
> And I reply'd, 'My Lord'.

The ways in which the two men married and were ordained were significantly different. Donne threw away a career because he loved a girl with passion. He became an unemployed father of a rapidly expanding family but refused the offer of an exceptionally good income as a parish priest, condemning himself to seven more years of anxious job-hunting, the jobs he wanted being rather grand. Herbert seems to have decided to become a husband and a priest at more or less the same time; he was then aged 36 and according to Izaak Walton proposed to the lady only three days after meeting her. He never became a father but he accepted the position of rector in a country parish, Fugglestone-cum-Bemerton; it had about four hundred inhabitants, almost all of them peasants. It was not a wilderness: it was near Salisbury Cathedral where he enjoyed Evensong twice a week and also near Wilton House, the seat of the Earls of Pembroke who belonged to a much richer branch of the Herbert family. But he wrote a little book about the duties of a parish priest as a 'mark to aim at' and seems to have found a genuine fulfilment as an obscure pastor; none of his sermons has survived but the happiest of his poems seem to date from this time. He died of tuberculosis in 1633, after two and a half years in the priesthood.

His little book in prose, called *A Priest to the Temple*, was not published until 1651, at a time when the Church of England had been overthrown, but in that situation the idealism about pastoral care and devoutly careful worship answered contempt for the Church and the book's influence continued for some three hundred years. And a small volume of his poems, *The Temple: Sacred Poems and Private Ejaculations*, became a book which many treasured when it had been published by the Cambridge University Press soon after his death in the year which also saw the first edition of Donne's poetry. Like Donne he was a poet brilliantly inventive technically and a frequent user of 'conceits' but unlike him he kept his cleverness and learning well under control, liked to use natural and homely images, disciplined his emotions by a glad submission to the Bible and the Church, and even when his subject was not heaven could express pure joy in his religion. Reaching a simplicity which Donne never achieved, he dedicated himself to 'Jesus my Master' with his 'utmost art' as a poet of a plainly holy love and as a courtier serving an invisible king in a tiny parish. And unlike Donne, when dying he entrusted his poems to a friend, with the hope that they would be published in order to edify.

Soon after his own ordination Donne sent George Herbert a Latin poem ending with best wishes for favour from the royal court. Later he became aware of the younger man's spirituality and they seem to have exchanged copies of their poems in English, although the only strong evidence for this is somewhat ridiculous. In 'To Mr Tilman' Donne complained that 'Gentry' refused to serve the Church

> As if their day were onely to be spent
> In dressing, Mistressing and complement. . .

This poem seems to have been sent to George Herbert – and to have been obliquely aimed at him while he hesitated about a descent in the class system through ordination, for in one of his own poems ('The Church Porch') Herbert included the advice that a young gentleman should not waste his time dressing up before paying visits and compliments to young ladies. Alternatively, Donne may have borrowed the line. However, it seems clear that he felt closer to George's elder brother Edward, with whom he exchanged whole poems in friendly competition.

Edward (who became Lord Herbert of Cherbury) was very much a man, outstandingly handsome, a tough and brave soldier, eager to fight duels with men who might be said to have insulted him and to make love to women who were known to admire him; he recorded his exploits in a boastful autobiography. He was also energetic in the field of religious controversy: while ambassador in Paris he wrote a book of philosophy and later he ventured into theology, with conclusions very different from his brother's since while thinking the existence of God obvious he regarded Christianity as no more than the best of the available religions, was not enthusiastic about Jesus, and cared little for priests. In a verse-letter of 1610 Donne assured Edward Herbert that although himself a writer not a soldier he admired a military man ('Actions are authors') and on the day of his ordination he wrote to him affectionately, trusting that their friendship was not over. Less solemnly he once wrote a short 'Essay of Valour' which teased the gallant soldier who easily impresses women. This macho, man-of-the-world side to Donne was a part of his complex character. It made him unlike George Herbert.

Ben Jonson was born in the same year as Donne and was in some ways like him in character. He was assertively masculine and never at a loss for words; he was very much a Londoner and for many years drank and talked with Donne; he looked to the court of James I for patronage; and he could write in a style so like his friend's that when a collection of his poems called *Underwood* was published in 1640 it included four which have also been attributed to Donne. But Jonson's writing was much more varied in subject and tone, and one reason was that as a professional writer (in a profession which had not existed before the 1590s) he had to apply his skill to any job which came his way. He could not afford to be always writing about himself. Nor could he afford to be too clever. It seems, however, that he had no wish to be. It was more in his nature to be comic or sad with a warm-hearted humanity, and to write poems which were simply beautiful or simply affectionate. He was as clever as Donne but not an intellectual.

Jonson's father was an Anglican clergyman who died before he was born, and his mother then married a man slightly lower in the class system: a bricklayer who had a cottage near the site which is now Trafalgar Square. With that home the boy was able to get an education locally – in Westminster School like George Herbert – but not a decent job. If he was to rise above his early years in his stepfather's trade and in the ranks of the army, he had to make money as an actor and as a writer of plays. What he wrote for a theatre had to please first the manager and then the audience, and in order to please it had to represent life as known to the audience, with attacks on the classes above. Before long, however, the highly talented young man saw a more profitable market for his words: scripts were needed for the 'masques' performed regularly in the royal court. What was most important in these entertainments celebrating the government's current policy was the dancing, in which the queen herself performed when more or less sober. The king watched and as the history of his reign demonstrated a good dancer could be rewarded far more handsomely than any script-writer. Jonson wrote what was needed and in 1616 included his scripts along with plays and poems in an edition of his *Workes*, in a year when the king's own literary works also appeared in a collected edition. That unprecedented volume was the height of a professional's career but it left the author still vulnerable. Even when under the patronage of King James his indiscretions could get him into trouble and under the stricter King Charles he was permanently out of favour, left to years of illness and renewed poverty.

Donne thought that his proper place would be among the courtiers who watched the masque. He was willing to criticize poems submitted to him by Jonson, and to write in praise of his friend's *Volpone*, but he had no intention of living in the ungentlemanly world which mere playwrights inhabited. Jonson, who was often drunk and often quarrelsome, once killed an actor and escaped a hanging only because he could translate some verses of the Latin Bible and so take advantage of the 'benefit of clergy' which remained as a strange survival from the privileges of the clergy in the Middle Ages. Whereas Donne wrote short poems about his experiences as a gentleman volunteering for naval expeditions during the war with Spain, Jonson wrote a long one about a voyage through an open sewer in the centre of London, the Fleet Ditch: it was an allegory of the life which he knew. He shared this low life with Christopher Marlowe, the first of the great playwrights but also not a real gentleman. A cobbler's son, Marlowe earned money by acting as a spy for the government but while drinking would say things which could get him into deep trouble as an 'atheist'. In the end he was killed in a tavern, during a fight which may have been arranged by the government. His most famous plays had been about the intoxications of power and knowledge but the reality was that playwrights knew that they could not hope for security. The custom was that the writer of a play was paid a single fee which was not large; most of the actors were paid a labourer's wage and the profits were kept by the small group of 'sharers' who also retained the manuscripts of the plays; Shakespeare's plays were not collected for publication until seven years after his death. In his second 'satyre' Donne mocked the dramatist who

> gives ideot actors meanes
> (Starving himself) to live by his labor'd sceanes . . .

And how does Donne look in comparison with Shakespeare?

As a shareholder in theatre business Shakespeare was more than a mere writer or actor, and that was the main reason why he was able to afford the best house in Stratford-on-Avon and recognition as a gentleman by the College of Heralds. He was also indebted to James I as his royal patron (as Donne and Jonson were and as George Herbert tried to be). And he was a genius who was interested in humanity – and who, as Harold Bloom has suggested, in a sense 'invented' it by the richness and depth of his understanding: into his plays he put men and women of every class and temperament, in every kind of situation, and he always allowed them to speak for themselves. But he never found his own life so interesting that he had to make a drama out of it. His sonnets are more self-revealing than anything else that he wrote, and they reveal a hard struggle for self-fulfilment not entirely unlike Donne's, but they were not reprinted in his lifetime and it has often been thought that this was because their author thought them too personal. Whether or not that was so, C. S. Lewis was surely right about the poetry of love: 'in Donne's most serious lyrics . . . we have a poetry which is almost exactly opposite to that of Shakespeare's *Sonnets.* In Shakespeare each experience of the lover becomes a window through which we look out on immense prospects – on nature, the seasons, life and death, time and eternity. In Donne . . . a particular man is mocking, flattering, browbeating, laughing at, or laughing with, or adoring, a particular woman.'

For Donne nature was to be kept in the background, philosophy was to be used and forgotten like a piece of furniture on the stage, and the most interesting bit of humanity in the comedy or tragedy was always himself. One climax in the drama of his life was his sensational marriage six years after the probable date of the first performance of *Romeo and Juliet.* Then came years of Hamlet-like indecision, even of Lear-like suffering which caused a Hamlet-like temptation to suicide, with the consolation of a romance somewhat like the world-losing love of Antony and Cleopatra. Then he moved on into a world of explicitly religious emotions and theological arguments into which Shakespeare never entered although many references in his plays show that he was familiar with the Bible and with the Book of Common Prayer. And as Donne preached many listened – with a response which encouraged him to go on preaching until he was very near death, and to preach after death in a highly unusual monument with a statue of himself as a shrouded corpse and a long inscription about his life, all carefully planned.

The monument to Shakespeare is on a wall of his parish church and there he is as silent as he had been during many a sermon. The bust depicts a happy, well-fed man holding a quill pen in order to show what he did before retirement. Beneath it are inscribed a Latin couplet and six lines of verse in English praising 'all that he hath writ' without mentioning anything specific and saying, with a breath-taking inadequacy, that his name 'doth deck this tomb' far more than the money spent on the monument. It is clear that William Shakespeare, the greatest man in English history and arguably also in the literature of the world, had left no instructions as to how his life and work were to be commemorated; family and friends have had to do their best. Here the only writing by him – or phrased as a message from him – is a request, in a tiny bit of very simple verse, that his bones should not be moved so that the grave can be reused.

Although Donne's own personality was such that other people were left almost entirely silent as he retold the drama of his life, it does not seem exaggerated to say that in a limited way he is fit to stand comparison with Shakespeare. In *The Donne Tradition* (1930) George Williamson wrote that 'of all the explorers of the soul who come with the seventeenth century, Donne, and not Milton, deserves to stand nearest to Shakespeare. . . Love poetry could never be quite the same after him, and religious verse that is poetry descends from him. His was one of the prodigious intellects which take all learning for their province, and one of those even rarer minds whose very thinking is poetical.' At least we can think of Donne standing not far from the greater man. There is no record that they met but they had friends in common including Ben Jonson. Sir Richard Baker, Donne's fellow student both in Oxford and in London, remembered that he had been well dressed and 'a great frequenter of Playes' when a young man-about-town. It seems very likely that he attended early performances of Shakespeare's plays right up to *Hamlet* in 1601. In 1600 a plan for a book was registered with the Stationers' Company, *Amours by J.D. with certain other sonnets by W.S.* So far as we know the project was abandoned but it would be very surprising if the two never got together. The surprise would come if the two men met and Donne never talked about himself. Perhaps the collaboration came to nothing because Shakespeare could not stand his fellow poet's egotism.

The platform on which Donne usually performed was London, and during a sermon about the life and death of a rich merchant who had 'acted great and various parts in it' he observed that 'this City is a great Theatre' (7:274). He was commemorating William Cockayne, about whom much could have been said had the preacher been discussing economics. One of Cockayne's schemes had wrecked an industry on which England had depended for centuries, the manufacture of cloth to be 'finished' and dyed abroad. In 1613 Cockayne secured from King James a monopoly for a company which would undertake all the final processes in London, but foreign merchants refused to buy its products and the result was the loss of the export market. The economic depression which followed – and which was one of the motives for emigration to America – was caused mainly by overpopulation in England and war in Europe, but Cockayne had played his part.

However, what fascinated Donne was not economics but personality. He therefore spoke about Cockayne the prominent man of business who had joined the dead and was now remembered for deeds which could commend him to the divine mercy: bringing up a family, being active in charity, saying prayers as his best investment. As a young poet Donne would no doubt have mocked and denounced a rich man who had done so much damage by a scheme to make himself even richer, but now that he was a preacher he thought it his duty to concentrate on the individual in relation to eternity. Did he therefore deserve to be condemned himself, as a stooge of the rich? That question will have to be faced. What is obvious is that as he lived his own life and approached his own death Donne would perform his part with a great sense of the drama of the individual living and dying before spectators – and even as a young poet who felt free to despise his seniors, he attacked their characters rather than their policies.

He did not wish to perform in the London of the theatres and of cruder entertainments on the south bank of the Thames. The stage of his life was a narrow strip on the north bank, about two miles long but never far from the road which ran from St Paul's Cathedral to royal Westminster. He was born in Bread Street, a short distance from the cathedral where he was to preach and be buried. He studied law in Lincoln's Inn which was down the road, down Fleet Street and the Strand, and began his career in York House which was a little further down. When his career collapsed his prison was in Fleet Street, near the chapel where he had been married in secret. When his career slowly revived he took lodgings in Fleet Street and was then housed more handsomely in nearby Drury Lane, before moving to the Deanery of the cathedral whose decaying medieval bulk was London's only building to be really tall.

If we can understand the plot of the drama of Donne's life, played out in the great theatre of London, that will not answer all the questions. We do not know all the facts and we ought not to suppose that all the words which Donne left behind in writing which has survived refer directly to his life. In a sermon (4:87) he reflected on the power of preaching and poetry to describe a world which, however, actually exists only in the responses of readers. 'How empty a thing is Rhetorique? (and yet Rhetorique will make absent and remote things present to your understanding). How weak a thing is Poetry? (and yet Poetry is a counterfeit Creation, and makes things that are not, as though they were).' So we must not expect to agree about the significance of the 'bracelet of bright haire' which his imagination placed on the arm of a skeleton. Nor must we expect all our more sensible questions to be answered by facts more solid than that bracelet. But if the known facts can be gathered and the probabilities assessed, and if much thought can be added, we may find that the plot of the drama of this complicated man's life emerges; we may be able to understand what can be understood. It is a large but limited ambition.

It seems good to make this attempt now because interest in Donne, including discussion in the academic world, has grown and grown in recent years, especially (but not solely) in the USA. 1995 saw the first two publications in an American project to reprint all his poetry in ten volumes, devotedly giving all the variations between the handwritten sources and the printed editions (with the assistance of computers). 160 of his sermons were written out by him and published after his death by his son John, to be re-edited in ten volumes in 1953–62 as a tribute from California to his enduring position in the history of preaching. No Englishman's private letters had previously been printed on the scale which was thought suitable for John Donne, in a collection published twenty years after his death – and not many writers of any nation or age have continued to arouse such personal interest that a larger and more accurate edition of some two hundred letters was being prepared in America some 350 years later. In 1982 the

John Donne Journal was founded as a medium for scholarly articles about his life and work; many conferences have been held; and many American scholars have published books providing an analysis in depth. And all this re-editing and re-thinking has come from a continent which Donne never saw, although he was keenly interested in the new colony in Virginia and was a contemporary of the Pilgrim Fathers who founded New England. How wrong T. S. Eliot was when he wrote in 1931 that 'Donne's poetry is a concern of the present and of the recent past rather than of the future'! And how wrong he was to predict that another revival would prove short-lived, saying that 'his sermons will disappear as quickly as they have appeared'! As the twenty-first century begins it seems clear that an interest in Donne has become a part of any serious interest in the heights of literature in English.

2 At the dore

I tune the Instrument here at the dore
'A Hymne to God my God'

He was born at an unknown date during the first half of 1572. His mother Elizabeth came from a family which was religious to the point of martyrdom and which was also literary: in so far as the talents of this poet and preacher were inherited, the genes responsible were, it seems, transmitted by his mother. His father was a prosperous ironmonger who in fast-expanding London ran a business attached to his home, making and selling kitchen utensils. John, the eldest son, was introduced to the power of death when this father died before the boy's fourth birthday, to be followed by one sister next year and two others in 1582. His mother quickly made a second marriage, to a leading London doctor, John Syminges, and the family moved into a house which had a garden. His childhood seems to have been reasonably happy, with care about his education. When he thought he was near death in 1623, he was to remember that 'my parents would not give mee over to a Servant's correction'. When preaching he was to remark that 'a man can remember when he began to spell but not when he began to read perfectly, and when he began to joyne his letters but not when he began to write perfectly' (4:149).

It is frustrating that Donne, who could write well enough on many other subjects, left behind him very little evidence about the years before he became a student of law. However, his first biographer, Izaak Walton, recorded that having been well grounded while in London he was sent to other tutors in Oxford and Cambridge, and there seems to be no good reason to contradict this statement. It is known that in October 1584 he was admitted as a student in Hart Hall, Oxford, along with his brother Henry, who was a year younger. Their ages were young by the standards of that time, but not impossibly so. Boys were sent to school to learn 'grammar' when about seven years old and from that age young John would have had Latin beaten into him, either in a school or at home, before Oxford at the age of twelve.

In Oxford Henry Wotton became one of Donne's lifelong friends and he was probably the source of Walton's report that even before he entered Hart Hall the lad was already so well educated that he was compared with a scholar of the Italian Renaissance, Pico della Mirandola, 'of whom Story says, *That he was rather born, than made wise by study*'. He already had 'a good command both of the French and Latine Tongue' – and as Henry Wotton evidently found, he was also not slow to develop a gift for friendship. From an early age he had the knack of combining the solitary work of a reader and writer with active friendship, which he called his 'second religion': he knew that in fact no one is born wise – or becomes wise by meeting only books. Also, he needed an audience.

One of the attractions of Hart Hall was that it had no chapel from which absences could be noted by an authority on the lookout for dangerous 'Papists'. When registering for admission the two Donne boys stated their age as a year younger than was the truth and the explanation seems to be that the statutes of the university demanded that at or after the age of sixteen anyone wishing to proceed to a degree should take an oath accepting the supremacy of Queen Elizabeth over the State and 'in all spiritual or ecclesiastical things'. The boys had a firmly Roman Catholic mother who wanted their Oxford education to last a little longer than this Protestant law intended. In due course, when he was obviously of an age when his religion had to be declared, John

Donne was withdrawn from Oxford. Walton says that he went to Cambridge where he was a 'most laborious Student, often changing his studies but endeavouring to take no degree'.

Donne seems to have told him about Cambridge and it seems very likely that the build-up of knowledge and wit continued in the environment of the other university. Cambridge had no equivalent to Oxford's demand that the royal supremacy over the Church must be accepted by all students over sixteen but the colleges did not welcome Papists and Donne probably kept a low profile as an unregistered student, chosing his own tutors, books and lectures. But Walton was inaccurate in a comparatively minor matter. He says that Donne remained in Cambridge 'till his seventeenth year', which by his reckoning was 1590 (because he also made a slip by giving the year of birth as 1573 instead of 1572). The more probable dates are 1586 or 1587 for the move from Oxford to Cambridge and 1588 or 1589 for the start of foreign travel. Walton says that the travel began in 1597 and lasted for 'some years' but we know that at the turn of 1597–98 Donne began a job in London; so scholarly opinion is that the journey to see the world was undertaken immediately after the more academic education which could be provided by tutors in Oxford and Cambridge.

He had inherited from his father funds which could be used for education and travel and from his mother he must have gained a great sense of belonging to Catholic Europe; her own family's history included Catholic martyrs among whom Sir Thomas More was the most famous but not the last. What is certain is that Donne was deeply interested in Italy and Spain, knew their languages and read their books. It is also certain that by the age of eighteen, when he became a student of law, he had developed a self-confidence which would have been less likely had he remained a 'most laborious Student'.

Walton says that Donne often mentioned with a 'deploration' his disappointment that he had not been able to afford to proceed from Italy to 'the Holy Land, for viewing Jerusalem and the Sepulchre of our Saviour'; he had gone to Spain instead. There he would have had a problem which was not merely financial: England was at war with Spain until 1604 and narrowly escaped invasion by the Spanish Armada in 1588. But the difficulty would have vanished if he could present himself as one of the many refugees from Elizabethan Protestantism and it is highly probable that this is what he did in the year after the Armada. We know that in 1591 he could pose for a miniature portrait which depicted him as an eager Roman Catholic. The miniature has not survived but a clumsy engraving of it was used as the frontispiece to the 1635 edition of his poems. It is full of character. It has been suggested that the original picture was the work of a leading artist, Nicholas Hilliard (on the ground that Donne's poem on 'The Storme' includes a compliment to his skill), but it seems very unlikely that this fashionable painter would have risked losing the patronage of the queen and her court in order to glamorize an obscure but cocky young Papist.

It would not be surprising if the miniature was intended to please his mother. It would mark his return to London and her third marriage, to another staunch Roman Catholic (Richard Rainsford), before February 1591. The picture is of an eager youth who flaunts both his masculinity and his faith: his age is given as eighteen. His face, while not beautiful, begins to have power. His hair is long (this was the new fashion) although the moustache is not yet growing at the desired strength. His dark doublet (coat) is also fashionable, with padded shoulders, many buttons down the front and sleeves cut so as to show the shirt. Rather awkwardly he lifts a gentleman's short sword in order to get it into the picture. A coat of arms is also displayed, belonging to the ancient and rich Welsh family of Dwyn; this too may be a bit awkward, since he is a London ironmonger's son. But certainly it is a portrait of a swashbuckling crusader. His earring is a little cross, a sign that he is ready to fight any Protestant who objects to this 'Popish' symbol. The motto, presumably around the edge of the miniature, means 'Sooner dead than changed'. It is defiantly in Spanish although that language is being used only three years after the Protestant nation's great moment of danger from the Spanish Armada.

That portrait announces that a crusader is willing to join the Catholic martyrs in his mother's family, even if it means being branded as a friend of the hated and feared Spaniards. But does the young man actually mean that? Does he know that in the Spanish play these words were sung by a young woman who was going to transfer her affections to another lover? Had Donne lost his Catholic enthusiasm as well as his virginity while abroad? We cannot know – but another portrait, also by an unknown artist, shows that for him much had changed after a few years.

This portrait was painted in the pose of a man being martyred in the cause of the fashionable religion of love. He is no longer bareheaded. His black hat is very large, as was expected when a young gentleman wished to conceal from the world his disappointment in love, although in Donne's case the hat is lifted back so as to reveal his face, which seems not utterly tragic. His lips look sensual under a carefully tended moustache. An expensive, transparent shirt falls over an elaborate lace collar with a tie which is embroidered. One hand is fully visible, displaying fingers which seem long enough to caress a woman acceptably (and are too long to be accurate work by the painter), but the other hand is half-hidden in the darkness and covered by a fur glove. The Latin motto around the top of the picture means 'O Lady, lighten our darkness'. It has been suggested that this is a serious prayer addressed to the Virgin Mary, but the pose in this portrait is far from devotional and the words are a deliberate misquotation of a prayer to the 'Lord' transferred from the service of Compline in the medieval

Sarum Breviary to Evening Prayer in the Church of England's Book of Common Prayer.

In 1959 this portrait in the possession of the Marquis of Lothian was recognized as 'that Picture of myne which is taken in Shadowes' and which Donne bequeathed to his friend Sir Robert Ker, an ancestor of the marquis. It had been hanging in the Deanery of St Paul's and Donne felt it necessary to explain in his will that it was painted 'very many yeares before I was of this profession'. In his old age Thomas Morton, then Bishop of Durham, recalled seeing this portrait at an earlier stage in a 'chamber' of Lincoln's Inn occupied by a 'dear friend' of Donne's, almost certainly Christopher Brooke. It seems that on Brooke's death in 1628 this picture of a fashionably melancholic lover was moved to the Deanery. (The dean's wife would not have cared for it but she had been dead for eleven years.) It is interesting that Donne was not ashamed to display this relic of his unclerical past; out of that past, as out of shadows, the great preacher had come.

By the time this portrait was painted he had left behind any thought of being a Catholic crusader and martyr. Instead, what had endured from his time in Italy, and had grown during his time back in London, was his willingness to play a role which was fashionable in Italian Renaissance poetry, the role of the lover left to sulk in the dark by a coldly unattainable mistress. It was a role inherited from the medieval tradition of songs of 'courtly' love – which by convention was never consummated, one reason being that the mistress was usually married to someone else, someone with the power to punish. This was the role played famously by two poets, Boccaccio as he flirted with the noble Fiametta and Petrarch as he lamented snubs by Laura or her death. In England the 'Petrarchan' tradition in this style of poetry went back to Chaucer's adaptation of Boccaccio in *Troilus and Criseyde* but it was given a boost in the Elizabethan age when actual or would-be courtiers had to express a devotion to the Virgin Queen.

So the pose in this picture belongs to a convention – yet the sadness may also be heartfelt, giving us a glimpse of the first great love of Donne's life. The probability that this portrait hung in Christopher Brooke's chamber can be linked with the verse-letter 'To Mr C. B.'. There Donne laments that the 'Saint of his affection' who is his 'Sunne', 'thrice-fairer' than the sun which warms the world, has left London for a place which has already been reached by 'sterne winter'. The poet is in 'amorous paine' because he feels that the lady is being cold towards him and no expression of his own hot love seems able to touch her:

> Yet, love's hot fires, which martyr my sad minde,
> Doe send forth scalding sighes, which have the Art
> To melt all Ice, but that which walls her heart.

Presumably this letter was sent to Christopher Brooke because he was then near the lady and in a position to influence her in Donne's favour. It seems possible that she was Brooke's sister, now living in York where Brooke's father was a rich merchant – and also possible that the picture was sent to her and, when the affair ended, passed by her to her brother. If it was, the rejected Donne seems to have grown sentimental rather than angry, since his friendship with Christopher Brooke survived the display of the picture. Or did Donne give Brooke the picture in order to reinforce the plea in that verse-letter?

The verse-letter 'To Mr I. L.' (who cannot be identified) almost certainly refers to the same lady. She is worshipped as 'my Sun' and she has gone to 'your North parts', leaving Donne in a London where he experiences 'no Sommer' but 'pestilence' instead. In contrast, I. L. is 'in Paradise', enjoying not only the company of Donne's own beloved 'Sun' but also 'thy lov'd wife' and an estate rich in pasture and woods – and so the despairing Donne sends a plea similar to that made in 'To Mr C. B.': 'helpe thy friend to save'.

Another piece of evidence that Donne was influenced by this tradition of Petrarchan love, adoring the unattainable, is that he copied an Italian motto from Petrarch into many of the books which he owned: it announced that his role in life was contemplative, not active. But in the 1590s he could not be expected to confine himself to contemplation. He was bursting with energy and had to prepare to earn his living. Also, he did not intend to be entirely inactive in his relations with women.

He was admitted as a student of law in Lincoln's Inn in May 1592, on financial terms which show that he had already spent a year in a preparatory college, Thavies Inn. The four 'Inns of Court' in London were in this period the leading centre for higher education in England, since Oxford and Cambridge were still basically medieval in their syllabus for undergraduates and heavily theological in the interests of the resident graduates, and there was no other university in England. But the young men who went there (often after an Oxbridge spell without necessarily taking a degree) were a mixed lot. Probably most of them wanted to meet marriageable women although they were still on the young side for marriage, and probably most of them also dreamed of attracting attention in the court of Queen Elizabeth, partly because they were patriotic subjects of a woman who had become the centre of a national cult but mainly perhaps because they hoped for the wealth which could follow royal favour. But there was a mixture in the students' social origins. Some had been born into privilege. While in London they would acquire some knowledge of the law which would be useful when they were landowners and magistrates, but their main interest probably lay in their pleasures. These would include the development of social skills such as making love, making a disturbance and making or appreciating music and poetry. Other young men were, however, more genuine students because they knew that their more limited financial prospects meant that they must acquire the knowledge of the law and the eloquence in court which they would need if they were to make a success of being professional lawyers. In Lincoln's Inn there were about forty students of one kind or the other.

Donne did not completely belong to either set in this small community where about a hundred lawyers were also based. He did study law. In his fourth 'satyre' he included a nightmare when

> mee thought I saw
> One of our Giant Statutes ope his jaw
> To sucke me in . . .

but it would be in character for him to enjoy arguing about the law more than merely memorizing what a long law contained. The art of argument formed a great part of higher education in that age. In the universities the young were required to take part in disputations three times a week, as a test of what they had already learned in their studies of logic and rhetoric, and in the Inns of Court students spent much of their time either listening to the arguments of barristers in courts or holding their own 'moots' where they had to argue for or against a given plea. It was also hoped that they would talk about law at dinners which were compulsory. We know from what he wrote that the young Donne loved an argument. He wrote 'paradoxes' setting out unconventional opinions which he defended – as he claimed, in the expectation that someone else would defend common sense. (One of his paradoxes was 'that a Wise man is knowne by much Laughinge'.) In his love poems he was very prone to argue, although the woman concerned was very seldom allowed to reply.

Moreover, Donne seems to have learned from his enjoyment of arguments that it would strengthen his position if he did learn what the law said. While formally enrolled in Lincoln's Inn he seems to have postponed most of that labour, but when he was unemployed in the early 1600s he resumed his study of law – to such effect that Walton thought that he rapidly acquired 'such a perfection as was judged' to be comparable 'with many who had made that study the employment of their whole life'. No doubt Walton was exaggerating but we do know that as late as 1612 Donne consulted a senior friend (Thomas Morton) about an idea that he might resume his study and become a full-time ecclesiastical lawyer. He dropped the idea after discouragement but claimed in a letter that the study of the law remained his favourite 'entertainment'. In the 1620s he became a part-time ecclesiastical judge, sitting on commissions which decided cases known to modern researchers.

However, any serious interest in the laws lay in the future. In the 1590s he was more anxious to be a gentleman and spent money and time in being one, knowing that the course in the Inns of Court, which usually lasted for about seven years, did not involve either formal examinations or a tutorial system. In his first 'satyre' we are given a glimpse of his wide reading in his study, separated by a wooden partition from the 'chamber' which he shared with Christopher Brooke:

> Leave mee, and in this standing woodden chest,
> Consorted with these few bookes, let me lye
> In prison, and here be coffin'd, when I dye;
> Here are God's conduits, grave Divines . . .

together with more secular literature: the works of Aristotle 'the Philosopher' who was also 'Nature's Secretary', the writings of statesmen and the 'gathering Chronicles' of historians, together with 'Giddie fantastique Poëts of each land'. The Latin poets almost certainly included Horace, who was to some extent imitated in this 'satyre'. No law books were mentioned.

Donne was later to criticize himself for having neglected legal studies in his youth; he blamed his 'immoderate' desire for wider knowledge. But his contempt for lawyers could be fierce. In his second 'satyre' he dismissed 'men which chuse Law practise for meere gaine' as worse prostitutes than 'imbrothel'd strumpets'. He mocked them for being unable to woo a woman with any words except legal jargon. (He had a particular lawyer-poet in mind.) He denounced them for taking bribes and uttering lies which would enable them to accumulate estates while the 'old landlords' were left to decline and 'winds in our ruin'd Abbeys rore'.

The young Donne must have spent time writing about lawyers which he ought to have spent reading laws, but this was surely excusable, for in the 1590s it was fashionable for young poets to mock the corrupt older men who had got the jobs in the law courts and at the royal court – and Donne was ahead of the pack. He must have seen that he had it in him to be a poet equal or superior to any contemporary. The first volume of Spenser's *Faerie Queene* was published in 1590, and Sidney's *Astrophel and Stella* in 1591. Shakespeare's less fanciful *Venus and Adonis* and *The Rape of Lucrece* followed in 1593–94. Marlowe's *Hero and Leander*, even closer to Donne's own earthy eroticism, was not printed until 1598 but seems to have circulated quite widely before that. Although (like a courtier such as Sidney) Donne was not interested in being printed in his lifetime, it is highly probable that he thought he could write as least as well as any of his contemporaries, with a style of his own, rejecting the Spenser–Sidney belief that the purpose of poetry was to 'delight' by sweetness and to 'teach' by high morality. The temptation to quote his love poetry must be resisted for the time being but here it can be said that his originality entitled Donne to laugh in his second 'satyre' at second-rate poets. These, he said, 'digested' the work of the masters whom they imitated, but they produced as their own work only 'excrement'.

Bishops would have agreed with Donne's estimate of the work of one fellow poet in the Inns of Court, John Davies, although no doubt they would have avoided the reference to dung. Davies dedicated to his friend Richard Martin a poem called *Orchestra*, a celebration of the decorum in the dancing of that age, but in 1598 he was expelled from the legal profession because in a fit of rage he violently assaulted Martin. Next year Davies made another mistake: he arranged for his *Epigrams and Elegies* to be printed. They were excessively improper; the bishops were scandalized; the hangman was ordered to burn them publicly; and the censor was told to forbid the publication of any further pornography.

Ben Jonson, who unlike Davies was a major poet, told William Drummond that Donne had written 'all his best pieces' by the age of 25. Jonson could be imprecise about dates, and could not be sure of knowing everything which Donne had written, but having been born in the same year he had reason to be jealous of what his contemporary had achieved: in 1597 he was imprisoned for his share in the writing of a low comedy which the authorities had found offensive, and in 1598 he was so dispirited that he made a brief return to his first job, as a bricklayer. Next year he bounced back into writing plays – and he dedicated one of them to the Inns of Court, 'the Noblest Nurserie of Humanity and Liberty in this Kingdom'.

Clearly Donne found the freedom in Lincoln's Inn a 'Nurserie' for his growth as a poet (if not as a lawyer), but it was not a nursery isolated from the sorrows of the world. For much of his time there it was surrounded by a London being massacred by epidemics. A verse-letter 'To Mr T. W.' reported that in every street 'Infections follow, overtake and meete'. In its context that sounds as if this young man did not expect to meet his own death and another such letter 'To Mr E. G.' claimed that 'by staying in London' Donne was bored rather than distraught. The theatres and the streets had no life in them and the only amusements on offer were the unsubtle sport of the baiting of a tethered bear by dogs – plus such fun as could be provided by the course in law:

> Our Theatres are fill'd with emptines.
> As lancke and thin is every street and way
> As a woman deliver'd yesterday.
> Nothing whereat to laugh my spleen espyes
> But bearbaitings or Law exercise.

But in 1593 Donne's public face had to be brave because, as he told a closer friend, Rowland Woodward, in his personal life he experienced 'Griefe which did drowne me'. His sorrow tempted him to write bitterly 'satirique' poetry 'in skorne of all'. For his only brother died tragically.

In his first published book, the *Pseudo-Martyr* of 1610, Donne lets us see the family in his background. He then recalled how difficult it had been for him to 'blot out certaine impressions of the Romane religion' because in his early years a family which 'by nature had a power and superiority over my will', and later tutors who had impressed him 'by their learning and good life', had naturally enough made him think of himself as a Roman Catholic. In 1610 he was still willing to make public his pride in members of his family who had been courageous in their refusal to deny their faith. He was 'derived from such a stocke and race, as, I beleeve, no family (which is not of far longer extent and greater branches) hath endured and suffered more in their persons and fortunes, for obeying the Teachers of Romane Doctrine, than it hath done'. Indeed, 'I have been ever kept awake in a meditation of Martyrdome'.

In his unpublished book *Biathanatos* he called the martyred Thomas More, whose sister was his own mother's great-grandmother, 'a man of the most tender and delicate conscience that the world saw since St Augustine'. Like More, Donne's grandfather John Heywood had incurred the wrath of Henry VIII. He had been imprisoned in the Tower of London, told that he was to be dragged through the streets to execution as a traitor, and fastened to a wicker hurdle for this grim purpose, before being reprieved. Perhaps this had been a sick joke, for the victim was a comic entertainer well known for his witty sallies which in happier circumstances had entertained the royal court. When Elizabeth I made England officially Protestant, John Heywood fled abroad. Donne's great-uncle Thomas Heywood had been seriously executed; his uncle Ellis Heywood had been forced into exile; and another uncle, Jasper Heywood, had been the leader of the Jesuit mission to England and had very nearly joined his fellow Jesuits in a very painful death.

In Oxford Ellis and Jasper Heywood had been promising scholars before accepting a vocation as Catholic priests. In 1610 Donne remembered being present at 'a Consultation of Jesuits in the Tower' and almost certainly the occasion had been when his mother took him along with another Jesuit in order to visit the imprisoned Jasper and to discuss a petition to the Crown for toleration. The government felt too threatened to be tolerant: captured Catholics could be tortured severely, taken through the streets amid derision, hanged, cut down alive and butchered by the hangman, and in the reign of Elizabeth almost three hundred people suffered all or most of these cruelties. It seems that the reason why Jasper was allowed to go into exile rather than subjected to this fate was twofold: he had been less hotheaded than the Catholics who were actively planning to support a foreign invasion, and the savagery in the public executions of priests had aroused indignation abroad, causing Elizabeth's chief minister (Burghley) to write a defensive pamphlet about *The Execution of Justice in England.*

For John Donne the year 1593 started well. He was assured of his popularity with his fellow students when they elected him as Master of the Revels and he could look forward to receiving and spending the remainder of his father's legacy to him: in June he would be 21. But early in May came tragedy. His brother Henry, who was now in Thavies Inn preparing to join him in Lincoln's Inn, was loyal to their mother's strong faith. He showed this when a Catholic priest, William Harrington, visited him in his chamber. The young man confessed his sins, presumably in the knowledge that this had been made an act of treason under a law of 1571. Presumably after a tip-off by an informer, government agents arrested both men. As previously instructed, Harrington denied being a priest even under torture, but in his own pain Henry made the fatal admission. No doubt full of self-condemnation, he was imprisoned and soon died from the epidemic then raging in the sordid cells. Next February Harrington was executed publicly and barbarously: he struggled with the hangman before being disembowelled.

Whether or not John Donne had already drifted far away from his mother's strong faith while enjoying the pleasures of Italy, Spain or London, it seems probable that the shocks of these terrible deaths in 1593–4 clinched his decision not to be identified with his family's martyr-making legacy. He would no longer 'bind my conscience to any locall religion' (as he was to put it in 1610) if the religion of his inheritance meant being regarded, certainly penalized and possibly executed, as a traitor to his country.

The plague which had killed his brother gave Donne some free time during the second half of 1593, when the normal activities of Lincoln's Inn were suspended, and he seems to have plunged into theological study, purchasing and heavily marking the recently published long defence of Roman Catholicism by Cardinal Bellarmine. He could show a heavily marked copy to an Anglican clergyman who interrogated him. Later he could say that he had 'surveyed and digested the whole body of divinity controverted between ours and the Roman Church' before deciding that the Church of England was 'ours'. Meanwhile he conformed to the government's religion outwardly, his comments on Bellarmine seem to have satisfied his Anglican examiner, and the principle which governed his private thoughts was stated in his third 'satyre', a poem which no doubt he kept private: 'doubt wisely'.

His name disappears from the records of Lincoln's Inn at the end of 1594. He was a student there that autumn and was elected Steward of Christmas, but he paid a fine and declined that responsibility for the festivities. (It was the first Christmas to be celebrated in the traditional style since 1591; at last London had a brief freedom from plague.) More importantly, he had decided not to complete the long course required before admission to the legal profession. The only surviving trace of his life in 1595 is that in July he employed young Thomas Danby as a servant, but after eighteen months Danby vanished together with some of Donne's clothes. The probability is that Donne was living in lodgings near the Inn, spending his time as he wished and also spending his inheritance from his father, which had been increased by the share previously reserved for Henry. This was a period when he was free to write and to add to the experiences which directly or indirectly equipped him to write about sexual relationships.

What he wrote was not mere 'excrement' but its coarseness is shown up if we compare it with Shakespeare's light-hearted masterpiece, *A Midsummer Night's Dream*, which was certainly written about this time and may have been first performed at an aristocratic wedding in 1594. It is of course a celebration of marriage, full of joy as well as humour. There is a great contrast between this play and a poem which Donne seems to have written for performance during the students' revels at midsummer in 1595.

His 'Epithalamion made at Lincoln's Inn' was a 'marriage song' superficially like Shakespeare's play, and there seem to be mocking references to Spenser's lushly romantic *Epithalamium*, published in the first half of 1595. Unlike plays and poems which went down well at the court of Elizabeth (where it was the custom for courtiers to pretend that they were in love with the Virgin Queen), Donne's poem is crudely for men only. Unlike more formal plays and poems which invoked divine blessings on the happiness of lovers who married, this 'marriage song' gloats over the deflowering of a virgin who is not allowed to speak, partly because the words accompany a charade in which the part of the bride is taken by a man. This script appears to be designed to raise cheers from tipsy and hormone-infested young bachelors who recite the refrain

> *Today put on perfection and a woman's name.*

At first the girl is told that 'your solitary bed nourseth sadnesse' and is a grave for 'that warme balme-breathing thigh'. Then 'Daughters of London' (who, it is hoped, will be 'our Golden Mines' when they marry these young gentlemen) are invited to attend the marriage of a girl who is 'faire and rich'. After further remarks about her sexually available body, the bridegroom comes and she is sacrificed

> Like an appointed lambe, when tenderly
> The priest comes on his knees t'embowell her.

Thus Donne demonstrated that he was one of the lads, but he had still to prove to his little social world that he was a Protestant fit for employment by the Crown. This he did by becoming one of the gentlemen who volunteered for active service in naval expeditions in 1596–97, episodes in the long war between England and Spain. Sending a verse-letter to a friend, he said frankly that his motives were mixed, for he himself did not know

Whether a rotten state, and hope of gaine,
Or to disuse me from the queasie paine
Of being belov'd, and loving, or the thirst
Of honour, or faire death, out pusht me first . . .

By now he needed money and hoped to have a share in the prizes to be gained by looting Cadiz or capturing some of the fleet bringing to the Azores treasure from the mines controlled by the Spaniards in South America. But his fifth 'elegie' sounded heroic. It seems to have been addressed to a mistress, real or imaginary, before embarking on the voyage into Cadiz and danger. He hoped to find her still faithful when he returned 'weather-beaten' with 'Sun-beams tann'd', perhaps with hands torn by having to row with 'rude oares', perhaps with the 'blew staines' of gunpowder on his skin, perhaps with his whole body a 'sack of bones'. He may have genuinely hoped to impress a woman when he returned as a veteran of war, but he does not impress modern readers by the brutality of his short poem which gloats over the burning of the Spanish flagship, when some men 'leap'd forth' and were killed by the English guns and others who remained on board were drowned when the ship went down. The behaviour of the English troops when they briefly occupied Cadiz was also brutal; their vandalism was directed with a special zest against the images of Popery.

More impressive poems reported to Christopher Brooke two near-disasters during the second (futile) voyage, to the Azores. One was a storm when winds and waves roared, the sun was hidden by clouds and rain, and the sails were torn into rags looking like the strips of flesh on the corpse of 'one hang'd in chaines, a year ago'. Another was very different: the English fleet was becalmed, with the ocean as smooth as a mirror. Some of the sailors hung out clothes to dry and some dived into the hot sea, to find it a 'brimstone Bath' which made them 'parboyl'd wretches'. No one had the energy to clean the ship, so that 'feathers and dust' lay 'in one place . . . today and yesterday'. Donne thought about poetry during these experiences at sea and he described them in imagery to be expected not from a sailor but from a very urbane and very superior observer. His earliest letter to survive was written in Plymouth in 1597. It complains about the 'stinke of 150 land soldiers' and 'so very very bad weather' during the voyage which had landed him back in a port where prices were too high.

He had learned that he was not cut out to be a military hero. His poem 'Love's Warre' exhibited a total lack of patriotism (which may have been one reason why it was not printed before 1802) but was realistic about the field in which he might still hope to make conquests. He has no wish to serve in the wars in the Netherlands or in Ireland, or in any more naval expeditions:

> Long voyages are long consumptions,
> And ships are carts for executions.

He prefers the 'more glorious service' of love, not war:

> Here let mee warr; in these armes let mee lye;
> Here lett mee parlee, batter, bleede, and dye.
> Thy armes imprison me, and myne armes thee,
> Thy hart thy ransome is: take myne for mee . . .
> There men kill men, we'll make one by and by.

These expeditions had brought him more than an experience of war and a renewed appetite for peaceful pursuits in and out of bed. During the second voyage he made friends with a fellow volunteer who was the son of Sir Thomas Egerton, Lord Keeper of the Great Seal, Master of the Rolls and a Privy Councillor close to Queen Elizabeth whose messages he communicated to the House of Lords (before being made Lord Chancellor in 1603). Through this friendship a door was opened into the great world, for Donne was employed as one of the great man's secretaries. He was now at last an insider. In his second 'satyre' he said that both Papists and poets seemed to be 'poore, disarm'd, . . . not worth hate' and he had belonged to both categories. Now he had his foot on the ladder of promotion and Egerton made a specially suitable patron, partly because he was fond of poetry and poets and partly because he had himself been listed as a 'recusant' or non-conformist Papist as recently as the 1570s. So Donne was now an established civil servant and a letter which has survived from Sir William Cornwallis, in verse suggesting a visit to a theatre, was addressed 'to my ever to be respeckted friend Mr John Done'. He was especially excited to be involved in plans to reduce the corruption and delays in the law courts. In his fifth 'satyre', which he probably showed to a delighted employer, he added to a denunciation of the law courts contempt for the dishonesty both of their officers and of many of the plaintiffs. But whereas the Roman poet Juvenal had ended his satire attacking lawyers with a lament that nothing could be done, Donne expressed delight that Queen Elizabeth was now willing for the abuses to be brought to her attention, and that Egerton was the ideal reformer:

> Greatest and fairest Empresse, know you this?
> Alas, no more than Thames' calme head doth know
> Whose meades her armes drown, or whose corne o'rflow:
> You Sir, whose righteousnes she loves, whom I
> By having leave to serve am most richly
> For service paid, authoriz'd, now beginne
> To know and weed out this enormous sinne.

Like many others, he seems to have been full of genuine admiration for Egerton. He was to send a copy of his first published book to the great man with a letter saying that 'those poor sparks of Understandinge or Judgement which are in mee were derived and kindled from you'. That tribute does not seem to be an example of the artificial flattery of which he was capable; the poetry which he had already written was proof of his 'wit' or cleverness but his life so far had left room for the development of wisdom, and he had been lucky to be given the education provided by daily contact with a wise and honest senior who truly deserved to be 'respeckted'. But letters surviving from these busy days show that his mind was not wholly absorbed in reforms of the law courts. He found time to write a good deal of poetry. He also enjoyed gossip about the royal court, although in his fourth 'satyre' he expressed a lofty scorn for a courtier:

> Of triviall household trash he knowes; He knowes
> When the Queene frown'd, or smil'd, and he knowes what
> A subtle States-man may gather of that;
> He knowes who loves; whom; and who by poyson
> Hasts to an Office's reversion . . .

With the support of that 'subtle States-man', Egerton, he seemed to be hastening to wealth himself, and as a first instalment he accepted a grant by the queen of some land in Lincolnshire. His acceptance has been thought to be out of keeping with his morally severe denunciations of lawyers and courtiers who built up estates out of corruption, but actually he was given only the rent received from land which belonged to his grandfather John Heywood, then a 'Papist' in exile, and it is probable that he handed the money over (a practice which the government allowed). Anyway a grant of land would have been part of a system which rightly or wrongly seemed to be incurable. A poet could mock the courtiers (as both Donne and Ben Jonson did) but could look to the court for rewards: the mockery was a standard practice, but so was a poet's need to live.

For centuries the main function of a king had been to lead the nobility with an eye on the need to defend, and if possible expand, the realm. For such government as there was, he had been served by literate and numerate 'clerks' mostly supplied and rewarded by the Church. He had relied on the chief landowners being able to produce soldiers, and on the richer laity and clergy being willing to produce subsidies, to respond to an emergency. Now there seemed to be a continuous emergency, for in an age of inflation the Crown needed not soldiers in person but more and more money, yet Parliament was never willing to vote for adequate taxation. One answer seemed to be the sale of offices under the Crown. From the Church the Crown now needed not 'clerks' but yet more money, so that clergymen wishing to become bishops were expected to hand over money or at least to agree that estates which had financed their predecessors should now support laymen favoured or used by the Crown. Laymen appointed to positions in the royal court or the government were still paid only minimal salaries. They were expected to reimburse themselves either by receiving grants (of land or commercial privileges) from the Crown, or by welcoming bribes from individuals. The corruption could make the Crown's agents liable to being deserted by the Crown: thus King James was to abandon Francis Bacon, his extremely clever Lord Chancellor, when the House of Commons was determined on his fall. A similar fate was to overtake the Earl of Suffolk, who while Lord Treasurer and embezzler-in-chief had built himself a palace at Audley End. But discreet corruption did not cause too much scandal: thus Robert Cecil, now Earl of Salisbury, was to build himself two palaces while in charge of the administration and died at the height of respectability, having given one of these palaces to the king. Under this system, everything depended on access to the Crown's favour.

Everyone knew that the system was corrupt and the young Donne was only one of the many writers who said so, in private or more dangerously in public, but no one clearly saw any realistic alternative – and Donne was only one of the clever young men who were willing to join the system. At the time his conscience may have troubled him, and later on, when he looked back from a pulpit, it clearly did. 'We make Satyrs', he preached, 'and we looke that the world should call that wit, when God knows that this is great part self-guiltinesse and we do but reprehend things which we ourselves have done; we cry out upon the illnesse of the times and we make the times ill' (7:408). However, in October 1601 Donne seems to have had no difficulty about accepting an offer of a seat in Parliament: he was one of the two members 'elected' to represent a small borough in Northamptonshire which was controlled by the Lord of the Manor, Egerton's son John.

He felt close to the top of politics when the Earl of Essex, formerly his commander in the war ('Our Earle' in a poem), formerly also the queen's favourite, disobeyed her by leaving his command of the army in Ireland without her permission, burst into her bedroom unannounced, fell very sharply from favour, was confined to York House as Egerton's unwilling guest, was allowed back to his own house, staged a farcical mini-rebellion, and was executed. Donne does not seem to have been greatly moved by the fate of Essex, who with his fellow-commander and great rival Ralegh had once seemed to embody the ambition and glamour of Elizabethan England immediately after the defeat of the Armada. But now there was another age and Donne called it an 'age of rusty iron' in his fifth 'satyre'. At Christmas 1599 he wrote to his friend Henry Wotton that the impetuous earl and the new age could not reach an understanding. Essex was not 'mist' in the circle which now had power and 'he plods on to his end'. That was also to be true about Ralegh, who was to be imprisoned for thirteen years and executed for treason in the next reign.

As Essex met his end Egerton's secretary was not going to stick his neck out – whereas Wotton, who had been employed by Essex, got in a panic and fled abroad. What did concern Donne was the general atmosphere of depression and intrigue as Elizabeth decayed towards death without naming any successor and without appointing anyone who had the combination of efficiency with charisma needed to be virtually her deputy in her old age. Robert Cecil, the son of the Lord Burghley who had been her indispensable chief minister in many happier years, had taken over from his father and was to keep the administration going until 1612; he was a tirelessly industrious worker but also a man on the make financially and a hunch-backed dwarf. The 1590s were a time of epidemics and bad harvests; the towns were almost as full of disease as of people and in the countryside about half the population lived below the level of decent subsistence. It was a time of an expensive and inconclusive war with Spain. And it was a time when the joyless creed of Calvinism was accepted by the more active of the clergy in the Church of England. This was the 'age of rusty iron' which inspired Donne to begin a long poem about evil in the history of the world.

It has often been thought that this poem, which after 520 lines was never completed, was to have ended with an attack either on the queen or on Robert Cecil. (Sir Herbert Grierson went so far as to say that it was 'obvious' that Elizabeth was Donne's target, but on p. 152 I shall argue that an error introduced by an editor or printer accounts for one reference to the target being 'shee' not 'hee'.) This seems very unlikely, for an ambitious civil servant such as Donne would have been mad to risk writing such an insult even if he kept it from the printer – and what he wrote included an 'Epistle' to the reader. Ben Jonson told William Drummond that the poem was to have ended by attacking John Calvin and this seems much more likely. It was safe to insult the Reformer: he was a foreigner and (since 1564) he was dead. It would be understandable if Donne wanted to express forcibly his strong disapproval of Calvinist influence over the Church of England. He was still enough of a Catholic to refer contemptuously to 'arguing' as 'heritiques' game' and to 'Luther and Mahomet' as evil figures in the part of the poem which he did finish, and Calvin would have seemed even more deplorable: Donne must have hated the destruction of order and beauty in church life and the cruelty of the doctrine that the great majority of the human race had been predestined by God to hell. Presumably the evil soul could migrate to Calvin after Luther's death (in 1546) – or possibly Donne, who was never entirely logical, did not fully think out the consequences of making both of these contemporaries 'prisons of flesh' to this one soul.

Calvin would fit the sarcastic passage in the poem which promised that 'the crowne and last straine of my song' would concern the evil influence over England of

> the great soule which here amongst us now
> Doth dwell, and moves that hand and tongue and brow,
> Which, as the Moone the sea, moves us . . .

Although Elizabeth was no Calvinist she had appointed and supported an Archbishop of Canterbury, John Whitgift, who in 1595 had been the chief architect of nineteen doctrinal statements called the Lambeth Articles. These constituted an attempt to push the Church of England into the official adoption of an extreme form of Calvinism. Since the Thirty-nine Articles had been accepted in 1571 as the Church's doctrinal position, already there had been a move quite far in this direction. Article 17 had affirmed the belief that by predestination God had decided to deliver some people 'chosen in Christ' from the 'damnation' awaiting 'mankind' – and had made this decision 'before the foundations of the world were laid'. However, it had not been made clear whether this was God's general policy or the choice of specified individuals before they were born, to be saved or damned. The Lambeth Articles were not so reticent: their teaching was that God had made a very long list of those destined to the torments of hell and had made that list before he made the world. The only question left unsettled was whether such a God could accurately be called good.

Five years after the Lambeth Articles Donne may well have feared that the Church to which he was obliged to conform was being tied to this repulsively cruel doctrine. He probably did not know that the queen refused to be impressed by her archbishop's tough theology although she used him as a tough administrator. He no doubt expected the ageing Elizabeth to be succeeded on the throne of England by a king from Scotland, the most thoroughly Calvinist country in Europe, but he cannot have been sure that this next Supreme Governor of the Church of England would leave the somewhat ambiguous Thirty-nine Articles untouched and try to make Scotland more Anglican. Least of all can he have expected King James to become his own patron after his ordination as an Anglican priest. Around 1600 he may well have thought that the 'great soule' of Calvin was gaining power over the mind of England, as a climax in the history of evil. It would not be surprising if this prospect helped to make him feel as gloomy as any Calvinist.

His poem was called *Metempsychosis* (Greek for 'transmigration of the soul') and had 'The Progresse of the Soule' as its sub-title. The tone is cynical and the view of the world is bleak. It is possible to gain a different impression after a careful study of the poem; one scholar who edited it with a commentary, Walter Milgate, found in it the 'high spirits', 'the grotesque fun and the sardonic humour', of a merry wit who enjoyed writing a 'mock-epic'. But probably few readers have found the poem amusing. Donne was never lyrical about nature but here he was relentless in the description of nature as a vast battlefield. There is no supervision by a commander; *Metempsychosis* was the nearest that Donne came to atheism. Endlessly one creature kills another, before being killed. Details in this poem can vividly represent a creature, its birth, its skill and its fate, but the 'progresse' of the sub-title is lacking both in the sordid process itself and in the poet's account of it. There seems to be an anticipation of the gloomiest emotions about the discovery of evolution 'red in tooth and claw' by the Victorians. But Donne was not a Darwinian scientist; he was a poet who at least in some moods (when he was alone in the evening after work?) was depressed by the 'age of rusty iron' and worried about his own future in a world of ruthless rivalries between competitors and factions. In the poem he addressed questions about himself to 'Great Destiny'. Would the new century bring him 'steepe ambition' or 'sleepie povertie'? For the time being he had enough ambition and self-confidence to boast:

> For though through many streights, and lands I roame,
> I launch at Paradise and I saile towards home

– 'home' being presumably Paradise itself in the long run, but more immediately London, where he hoped for steep promotion. At any rate the poem was intended to reach port with 'anchors laid' in the Thames.

From his wide reading he had picked up a notion which he now used as his poem's central 'conceit': the idea of the transmigration of a single soul through plants, beasts and people. The soul making this journey was the soul of evil and it began in the apple which infected Eve and Adam. Then it travelled through a mandrake (a legendary plant which fascinated Donne), a sparrow, a swan, a fish, an oyster-catcher, a whale, an elephant, a mouse, a wolf, a dog, an ape, the 'silly' Siphatecia who is raped by the ape, and Themech, 'sister and wife to Caine'. Some unity is given to this drama without a plot by the frequent references to sexual intercourse. Promiscuity is not condemned in the passage about the cock sparrow, and the wolf is not rebuked for the rape of the dog, but when human beings are involved there is a flicker of morality. Thus when Adam takes the fatal apple from Eve it is said that

> Man all at once was there by woman slaine . . .

About Themech their daughter it is said that she made a suitable 'sister and wife' to their son Cain the first murderer, for

> she knew treachery,
> Rapine, deceit, and lust, and ills enow
> To be a woman.

The date when the poem was abandoned was given as 16 August 1601. It was dedicated, it seems sarcastically, to 'Infinity' and it ended with what seems to be a reference to his own very uneasy position. Donne reflected that since he was the first murderer Cain was 'cursed' – yet according to the Bible most of 'those arts whence our lives are blest', 'plowing, building, ruling and the rest', were invented by Cain or his descendants. So was Cain good or bad? The truth was complicated and it had to be left to public opinion, not a reliable judge, to decide the difference between good and evil:

> Ther's nothing simply good, nor ill alone,
> Of every quality comparison
> The onely measure is, and judge, opinion.

No doubt Donne grew tired as he contemplated the almost infinite number of years and poetic lines (rhyming) through which the soul of evil would have to travel as it moved from Eve's apple to whoever was intended as the poem's climax. Near the beginning of the poem he had expressed a fear that its completion would take him thirty years ('sixe lustres') and bring 'expense of braine and spirit', and as he wrote he may well have seen more clearly that the whole project had been a mistake. But almost certainly the end was so abrupt because the poet had been overwhelmed by an event: he had fallen deeply in love. And he was afraid that because the woman he loved came from a very wealthy family, he would be treated as a criminal, almost as another Cain.

In a sense the Anne who was his Eve killed him, because marrying her was to kill his career when 'opinion' judged that their marriage had been a crime against the structure of society. But in August 1601 he saw no point in trying to write the rest of *Metempsychosis.* He was revising his fashionably male cynicism about what it means 'to be a woman', at least in one instance. He was now determined to marry this glorious woman, whatever the opinion of society and whatever the cost to him.

3 Winter-seeming

So, lovers dreame a rich and long delight,
But get a winter-seeming summer's night.
'Love's Alchymie'

He had fallen in love with his employer's niece, Anne More. It was a romance wide open to condemnation, for she was his superior in the class system, and having spent all the capital left to him by his father he had no money with which to maintain her in the grand style to which she was accustomed. Moreover, it could be said that he had taken advantage of his employment in a position of trust in order to seduce an innocent girl – as he had (rumour said) treated other women in his history. He was almost thirty years old, some five years past what was then the average age for men getting married, and she was approximately half his age, having led a very privileged and sheltered life. He must have understood how society was likely to react. Yet it was a romance and it would be natural for him to hope that he was entering a 'rich and long delight'.

They were married in secret not long before Christmas 1601. He must have known the legal situation, which was that the Church had retained from the Middle Ages jurisdiction in matrimonial cases. The ecclesiastical courts were therefore able to decide that any marriage was valid if the partners had freely consented and had consummated their union, if the man was over fourteen years of age and the woman over twelve, and if a priest had officiated. But in this case it would be folly to rely on an exemption from the rules being granted after the event, for this marriage was highly irregular. The canon law of the Church of England, soon to be restated in the revised code of 1604, prohibited marriages of persons under the age of 21 without the consent of their parents and of all marriages without announcements ('banns') in the parish churches of both partners on three Sundays, and the insistence on 'the banns of all that are to be married together' was plain in the Book of Common Prayer. It was also contrary to the custom of the Church to marry during the solemn season before Christmas (Advent). But even more to the point was the fact that Donne had defied the conventions of the society to which the Church belonged. And what happened was what Donne must have feared. When told about the secret wedding about two months later, Anne's father exploded in anger. He refused to part with the large financial dowry which would normally have accompanied such a bride. Instead, he demanded that the marriage should be annulled. His influence was such that the bridegroom, the officiating priest and the rising lawyer who had acted as witness were all thrown into prison, and Egerton dismissed his scandalous secretary. (The details will be discussed on pp. 254–9 and 283.)

Donne was shattered. In 1599 he had boasted to a friend: 'I have alwayes been either so strong or so stubborne against any assault of fortune, that she hath rather pickt quarrells with my friends than with my self.' Now he needed all the friends he could get to sustain him with money or at least encouragement. After a time the Archbishop of Canterbury's court accepted his marriage, his father-in-law's rage diminished and in 1606 money was produced for the modest support of Anne and a frequently growing brood of children. Moreover, Donne found new patrons in wealthy friends who came to the rescue or aristocratic ladies who were interested in flattering or teasing poems. For ten years, however, he had no patron who could afford to be lavish and until his ordination as a priest at the start of 1615 he had no regular job.

This may seem strange because he was so able, but in the universities student numbers had been enlarged, mainly in order to train Protestant preachers or civil servants. England was now oversupplied with graduates who had no wish to preach but who did compete for the kind of job which Donne needed for the exercise of his talents and the upkeep of his family. Almost all such positions were in the gift of the Crown or of the leading courtiers, and it was not surprising that appointments went to men who had not scorned society's conventions. This was particularly true about any job for which a half-trained lawyer and secretary such as Donne might apply. And one of the many reasons which he could have given for not 'going into business' was that really profitable commerce depended on monopolies granted by the Crown to favourites. Industry above the level of the cottage (or Donne's father's manufacture of kitchen utensils) scarcely existed: Francis Bacon's *Advancement of Learning* was published in 1605 with its vision of a brave new world transformed by science-based technology, but Bacon himself remained a lawyer – and a corrupt one.

It may also seem strange that, given empty days and years, Donne did not dedicate himself to the development of his gifts as a poet by tackling a large subject and producing the masterpiece which *Metempsychosis* was not. We may think of Edmund Spenser's *Faerie Queene*, achieved in the 1590s, when that poet had far less leisure than the unemployed Donne, or of George Chapman's magnificent translation into English verse of Homer's *Iliad* and *Odyssey*, completed in 1615 after labour covering some twenty years during which small sums of money had to be earned by writing many second-rate plays. But here we are reminded of the limitations of Donne as a poet, recently demonstrated by the failure of the over-ambitious *Metempsychosis.* He was best in short bursts of inspiration and about his own feelings, and he always thought of the main work of his life as being other than writing such poetry. He therefore felt miserable when he had no job which would stretch him in the ordinary business of the world and he occupied his empty hours by writing books in prose – books which fell below the level of the short poems which he also wrote as expressions of his depressed confusion. In the future he was to be fulfilled as a preacher, with a style which combined prose and poetry in outbursts sustained for an hour and with subjects which called for the powerful statement of his own feelings and convictions yet challenged him to submerge (or at least to conceal) the ego in concentration on God. He was to say that his marriage had made him seek God as never before and that his consequent experience of adversity had brought him treasure. But meanwhile he was at a loss.

Donne had sworn to Anne's father, and no doubt also to Anne herself, that he would do his utmost to support her and any children, but as the months and years passed he had to admit that he had become an outsider. The arduous education, the legal training, the abandonment of Roman Catholicism, the expensive volunteering for the Protestant naval expeditions, the work as a civil servant close to the centre of power – all this had come to nothing. Great Destiny had handed him 'sleepie povertie' and being unemployed he had to accept the offer of accommodation which came from his wife's cousin, at Pyrford in Surrey.

In 1603 Elizabeth I died and James VI of Scotland became also James I of England, but so far as we know Donne felt too dispirited to mark the new beginning with a poem. In the excited first months of his reign James created more than nine hundred new knights who could hope for new prosperity, and these included a considerable number of Donne's friends. Among them was Henry Wotton, who was sent to Venice as the English ambassador, at a time when it was hoped that this republic would reject the papacy and ally itself with the Protestants without losing its fabulous wealth and glamour. Wotton's association with the very foolish

Earl of Essex might have done permanent damage to his career, but the Grand Duke of Tuscany had sent him from his exile in Florence to warn King James about a plot; now he could enjoy Venice as his reward.

Another person favoured by the new king was John Davies. He had been readmitted to Lincoln's Inn and to the legal profession less than a year before the dismissal of Donne by Egerton; the Lord Keeper had used his influence in support of Davies, who dedicated poems to him (and also to the old queen and the new king). Donne's fellow poet, who had hurried up to Scotland in order to greet James, was sent to Ireland as the government's chief lawyer; he arranged the transfer of lands to Protestants in Ulster, became Speaker of the parliament, built up a fortune and had a daughter who was to become a countess. He was to die when he had just been appointed Lord Chief Justice. Donne was to preach at that funeral – but the new reign brought no job to him.

The unemployed ex-secretary might have given way to bitter jealousy. Instead he sent Wotton an assurance of good will which congratulated him on the 'activity' to which he had been appointed by 'our good and great King's lov'd hand and fear'd name'. This generous poem ended:

> For mee (if there be such a thing as I)
>   Fortune (if there be such a thing as shee)
> Spies that I bear so well her tyranny
>   That she thinks nothing else so fit for me;
>
> But though she part us, to heare my oft prayers
>   For your increase, God is as neere me here;
> And to send you what I shall begge, his staires
>   In length and ease are alike every where.

When friends saw that Donne was unemployed, ordination in the Church of England was suggested, knowing that he was at heart the man who wrote that poem – and, moreover, that he had an interest in theology. A 'probleme' which exercised his wit was 'Why doe young laymen so much study divinity?' The question was a bit of a joke and the suggested answers were also attempts to be funny, but there was some serious material beneath the surface. Perhaps young laymen think that it is their duty to work at 'divinity' since the clergy are too preoccupied by their hunts for larger incomes ('tending busily Church preferment') to have time for serious theology? Perhaps these young men want to expose the arrogance of the professional preachers who claim to be able to penetrate 'God's secrets'? And perhaps arrogance motivates the young men too, so that what they produce is not really 'divinity' since it has little or nothing to do with God? In this period of enforced leisure Donne was an attentive student of theology, seeking the truth like a man climbing to the top of a mountain, not a man who could talk confidently about God. It is not surprising that he despised those who could: the professionals who (as he wrote privately in a letter) 'write for Religion without it', the enthusiasts who know more than humanity can know, the amateurs who rush in where angels keep their distance.

Another problem was that the lifestyle of the average parish priest held few attractions for a gentleman who was a Christian believer but not keen to be a martyr. Many vicarages resembled small farmhouses, with manual work on the 'glebe' needed to supplement the meagre 'tithes' received from parishioners. In the 1630s Archbishop Laud was to conclude after an investigation that half the clergy lived in real poverty and in the 1620s Donne was to describe how the clergy could look while he pleaded that they should be given more respect. He said that 'Ministers may have clouds in their understanding and knowledge (some may be less learned than others), and clouds in their elocution and utterance (some may have an unacceptable deliverance), and clouds in their aspect and countenance (some may have an unpleasing presence), and clouds in their respect and maintenance (some may be oppressed in their fortunes) . . .' (4:83).

It was an age when favoured clergymen were allowed to draw incomes from more than one parish without residence, on the assumption that no one parish would produce the money needed to maintain such an exceptional clergyman on terms of equality with the gentry – but to obtain this privilege a man needed the patronage of the great and at this time Donne was totally unable to imagine himself as the royal chaplain and court preacher that he was to become. One of the 'problemes' which he set himself, it seems in this period of his life, was 'Why are Courtiers sooner Atheists than men of other Conditions?' The answer which he reached was that 'a familiarity with greatnesse' breeds 'a contempt of all greatnesse'.

In his second 'satyre' he had attacked lawyers who 'lye in every thing': they are

> Like a King's favourite, yea like a King.

And in his fourth 'satyre' he had painted a lurid picture of the royal court – of the court as it had been under a decaying queen, but under the new king the vices of the courtiers became more open, because his servants could imitate a monarch who combined the mind of a genuine scholar with a lifestyle far more coarse than Elizabeth's. Donne had described the courtiers assembling for worship of the monarch: to him it had seemed a 'Masse in jest'. They gathered from riding, from playing handball or tennis, from eating or a visit to the brothels, and like 'Pirats' they were looking out for 'Ladies' whom they could 'board'. Donne had no intention of trying to preach to such a flock: 'Preachers which are Seas of Wits and Arts' might attempt to 'drowne the sinnes of this place' but 'for mee . . . it enough shall bee to wash the staines away'. Merely to be in such company during a visit was 'Purgatorie', even 'hell'. In secret and in Latin he drew up a mock catalogue for a courtier's library: each title in it was a shrewd blow. And in his third 'satyre' he had mocked the Church of England with its 'vile ambitious preachers' such as the royal chaplains.

The laws defending this Established Church were not only cruel (his brother had died because of them) but also new ('still new like fashions' because as recently as 1558, under Queen Mary, the laws had enforced Roman Catholicism). Indeed, they were an insult to God because as Supreme Governor of the Church the monarch had usurped a place which belonged to Christ alone. It seems clear that these had been his real feelings in the reign of Elizabeth (although as a rising civil servant presumably he had kept them to himself and a small circle of friends), and a contempt for the royal court and for the State Church must have been a factor in his mind in the early stages of the new reign.

A combination of factors including that contempt seems to lie behind his refusal of an invitation to move to the financial security offered by a rural parish near York which, because it was large and fertile, provided exceptionally good 'tithes' (a tenth of the produce or other income of the parishioners). This opportunity was offered in 1607 by Thomas Morton, who had enjoyed this income but, having no family, felt no need for it now that he had been appointed Dean of Gloucester. He agreed with the patron (the layman who had the right to appoint in the parish) that the position should be offered to Donne, who (it seems) had helped him to write *Apologia Catholica*, a defence of the Church of England against the papacy and the Jesuits. But Donne said no. One reason may well have been that the life of a parish priest in Yorkshire did not appeal, but Morton had not spent all his time in the parish; the government had encouraged him to be absent often in the course of his writing and speaking as an Anglican apologist. Donne seems to have been willing to provide Morton with material from Roman Catholic sources but not willing to share his Anglican commitment. So for one reason or another he declined the offer – and he could plead unworthiness without much fear of being contradicted. No one who had been sacked by the head of the legal profession for seducing a girl could be blamed for not quickly becoming a parish priest.

Instead he applied for jobs which depended on the king's favour or acquiescence but did not involve Anglican ordination. What they did involve was a longing to end his unemployment – an emotion which temporarily overcame the fact that these positions would have been almost as unsuitable as a rural parish in Yorkshire. Not all his applications can be known now, but the evidence is that this man who had written so scornfully about courtiers wanted to become one, in the household of Queen Anne; that this man who had been so proud of his outspoken independence wanted to join the English civil service in Ireland, where the army of occupation faced rebellion by the 'natives'; and that this man who had been so glad to get ashore after the storm in 1597 wanted to be secretary of the Virginia Company which was trying to plant England's first colony overseas. Less strangely, Donne believed that he was well qualified to follow Henry Wotton as the English ambassador in sophisticated Venice. After each revival of hope, however, he was rejected.

In 1606 he felt able to afford to rent a 'little thin house' in Mitcham and he also hired a small apartment in the centre of his beloved London: it was only an hour's ride away. He took that ride so often that he could boast that his horse knew the direction and he could relax, 'inverted into my self'. He belonged to two clubs which met each month in London taverns, and as he reminded George Gerrard 'that which makes it London is the meeting of friends'. The club meeting in the Mitre enabled him to make or maintain friendships with men of the kind that he had sat with him in the House of Commons but the friends who met in the Mermaid were more literary. Writers such as Jonson, Beaumont and Fletcher gathered for an evening of competition in drinking and wit. Beaumont's lines have often been repeated:

> What things have wee seene
> Done at the Mermaide? heard words that have keene
> Soe nimble and soe full of subtill flame
> As if every one from whom they came
> Had meant to putt his whole witt in a Jeast . . .

For Donne political gossip in the Mitre or jesting in the Mermaid made a precious change but for the most of the time letters had to compensate for absence from friends; 'letters', he claimed, 'mingle Soules'. In one he wrote about the emotions which could overcome him. When dejected by sadness he tried to 'kindle squibs' as if his friends were around him exchanging firecrackers of wit, but even when he had company and was 'transported with jollity' he would think of his misfortunes, his advancing years and his duties as a husband and father, and these thoughts would drag him down as if leads had been attached to his heels.

The house in Mitcham, where he spent most of his time, was needed for his family but he also used it for long periods of reading and writing. Within four years the literary fruit had appeared in the shape of two books stuffed with arguments and quotations. The reading was so intense that after his death papers were found in his Deanery which contained (in Izaak Walton's words) 'the resultance of 1400 Authors, most of them abridged and analyzed in his own hand' and many of these notes (now lost) must date from that time of enforced leisure in the cottage. He wrote to a friend that 'I shall die reading' and be buried in the cellar beneath the study, a 'vault' from which 'raw vapors' already arose. His letters included many such complaints about a house which was his 'hospital' or 'prison'. He once wrote that 'I am oprest with such a sadnes as I am glad of nothing but that I am oprest with it . . . By all this labor of my pen my mind is no more comforted than a condemned prisoner would be to see his chamber swypte & made cleane.' In another letter he moaned: 'When I must shipwrack, I would do it in a Sea, where mine impotencie might have some excuse; not in a sullen weedy lake, where I could not have so much as exercise for my swimming.' He complained of the 'barbarousnesse and insipid dulnes of the Country' and in a poem sent to Henry Wotton he viewed the pleasant greenery of England as a 'desert' where 'men become beasts'. The countryside in spring increased his depression: 'Every thing refreshes and I wither.' In his exile from London he felt 'rather a sicknesse and disease of the world than a part of it'. The contrast with poets who have delighted to paint rural scenes in words which reflect the loveliness, or with the succession of poet-mystics who have found God in nature, could not be greater. But as a reward for this self-inflicted course of intense study, he was able to claim that 'it will please me a little to have had a long funerall, and to have kept myself above ground without putrefaction'.

In a later year he seems to have been thinking about himself in the past, as well as about others who had made no solid contribution to the world, when he preached about the man 'who never comes to the knowledge and consideration, *why* he was sent into this life?' He warned such a man: 'Thou passest out of the world, as thy hand passes out of a basin of water, which may be somewhat the fowler for thy washing in it, but retaines no other impression of thy having been there' (4:149). He did not really believe what he had told Wotton, that his one ambition had become the achievement of contentment, of building 'thine own Palace' within the self as a snail is happy within a shell, of being as inconspicuous as fishes which 'glide, leaving no print where they passe'. In his rural exile he was a fish out of water.

One of the books which he wrote in Mitcham, in or around 1608, was about suicide. In substance as well as style it was too agitated to be clear but it did show that Donne was wrestling with a question: would God forgive him if he decided to end his life?

Eleven years later, when he was going abroad and thought that he might die there, he entrusted this book in manuscript to Sir Robert Ker with the instruction 'publish it not'. 'Reserve it for me if I live, and if I die, I only forbid it the Presse, and the Fire: publish it not, but yet burn it not; and between these, do what you will with it.' If Ker showed it to others, he was to point out that it was 'a Book written by Jack Donne', not by the Doctor of Divinity who had become a leading preacher. He knew that it would cause a scandal if printed in his lifetime because he had refused to conclude that under all circumstances suicide should be reckoned a sin and a crime. Indeed, in the preface he confessed that he had often had this 'sickeley inclination' himself, feeling that 'I have the keyes of my prison in mine own hand'. Writing to Henry Goodyer, he recalled that he had sometimes desired death even in the years of hope 'when I went with the tyde', but the temptation was stronger now. He wanted to 'do something' but 'that I cannot tell what, is no wonder. For to chuse is to do: but to be no part of any body, is to be nothing.' Actually, he could not 'chuse' to belong because no one wanted to employ him. When he talked himself out of despair, it was with the thought that people have within themselves 'a torch, a soul, lighter and warmer'. Changing the metaphor, he reflected that 'we are therefore our own umbrellas'. But his torch did not burn steadily and his umbrella leaked.

The book with the unappetising title *Biathanatos* ('violent death' in Greek) was one long muddle, showing that its author did not know what he really thought. A multitude of quotations displayed Donne's learning in the branch of theology then called 'moral divinity' but not all of the references given were accurate and none of them was integrated into a coherent and convincing argument. It has been suggested that this big book was intended as nothing more than a parody of the tortuous style of 'moral divinity' – although spending so much labour on an unobvious joke seems unlikely, even when an author is so unusual as Donne. It seems more likely that the book was what he called a poem (or collection of poems) which he sent 'To Mr T. W.': 'the strict Map of my misery'. But he saw no escape from this misery: he could not get a job and he could not think of an argument which would justify his suicide.

Although he condemned suicide 'onely or principally' intended 'to avoyd temporall troubles' he never discussed at any depth the problem which interested him personally, which was whether a severe mental depression ever made suicide excusable. Nor did he consider cases of severe mental illness. Nor did he think carefully about voluntary euthanasia during the agony of the terminal stage of a physical illness. Instead he wandered around possible situations in which 'self-homicide' could be followed by 'a charitable interpretation of theyr action' – and he drifted towards the conclusion that it should be forgiven when 'the glory of God is respected and advanced'.

He made the self-sacrifice of Christ the supreme example in this category but he damaged his case by arguing not only that Christ put himself into the hands of his enemies by going to Jerusalem but also that he freely decided when to die on the cross. He could quote Fathers of the Church who had drawn this conclusion from the belief that being sinless, indeed divine, Christ was naturally immortal as Adam and Eve had been before the Fall, but of course the gospels presented Christ's acceptance of his death as being very different from suicide and his agony on the cross as having its natural end, with no escape. Donne had to admit the consistent tradition of Christian condemnation of suicide, and did so without thinking out how what had been condemned differed from the crucifixion which had been the centre of sixteen hundred years of devotion. He could not deny that theologians of the stature of Augustine and Aquinas had denounced suicide whatever the circumstances; Augustine had taught that Christian women should not kill themselves even when the alternative was rape by a barbarian. Since the fourth century teachers of the Church had disagreed at length with the Roman approval of heroic suicides and (at least) since the sixth century Christian burial had been firmly denied to people who committed that sin. Nor could he deny that English law treated an attempt at suicide as a specially grave crime which had to be punished with a special severity, although he claimed that the reason was that so many of the English wanted to commit this crime. (Suicide remained a crime until 1961.) Nor could he deny the general agreement that the laws of Nature and of Reason encouraged self-preservation. All that he felt able to do was hunt around for strange circumstances in which 'self-homicide' might be justified. He entirely missed the fundamental distinction made in Christian thought between a truly heroic death and suicide, which has been that the martyred hero would have chosen to act rightly even if death had not followed. He also failed to anticipate what has become the modern Christian attitude, that a suicide when the balance of the mind has been disturbed by great distress may not have been intended for God's glory but can be expected to receive God's mercy.

He claimed that pelicans and bees kill themselves, but spoiled the effect of this appeal to nature by the generalization that 'most vertuous actions are against Nature'. He drew attention to the praise for courageous suicides by defeated politicians in Ancient Rome or by widows in India, but again spoiled the effect both by admitting that he was writing for Christians and by adding ludicrous stories of suicides for trivial reasons. He pointed out that Samson was praised in the Bible for causing the death of Israel's enemies although this also caused his own, but he made the mistake of taking seriously a story that Judas Iscariot was rescued from his own suicide before he 'grew to so enormous a bignesse . . . that he was not able to withdraw himselfe out of a Coche's way, but had his Gutts crushed out'. He declared that his aim was 'to encourage Men to a just contempt of this Life' but he supplied no convincing answer to the traditional argument that to kill oneself shows a contempt for God's gift of this life. He suggested that 'in some cases, when we were destitute of other meanes, we might be to our selves the stewards of God's benefits, and the Ministers of his Mercyfull Justice', but he 'abstayned purposefully from extending this discourse to particular Rules, or instances, both because I dare not professe my selfe a Master in so curious a syence, and because the Limits are obscure, and steepy, and slippery, and narrow, and every Error deadly'. So he opted out of being useful. But one good thing about this book was that it was never printed in its author's lifetime.

When sending *Biathanatos* to a friend, Donne could claim that he had already shown it to 'some particular friends in both universities'. Their comment had been that 'there was a false thread in it, not easily found', but the book seems worth some attention precisely because it is a tapestry of false arguments, suggesting that around 1608 Donne was near to intellectual, if not to physical, suicide. A real opportunity to guide opinion sensibly had been missed. Although accurate statistics are impossible because many suicides were not reported and many records have been lost, modern researchers have concluded that the religious confusion caused by the Reformation caused the numbers to rise steeply and that after these tragedies the Protestant state enforced punishments which had not often been inflicted in the Middle Ages. A more charitable attitude was not thought to be 'Christian' until the eighteenth or nineteenth century, when the advocacy came mainly from outside the Churches. Before that, the blunt title of the theological response to Donne by Thomas Philipot in 1674 was typical: *Self-homicide Murther*. And since Donne's muddle was the only presentation of an alternative view to take account of theology, *Biathanatos*, first printed in 1647, was reissued in 1700.

A book which was quickly published, *Pseudo-Martyr*, also demonstrated the confusion in Donne's mind but it had a limited success. The number of copies surviving suggests that there was quite a large edition, sold from a bookshop in the courtyard of St Paul's Cathedral in January 1610. In contrast with the lack of current discussion about suicide, this book was a timely contribution to a public debate. After the Gunpowder Plot of 1605 a new oath had been imposed on Roman Catholics, not explicitly demanding their acceptance of the Church of England but making it clear that they rejected the right of the pope to release them from their allegiance to the king. If as instructed by the pope they refused to take this oath, they faced very severe penalties. The king himself published a defence of the oath, with a second book which reprinted the pope's instructions in the belief that merely to read them was to know they were wrong. There were, however, replies from the Roman Catholic side, to which the Anglicans including the great Bishop Andrewes responded. Donne expressed private contempt for at least one of these Anglican efforts (by another bishop) and rushed to do better. He used his accumulated notes to provide quotations and footnotes as impressive as those which had adorned the book on suicide; indeed, he recycled some of that material. But readers appear to have been disappointed and there was no call for a second edition. The only reply which was published came after a delay, in 1613. In it Thomas Fitzherbert was contemptuous, advising Donne to confine himself to writing poems 'wherein he has some talent, and may play the foole without controle'.

Donne was his own sharpest critic but he put his points in a private letter where he confessed that 'I think truly there is a perplexity (as far as I see yet) and both sides may be in justice, and innocence'. On the one hand, 'our State cannot be safe without the Oath', for the Roman Church maintains that its 'Clergie-men' are 'no Subjects, and that all the rest may be none tomorrow'. On the other hand, the 'Supremacy' which the Roman Church claims 'were diminished, if it were limited'. As kings are 'the onely judges of their prerogative', it is also the case that 'Roman Bishops' claim to be enlightened by the Holy Spirit. So may not the bishops as well as the kings be 'good witnesses of their own supremacie?'

In this private reflection Donne discerned the reason why it was at that time futile to hope that arguments which might be set out in a book could solve the problem. The problem was indeed soluble: the king always wished to halt the persecution of his Roman Catholic subjects provided only that they were loyal patriots who obeyed him, and in order to win this prize the leader ('archpriest') of the Roman Catholic clergy since 1598, George Blackwell, recommended that the oath should be taken. But in England public opinion was such that even James had to keep persecution as part of the law throughout his reign, and in Rome the official position was such that Blackwell had to be sacked. Many years had to pass before the average Englishman was prepared to acknowledge that Roman Catholics were decent citizens and before the papacy was prepared to see heretical rulers being obeyed. In England a turning point was to come in 1778, when the Vatican did not veto an arrangement initiated by the Catholic gentry resulting in prayers at Mass for the royal Protestants of the Hanoverian dynasty.

Considerable numbers of Roman Catholics took the post-1605 oath but the arguments which prevailed with them were not theological: they were more related to patriotism and a wish for a life without fines, exclusions and executions. The government offered such conformists little other encouragement. The oath was drawn up during the hysterical aftermath of the Guy Fawkes plot to blow up king and Parliament, when the men convicted of plotting were executed with great barbarity but amid the crowd's cheers outside St Paul's Cathedral, very near Donne's birthplace (he was then abroad). It included words at which any Roman Catholic would blink: 'I do from my heart abhor, detest and abjure as impious and heretical this damnable doctrine and position, that princes which be excommunicated and deprived by the Pope may be deposed or murdered by their subjects or any other whatsoever. And I do believe, and in my conscience am resolved, that neither the Pope nor any person whatsoever hath power to absolve me of this oath or of any part whatsoever.' So the pope must be treated as a heretic and the individual Roman Catholic as someone who was likely not to mean what he or she said on oath. Donne's mother and her new husband were among the Catholics who accepted punishment rather than say that.

Paul V was a pope who did not hesitate to excommunicate the senate of Venice and to demand that the French should withdraw a claim that only God could depose a king. He was preoccupied by enforcing discipline in his own Church, by canonizing the heroes of the Counter-Reformation as saints, and by adding to the physical splendours of Rome. He did not mince his words in his replies to King James. The dispute was between two monarchies both of whom claimed a right given by God to govern the Church and to decide what was moral in politics. And since he was so reluctant to admit in public the existence of this central problem, Donne also failed to say precisely where the frontier between the two jurisdictions ought to be drawn. In chapter 3 he wandered off into an attack on Roman Catholic doctrines and in chapter 5 he derided Franciscans and Jesuits for blind obedience to their spiritual superiors. Elsewhere he extended his case against the papacy into details of medieval and later history, getting into an argument about whether or not the council of Carthage had forbidden the clergy to wear beards in 525. The table of contents promised a chapter on the history of England but in the printed book this did not appear. Also missing was a promised chapter about France.

Donne now assumed that the 'Law of Nature' gave King James an obvious right to demand this oath from his subjects: 'To obey the Prince . . . belongs to us as men.' Obviously he was on strong ground when believing that government is better than anarchy, but obedience in this particular matter raised questions. In his third 'satyre' he had written very differently: God had not given to kings 'blanck-charters to kill whom they hate'. And in his book on suicide he had recorded his private opinion that 'this terme, the Law of Nature, is so variously and unconstantly delivered, as I confesse I read it abundant tymes, before I understand it once'. Then his attitude had been that 'a private man is emperor of himself' because 'the obligation which our conscience casts upon us is of stronger hold . . . than the precept of any superior, whether law or person'. And now his appeal to the Law of Nature had to avoid awkward questions.

He did not say whether that 'law' justified Henry VIII in executing Thomas More – or Thomas More and Henry's daughter Mary in burning Protestants. Nor did he dwell on the fact that the Elizabethan government had tried to end the pope's remaining influence in England not by an appeal to the Law of Nature but by the severe punishment of Roman Catholics, including executions with exceptional cruelty and publicity. Nor did he discuss the relevance of this mysterious law to France, where Henri IV had converted from Protestantism to Catholicism without much religious conviction and was murdered by a Roman Catholic, fanatical and perhaps mad, in this year 1610. He scored debating points but did not win the intellectual victory, for the propaganda war remained in the deadlock where it had been left by Lord Burghley and Cardinal Allen in the 1580s. Elizabeth's first minister Burghley (who like Elizabeth herself had conformed to Roman Catholicism under Queen Mary) had maintained that the purpose of the Protestant government was solely to eliminate traitors, while Rome's chief spokesman William Allen had maintained that the purpose of the Catholic mission in England was solely to feed souls. Theirs, too, had been a dialogue of the deaf.

Pseudo-Martyr was a success with the king, who allowed it to be dedicated to him. Whether he considered it superior to his own contributions to the controversy may be doubted, but it seems that it finally convinced him that Donne would be valuable to the Church of England if he could be persuaded to become a preacher. When the suggestion was put, however, the author pleaded unworthiness and continued to hope for a political job. Izaak Walton was to claim that James had begged Donne to write the book. No doubt there had been some encouragement (permission had to be secured for a dedication to royalty), but the book says that its author hoped to 'ascend' into the king's presence by writing and that he had observed that James had set an example because 'your Majestie had vouchsafed to descend to conversation with your Subjects, by way of your Bookes'.

The third book which came out of the study of the cottage in Mitcham was not long and did not pretend to be serious. Published in 1611, it was a satire on the Jesuits, *Ignatius his Conclave*. Undeniably the Jesuits had laid themselves open to criticism. Their mission to England during and since 1580 had handed the government a victory in the war of propaganda, for the mission could be denounced as a sinister band of priests, trained abroad, who had entered the country in disguise and were recruiting for supporters for a plan to welcome a foreign army and to cause a civil war. Protestant patriots reacted in the way to be expected: for example, blaming the Gunpowder Plot of 1605 on the Jesuits, who had nothing whatever to do with it. The Jesuits all denied that they were traitors, and some of them took their own patriotic acceptance of the Protestant government to the very brink of heresy, but the schools where they were educating the sons of English Catholic families outside England were subsidized heavily by the Spanish government. And within England many Roman Catholics deeply resented the Jesuits' trouble-making interference. These missionaries were the pope's agents, pledged to total obedience to his wishes and responsible directly to him, not to any local bishop or other authority; and what they were told to spread was the official message from the pope in far-away Rome that whatever the dangers might be there must be no arrangement with the Protestant government if any compromise carried with it any recognition of the Church which the government supported. For the clergy who were not Jesuits, the independence of this new and élitist Society of Jesus could be disliked because it created a more-Catholic-than-thou Church within the Church, and the tension became semi-public when there was a dispute between Jesuits and other priests who were imprisoned together in Wisbech. For the laity who faced poverty and imprisonment if they defied the government, with the risk of execution, the Jesuits' own heroism as martyrs was an attitude easier to praise in theory than to imitate in practice.

Donne could have written a devastating book about those Jesuits such as Robert Persons who by dependence on Spain had brought division and danger to the Catholic community in England. Instead he wrote a knock-about comedy, about the arrival of Ignatius Loyola (the founder of the Society of Jesus) in hell, intent on claiming the throne from Satan: the dispute produced a riot, ending only when the Jesuits were invited to make a new hell on the moon. This farce did not even glance at the serious questions raised by the true stories of Loyola himself (whose vision sent missionaries to India, China, Japan and both of the Americas, and in Europe created a large network of schools and colleges) and of his self-sacrificial disciples (including Donne's own uncles). It took no account of the existence within the Society of moderates such as Donne's uncle Jasper Heywood, who even before his imprisonment and release seems to have accepted Elizabeth's political authority. It included no hint that like many other Protestants including some Puritans Donne regularly used methods of meditation taught by Jesuits and scholarly books written by them. (He translated a lovely little poem by a Belgian Jesuit, Angelin Gazet.) It invited cheap laughs against this centrepiece of the Catholic Reformation and even cheaper applause when Donne also sent to hell innovators such as Copernicus (who saw the sun in its true splendour at the centre of our system of planets) and Columbus (who saw American soil on the other side of the frightening ocean). And Robert Persons, who ought to have been the target, was left in his grave in peace.

Donne had thought the public unworthy of a sight of his poetry. Now in giving the public the low-level prose of *Ignatius his Conclave*, he was stooping – and he knew it. In a preface which he half-disguised as 'the Printer to the Reader', he admitted that it was strange for an author of his 'gravity . . . to descend to this kind of writing'. He had, he claimed, been unwilling 'to have this booke published' – which had not prevented him from translating the book from Latin into English. In 1969 a Jesuit, Timothy Healy, was to make the perfect riposte. He bestowed great care and sympathy on the Oxford University Press edition of this scurrilous attack on the Society of Jesus, and in his introduction he claimed that Donne's main objection was to innovations in religion: the Jesuits had been attacked less for being bad than for being new. He quoted one of the most conservative passages in the sermons: 'Old doctrines, old disciplines, old words and formes of speech in his service, God loves best' (2:305). It will be less charitable but more just if Donne's words introducing *Ignatius* are now quoted against him: 'This Booke must teach what humane infirmity is.'

He was to stoop further as his debts mounted. In 1611 a very rich and ambitious gentleman, Sir Robert Drury, provided cash, a job as his secretary during a long foreign holiday, and on their return to London accommodation for the family in a recently built 'bricke howse' in Drury Lane. Donne saw no alternative to having Drury as his patron; indeed, he did all he could to secure this income and housing, in a contact that seems to have begun because his sister lived near the big country house of the Drurys. But like him, Sir Robert was never offered the position in the service of the Crown which he wanted and one reason was that he, too, had a reputation for indiscretion. So Donne's alliance with this politically unfashionable patron was not an avenue to political employment or to a career in the Church. Knowing this, in 1613 he approached Robert Carr, Viscount Rochester and the king's current favourite, saying that he had no existing obligations 'towards any other person in this State'. The response was encouraging: Carr needed secretarial help and, as Donne put it frankly in another letter to him, 'bought' the applicant. (Carr was related to Sir Robert Ker, already mentioned as one of Donne's close friends, but in order to prevent confusion the English version of the Scottish surname is used here.)

He had to pay a price in return for the favours of these patrons and in each case the price was high, costing him his reputation then or later. First we can see what resulted from his relationship with Sir Robert and Lady Drury.

He had to earn their favour by writing three poems, two of them the long poems called 'Anniversaries', consoling them for the loss of their only child, Elizabeth, who had died when aged fourteen. Donne first sent them a 'Funerall Elegie':

> To scape th'infirmities which waite upon
>   Woman, shee went away before sh' was one . . .
> Shee did no more but die; if after her
>   Any shall live, which dare true good prefer,
> Every such person is her delegate.

The parents were consoled and with their encouragement (expressed financially) he wrote at greater length about their daughter's physical and spiritual perfections and about the mourning of the world, which now felt that after her death it faced nothing but decay. These themes were familiar in poems marking the deaths of persons of distinction and Donne had handled them in the past: he was to do so again in the future and some other poets were to admire (and borrow from) his performance when consoling the Drurys. But people for whose opinion Donne cared were critical because the person now being commemorated was an obscure girl, because he wrote more than a thousand lines of verse allegedly about the cosmic disaster of her death, and because many of his lines consisted of flattery which was gross even by the standards of courtly poetry in that age.

Ben Jonson in particular rebuked Donne. As a professional writer he was willing to turn his hand to this kind of job connected with a funeral but it was his practice to say something substantial about the deceased. Donne did not attempt to describe Elizabeth Drury, partly because as he confessed 'I never saw the Gentlewoman'. Instead he very quickly linked her death with a much wider theme: the need to despise the world and to seek the joy of heaven. Jonson bluntly told his friend that 'if it had been written of ye Virgin Mary it had been something' but since it ascribed to the girl a place in the universe usually reserved for Christ himself this exercise in flattery was 'full of Blasphemies'.

Donne wrote to a more sympathetic friend admitting that at least the printing of these poems had been a mistake: 'I confesse I wonder how I declined to do it, and do not pardon myself.' He defied anyone to find faults in the dead girl but 'I cannot be understood to have spoken just truths'. He told Jonson (according to Jonson) that he had 'described the idea of a Woman and not as she was'. Whatever may have been meant by that much discussed phrase, a clearer response was made to the criticism: it had been the poet's intention, declared in both 'Anniversaries', to write further poems in an annual series but the decision was made to write no more. And it seems fair to say that the whole project was a great opportunity missed. The first 'Anniversarie' had a theme familiar in Christian literature (or at least, familiar before the eighteenth century): contempt for the world. The second had another: the consolation offered by the hope of heaven. But it seems that at this stage of his life the deepest concern in Donne's own spirituality was his relationship with Christ; this was to be expressed in his famous poem inspired by Good Friday in 1613. In the 'Anniversaries' Christ was never mentioned. Donne's masterpiece might have been a long poem about humanity's relationship with Christ but this was never written. (The 'Anniversaries' will be discussed further on pp. 218–22.)

Of all the people with whom Donne was associated in his life, Robert Carr was perhaps the most stupid and certainly the most repulsive. But because the unsavoury favourite of the king had 'bought' him, Donne was told to write a poem celebrating Carr's wedding. He was very reluctant and slow to obey, which is not surprising.

Carr's homosexual relationship with the king was breaking down; swollen-headed because of the money which James had showered on him, he refused to sleep any more in the royal bedroom. He was in fact bisexual (like James) and he fell in love with an aristocratic lady, Frances Howard. Unfortunately the lady was already married, in a marriage contracted for political reasons when the couple were scarcely in their teens. The king, being anxious to retain the services of his favourite, did his best to have her marriage dissolved, on the basis of her plea that her husband had been made sexually impotent by witchcraft. (It was later found that she had helped by administering a drug to prevent his arousal.) The problem was referred to a committee. Awkwardly, the

Archbishop of Canterbury (Abbot) proved obstinate: he sided with the husband, the young Earl of Essex who had inherited neither virility nor glamour from his father. The earl seems to have been somewhat incoherent when discussing his sexuality with the assembled bishops but he did mumble a claim that he would be happy to consummate another marriage: his present inability arose because he was incompatible with his wife. (He had good reason: Frances had been notorious even in the morally relaxed court of King James.) The unworldly archbishop therefore believed that the solution was to mend the marriage, or at least to make sure that the couple parted as friends. But the king added more co-operative (or was it realistic?) bishops to the committee; in the end it voted 7–5 as he wished.

Those in favour included the saintly Bishop Lancelot Andrewes, who had a conscience at least as active as the archbishop's. The king had talked to him privately but it seems probable that the main argument which persuaded him was of a pastoral nature: he had baptized the earl as a baby, his eyes were open to the character of Frances Howard, and he concluded that there ought to be an end to a hell of a marriage. Later he was to be pastorally sensitive to Archbishop Abbot, who while hunting accidentally killed a man instead of a deer.

Abbot's defiance of the king's wishes was not the only problem. Sir Thomas Overbury was a very able man who did not under-estimate his abilities and he had been secretary to the incompetent Carr. Knowing many secrets, he objected to the plan for the new marriage. Consequently he was offered a post which would have got him out of the way (as ambassador to Russia) and when he refused was imprisoned in the Tower. Since he remained critical and might prove talkative, he was murdered in September 1613, enabling the union of the happy couple to be celebrated in December. Almost certainly his murder had been planned by Frances Howard, although it had been necessary to add further poison to supplement the tarts and jellies which she had sent to his prison in her role as Lady Bountiful. It has been suggested that she was not telling the truth when she later admitted her guilt, and undeniably she was capable of lying, but had she been innocent every motive of self–interest would have encouraged her to play the role of a maligned heroine.

In 1615 a young man who was dying in Brussels confessed that he had been the apothecary's apprentice who had been bribed by Frances Howard to supply poisons, although the final blow had been delivered by a doctor whose prescription, when inserted into Overbury as medicine, did the trick. The story reached the ears of the king, who to his credit allowed justice to take its course (more or less). It was also relevant that by now James had developed another relationship with a handsome young man, George Villiers, who had been introduced into the royal presence by an anti-Carr group because with slender legs he was a superb dancer – and also had a brain. A trial for conspiracy to murder was arranged. Although her husband protested his innocence, Frances Howard did not deny that she had been the most prominent of those who had plotted the murder. The couple escaped the death to which other conspirators were sentenced (this seems to have been the bargain made before she pleaded guilty), but they replaced Overbury in the Tower, to be released in 1622 and pardoned shortly before the king's death. By a curious coincidence the governor of the Tower when they were imprisoned was Donne's father-in-law. (The governor who had had custody of Overbury was one of the conspirators and one of those executed.)

There is no evidence that before 1615 Donne knew of the guilt of Frances Howard, and his friendship with Overbury (who was also a poet) is shown by the fact that he contributed to a volume published in the victim's honour after the murder. The conduct of Frances Howard was so outrageously evil that it seems probable that he did not think her capable of it until the dying apprentice had revealed the secret. But it also seems probable that he was uneasy about Carr's marriage: he obeyed his patron's demand for a poem but what he produced was feeble. It began with flattery of the 'zeale and love', the 'sweet peace', of the court which honoured the king and his favourite. It continued with an apology that at present the poet was 'dead and buried' and therefore unable to join the court's celebration of the wedding – and with a hint that he expected a welcome at court in the future. It ended with the tactless thought that it would now be a 'divorce' even to think of the couple apart, 'so much one are you two'.

There was an anticlimax, for soon Donne was complaining that he had not been adequately rewarded.

The spiritual humiliation of these years of dependence first on Drury and then on Carr was all the more pathetic because in this period Donne was beginning to move towards his future as a Christian preacher. While in France he said in a letter about current religious controversies: 'I look upon nothing so intensively as these things'. On the first Good Friday after his return to England in 1613 he had the spiritual experience which he recounted in one of the greatest of his short poems (see p. 240). When he approached Carr seeking his support in a new career, it was with the declared intention of making 'Divinitie' his 'Profession', after 'much debatement within me' but also after the 'Inspirations (as I hope) of the Spirit of God'. He added that he hoped that the prayers which he would offer for Carr's happiness would be more 'effectual with God' if offered by a priest.

However, the humiliating confusion continued. He asked Lord Hay to hand this letter to Carr and in his covering letter he complained that 'my poor studies' had 'hitherto profited me nothing'. It was his thought that in the Church 'a fortune may either be made, or at least better missed', than in a lay profession. This was not an unworldly thought and the immediate sequel in

Donne's life was to show, after Carr's encouraging response, that the prospect of a financially rewarding career as a layman could rapidly eclipse any idea of dedication to 'Divinitie'. In another letter of this period he admitted that 'no man attends Court fortunes with more impatience than I do'. He could make a private joke about politicians who 'find matter of state in any wrinkle in the King's socks' but that did not prevent him from looking in the same direction. The fact seems to be that his personality was now divided more than at any other time: he was both an aspiring Christian and a grasping careerist. This was what he had implied when on Good Friday 1613 he had prayed that the Saviour might apply his 'corrections' and 'Burne off my rusts and my deformity'. He seems to have known that his deepest problem was that while he was now ashamed of the 'lust and envie' of his earlier years, and had good reason to believe that this record made it impossible for him ever to climb into a pulpit, his life since then had shown him still deformed. As a Christian he had still not risen to a spiritual level which could make him a convincing priest and preacher, and as a poet he had betrayed the integrity which had been his greatest pride in the 1590s. In his second 'satyre' he had mocked poets who flattered the great:

> And they who write to Lords, rewards to get,
> Are they not like singers at doores for meat?

When preaching years later he was to observe that sycophants contributed to the corruption of 'men of high degree': 'When I over-magnifie them in their place, flatter them, humour them, ascribe more to them, expect more from them, rely more upon them, than I should, then they are a lie of my making' (6:306–7). But it seems that at this sad stage of his life he saw little clearly except that he had to 'over-magnifie' rich patrons because he and his family needed the 'meat'. One of Donne's anxieties in this period was caused by trouble with his eyes. When he was supposed to be celebrating Christmas 1613 he wrote to a friend that he was 'almost blind'. But an earlier letter of that year had referred to a lack of another kind of vision: 'except demonstrations (and perchance there are very few of them) I find nothing without perplexities'.

In the early months of 1614 his association with a man such as Robert Carr almost led Donne into an indiscretion which could have prevented his ordination at the beginning of the next year. He told Goodyer that he was 'under an inescapable necessity' to print 'my Poems'. Presumably Carr had ordered this and the point was that the collection was to be dedicated to him. Donne was doing his best to limit the damage which might be caused: the poems would be printed 'not so much for publique view, but at mine own cost, a few Copies' to be sent to 'persons of rank'. But he was still extremely reluctant. For one thing he found it undignified to be the 'Rhapsoder of mine own rags, and that cost me more deligence to seek them, than it did to make them. This made me ask to borrow that old book of yours' – a manuscript which included poems of which he had not kept a copy. In other words, even on this small-scale publication would be against his wishes, after enduring the ridicule after the publication of his poems for the Drurys. 'I shall suffer many interpretations', he predicted, although he claimed that he was now 'at an end of much considering of that'. He might try to persuade himself that the book would be a suitable farewell to the secular world 'before I take Orders' but he must have known that erotic poems would shock many if he went on to preach as a priest, and that the poems flattering patrons would now upset those to whom they had been addressed, for they had not known how others were being praised with a similar extravagance. In particular he was worried about the reactions of the Countess of Bedford. Fortunately the project seems to have been cancelled, for no copy of a printed book of this kind has ever been found; presumably Carr had changed his mind. The way was open for Donne to be ordained without that burden from the past.

As a preparation for this possible step, he either wrote or completed a book which was for him a task more congenial than the collection of his embarrassing poems for the printer. It was a book designed to sort out the ideas he had gained from his religious meditations and theological studies over the years, and to add to the stock. Like the book on suicide it was written as if it must be ready for the printer but was not published. However, it could be shown to anyone (such as a bishop) who doubted whether he was a fit person for the pulpit. We do not know that it was ever used for that purpose, but we do know that he repeated some of its contents, consciously or unconsciously, when he began to preach. We also know that like *Biathanatos* or *Pseudo-Martyr* the book is more or less unreadable because of its dull style. It was not published until 1652 when some copies could be sold on the strength of his name.

These *Essayes in Divinity* were given a superficial unity, if not much impact, by being meditations on the first verses of the first two books in the Bible, assisted by an attempt to learn Hebrew which, we gather, was not entirely successful. Any deeper unity emerges only when we ask what essentially were his religious positions at this time when his mind was still considerably confused, and we have to admit that these positions were obscured because he felt the need to put on paper many thoughts less mature and less important. With good reason he prayed that the divine Spirit might 'now produce new Creatures, thoughts, words and deeds' after the 'shaking away' of 'confusion, darknesse, and barrenesse'. And after self-examination he believed that human reasoning could not replace that divine Spirit as the giver of wisdom, since 'you are the Children of the

Lust and Excrements of your parents, they and theirs the Children of Adam, the child of durt, the child of Nothing'. (He wrote about 'you' as if addressing a congregation – but even now he was not ready for that.)

One position which he was to occupy firmly, and develop strongly, as a preacher was this: God the Father has created the world out of Nothing; without that miracle nothing in the world would exist; and ultimately, without it nothing in the world makes any sense. In these *Essayes* he reflected that a summons to that position of worship was the great message of the book called Genesis. He did not deny the existence of evil in the world – the reality which had made him adopt a position of near-atheism in *Metempsychosis* – but for him now that fact was dwarfed by the obvious existence of the Creator, and evil was blamed on the rebellion of Adam and Eve.

The other position towards which he moved in the *Essayes* was a deep response to the work of God the Son. In the book called Exodus Moses led out of Egypt, and through the wilderness, a people which was very mixed to begin with and which had to pass through many trials before it could reach the promised land. In much the same way Christ had led a large and mixed company of people out of the 'Egypt of sin' and on through a wilderness of continuing temptations, all the way to the promised land. Out of his meditation arose what a later generation would call Donne's ecumenical vision, which was extraordinary in the setting of his age – a time of theological hatred and of war in the name of religion, Catholic versus Protestant. 'I do zealously wish', he wrote in these *Essayes*, 'that the whole Catholicke Church were reduced to such Unity and agreement, in the form and profession Established in any one of these Churches (though ours were principally to be wished) which have not by any additions destroyed the foundation and possibility of salvation in Christ Jesus; That then the Church, discharged of disputations, and misapprehensions and this defensive warr, might contemplate Christ clearly and uniformely.'

To Donne this emphasis on the supremacy of Christ over the divisions of Churches and the sins of Christians was to be of absolutely vital significance. It enabled him to see that in order to have a powerful religion it was not necessary to accept either the Roman Catholic or the Calvinist system, each of which restricted salvation to those who accepted the creed taught by its own clergy. Many active Christians in that age believed that this intolerance was necessary, but Donne did not.

However, still he hesitated to admit that his future lay in a pulpit. For two months in the spring of 1614 he was a Member of Parliament, nominated to Taunton constituents by a judge. His name had almost certainly been put forward by the Earl of Somerset, as Robert Carr had become. He served on four committees of the House of Commons but it is not at all likely that he added his voice to the opposition to the royal government which had its focus in criticism of the king's Scottish favourites. He was not going to end up in the Tower of London, which was how his friends Sir Walter Chute and John Hoskyns were punished. This 'Addled Parliament' was distinguished in that it did not pass any legislation whatsoever; its main result was to convince the king that he need not summon another Parliament for seven years.

After proving his loyalty in the Commons Donne wrote to his patron, asking him to 'admit into your memorie' that fact that he was now 'a year older' than when he had last been turned down for a job in the service of the State. He was 'broken with some sicknesse' but as honest as ever. So he begged Carr either to 'bid me hope for this businesse in your Lordship's hand' or to let him 'abandon all' in that field and 'pursue my first purpose' – ordination. We do not know what 'this businesse' was but once again no job was offered.

Ten years later Donne was to say in his *Devotions* that the king was not to blame: 'when I asked a temporall office, he denied not, refused not that'. But at least James must have assented to the frequent refusals and he now had no reason to want Donne in a political job since the married Earl of Somerset was falling out of favour, being replaced by George Villiers, who was to be made Duke of Buckingham. Villiers was superior to Carr in charm, in intelligence and in morals, and in the future Donne was to be helped by him; it seems significant that Charles the future king, genuinely devout and strictly heterosexual, became his close friend and relied on him as much as did the infatuated James. But in the autumn of 1614 Donne at last saw what had been obvious for some time: he must make a direct approach to the king with a clear decision that if he was offered a suitable opportunity to serve the Church he would take it. Sensibly, he wanted an opportunity which would suit his very unusual personality and gifts; in 1614 as when he had declined Morton's suggestion in 1607, he could not imagine himself as a normal clergyman in a parish.

In November he went to see the king and told him that he was now ready to take the course which James wanted for him, ordination. It seems that up to this point the royal wish had not been accompanied by any guarantee of a fulfilling career in the Church, for had Donne already been given a firm promise from the Supreme Governor of the Church, he would not have needed to beg for the patronage of the king's favourite, as he had done in that crawling letter to Carr in the spring of 1613. But in the autumn of 1614 he reported that he had 'received from the King as good allowance and encouragement as I could desire'.

He was also assured of support from Archbishop Abbot, but a whole world was ending for him. Although he did not make public his grief when his son Francis died this November at the age of seven, at the request of the Countess of Bedford he wrote a longish poem in honour of her brother, who had died at the age of 22. In it he announced that 'in thy grave I doe interre my Muse'. Both the countess and Henry Goodyer, who had been prominent among his patrons, were now themselves in debt after much extravagance, but other friends seem to have enabled him to make a fresh start financially. The mood in which he was ordained seems to be shown in his prayer added to the *Essayes in Divinity.* 'Thou hast set up many candlesticks, and kindled many lamps in mee; but I have either blown them out, or carried them to guide me in forbidden ways. Thou hast given me a desire of knowledge, and some meanes to it, and some possession of it; and I have arm'd myself with thy weapons against thee. Yet, O God, have mercy upon me . . .'

He was ordained both as a deacon and as a priest by the Bishop of London on 23 January 1615. In his *Devotions* of 1624 he was to thank God that King James 'first of any man conceiv'd a hope that I might be of some use in thy Church'. Previously, he recalled, he had been 'sicke of a vertiginous giddines and irresolution', so that he had 'almost spent all my time in consulting how I might spend it'.

4 Thou hast done

And having done that, thou hast done,
I feare no more.
'A Hymne to God the Father'

Looking back, Donne was to say that God the Holy Spirit had been active all through his long period of 'irresolution', keeping his ears open to the call to preach even while he was trying to place his feet on the ladder of secular promotion. Not all the 'I' and 'we' passages in the sermons are unadorned autobiography, any more than the poems are a prosaic record of his earlier life, but one passage does seem to refer to what he now saw as his spiritual journey. He reflected that to be genuine a divine command to preach 'must be a light; not a calling taken out of the darkness of melancholy, or darkness of discontent, or darkness of want and poverty, or darkness of a retired life to avoid the mutual duties and offices of society: it must be a light, and a light that shines; it is not enough to have knowledge and learning; it must shine out, and appear in preaching; and it must shine in our hearts, in the private testimony of the Spirit there' (4:109).

Donne had very thoroughly known for himself the darkness of melancholy and discontent, poverty and loneliness, and it is extremely unlikely that he ended his 'irresolution' about the priesthood because he was driven by motives which were exclusively high-minded. Like many other people who have been ordained as 'ministers of religion' he wanted to earn his pay and to support his family. But the commentators who have concluded that he was a fraud as a preacher would appear to have delivered one hostile verdict too many, for the fact that Donne wanted a job does not exclude the possibility that he had a vocation, either to be a servant of God in the spirit of his religious poetry or (if we prefer a secular way of putting things) to reach the public by using the talents which had been rusted by an almost unendurable period of unemployment.

After his ordination he remained interested in money: at the end of each year he compared income with expenditure, as no doubt had been the habit of his father the ironmonger. But his character was such that he not only wrote down a thanksgiving to God when his income was sufficient or more than sufficient: he also became dedicated to his new work – and highly skilled within a strikingly short space of time, as if all his life he had been preparing for the pulpit. He had not been a priest for two years before he was expounding the Scriptures and his own reflections Sunday by Sunday to an audience of lawyers and students of law, shrewd men who were trained to examine, dissect and contradict other men's arguments. Then and later he prepared his sermons by hard study and prayer; he tackled difficult subjects; he took trouble to express his thoughts in words often of the quality which he had attained in his poetry; he was far more coherent than he had been in his books about suicide and the Oath; he memorized what he had to say and took an hour to say it; later he could confidently re-create his spoken words in a text for the printer; and one of his messages, very properly, was that behaviour mattered more than anything said. If a clergyman was interested mainly in his income it was not necessary to go to all that trouble. In Donne's case there is plenty of evidence that many of those who heard him found him convincing, although not necessarily in every word. Being believers they would interpret this as the work of the Holy Spirit in his heart and theirs, and it does not seem to be our duty to say that they were utterly deluded because he was in fact pretending all the time.

But Donne also believed that King James had been the Holy Spirit's instrument in encouraging him to be ordained – and this belief, too, can seem strange to modern readers. Whatever may be true about the activity of God and about the right of a king to govern a Church (subjects on which no wise historian would wish to pontificate), the role of this particular king will be suspect. We have already seen him mixed up in the sordid affairs of Frances Howard, the biggest scandal of his reign but not the only one. So how was he mixed up with Donne? In a short piece of attempted humour in prose, 'The Character of a Scot at the First Sight', a younger Donne had ridiculed the uncouthness of some of the Scots who had followed James to England. He may well have had the same early attitude to James himself.

This is not a biography of James but it must be said that this king was no fool in his religious policy which included the encouragement of Donne. He had no personal glamour or natural dignity. He exposed himself to gossip, ridicule and failure as a king by his pathetic infatuations with a series of handsome young men, at a time when in theory sodomy was punishable by death. Of course Donne knew this; the sixteenth of the 'problemes' which he put to himself and his friends privately, probably in the 1600s, was 'Why are Statesmen most Incredible?' and in his answer referred to those 'by whome the Prince provokes his lust, and by whom hee vents it'. In that age of contempt for any sign of homosexuality it was not easy to believe in James as a model to his subjects. Physically he was very clumsy, in an England where physical elegance was expected of the élite; emotionally he had been damaged by an extraordinarily tough time, 1566–1603, between his birth and his move to England; and financially he had two great problems. One was that in reaction to those years of humiliations and fights in Scotland he was hopelessly extravagant in expenditure on pleasures when he had a chance in England. (He told Parliament that his first three years as King of England 'were to me a Christmas' and the rest of his reign was not very different.) The other was that in a period of roaring inflation he did not put the public finances in order by insisting on professionalism in control and audit and by making a long-term agreement with Parliament. The Great Contract talked about in the Parliament of 1610 came to nothing. An efficient businessman, Lionel Cranfield, was appointed Lord Treasurer in 1621 but sacked three years later when he argued that the country could not afford the war which was then demanded by the king's all-powerful favourite, George Villiers, against the whole previous policy of virtual pacifism.

A vision of James in glory was, however, painted by Rubens on the ceiling of the Banqueting House in Whitehall and it was a vision of the heavenly reward to peacemakers. It was his pride to have ended for ever wars between England and Scotland: he invented the idea of 'Great Britain' although in 1608 he had to admit that it would have to consist of two kingdoms with different laws. He was also proud to have stopped the long war between England and Spain; and he did what little he could to prevent or end the Thirty Years' War in central Europe, putting his trust in a characteristic policy not of military intervention but of royal marriages, first with a Protestant ruler in Germany, then with a Catholic princess in Spain and then with a Catholic princess in France. Peace had been secured between England and Scotland because Scotland's king had by birth the best claim to the throne of England, and perhaps royalty could bring peace to Europe.

He also had a vision of religious peace. In practice he was much more tolerant towards Roman Catholics than the Puritans wanted, and much more tolerant towards Puritans than some of the bishops wanted. His wife was a Roman Catholic convert and his son, Prince Henry, was developing as a Protestant hero before his death from typhoid fever. Early in his reign in England he tried to persuade other monarchs to join him in convening a General Council of the Church in order to reconcile Catholics and Protestants all over

Christendom. Inevitably that plan failed because it depended on the pope being willing to renounce much of his existing authority. The shrewd Henri IV of France advised James to become a Roman Catholic for the sake of peace, as he had done himself ('Paris is worth a Mass') – and to stop writing books. It was Henri who called James the most learned fool in Christendom. So the dream of being another Constantine faded. (The emperor Constantine had begun his career in Britain, had restored peace to the Roman world as the first Christian emperor, and had presided over the Church's first General Council.) But James was not completely deterred: he encouraged Pierre du Moulin's plan to unite all Protestants – another plan which was abortive – and he supported the Church of England's first contacts with the Eastern Orthodox. And in 1611 the fulsome dedication of the 'Authorized' or 'King James' Version of the Bible did point to a reality: James carried weight as a theologian as well as a king, he had insisted that all existing English translations were defective, and he had ordered that the new version should have no controversial footnotes. This Bible was to prove his most influential achievement.

He valued bishops because they could be his agents in keeping the Church in a peace which included submission to him but did not include a tight discipline. In 1610 he persuaded the Calvinist Scots to accept bishops consecrated in England. But equally, in England as in Scotland he valued preachers who were also scholars and his patronage of Donne was part of this policy. So despite his defects about which a younger Donne had been scornful, his record as a maker of peace and as a patron of religion was such that it did not seem totally and obviously shameful to accept his patronage.

We do not know exactly what Donne had been promised as royal encouragement, but the new priest was given two honours almost immediately: he was appointed one of the 48 chaplains to the king and was awarded a doctorate by a reluctant university in

Cambridge at the king's command. A cipher was entrusted to him for use in secret correspondence about developments in religion and politics abroad, taking advantage of his knowledge of other languages. Being a royal chaplain entitled him to draw income from two parishes without residence in either of them, and it must have been a help when the lawyers of Lincoln's Inn needed a new Reader in Divinity to take charge of their chapel. By the end of 1616 Donne felt financially secure – and he was also delighted to have work to do.

He made no apology for needing to be alert within the world of work and money. On the contrary, he preached that 'God hath not removed man, not with-drawne man, from this Earth; he hath not given him the Aire to flie in, as to the Birds, nor Spheares to move in, as to the Sun and Moone; he hath left him upon the Earth, and not only to tread upon it as in contempt or in meere Dominion, but to walke upon it in the discharge of the duties of his calling; and so to be conversant upon the Earth is not a falling' (6:69). God, he declared, 'produced plants in Paradise that they might grow; God hath planted us in this world that we might grow; and he that does not endeavour that by all lawful meanes is inexcusable' (6:308). Preaching to the court of Charles I, he was to issue a warning that 'he that stands in a place, and does not the duty of that place, is but a statue in that place; and but a statue without an inscription; Posterity shall not know him, not read who he was' (8:178). And he was to preach this gospel of personal growth through work on many other occasions, saying robustly that 'wee are not sent into this world to Suffer, but to Doe' (3:329).

He did something as a diplomat, obeying the king's command to take a leading part in a mission which was essentially flawed because the king's own purpose was not down-to-earth.

The mission was announced as a bid to stop the war in central Europe between Catholics and Protestants, a war which was to become unstoppable (until 1648) in August 1619, when the Protestants in Bohemia rebelled against their Catholic king, Ferdinand, and replaced him by the Protestant ruler of the Palatinate of the Rhine, Frederick. King James was anxious to make peace, partly in order to be seen to act as a peacemaker but also because Frederick was his son-in-law. But his position was complicated: he hoped that the daughter of the king of Spain would soon become his daughter-in-law, and the king of Spain was allied with fellow Catholics who were involved in the Bohemian crisis. James had, it seems, no clear idea about how peace could be made: as so often, he put his trust in the idea that somehow talk would make the problem go away. In February 1619, as trouble brewed, it was announced that a large and expensive mission from 'Great Britain', led by Viscount Doncaster, would conduct a charm-offensive and Donne was soon telling Goodyer that he had 'commandment from the King' to be one of its leading members as its chaplain.

Little evidence survives of what exactly he did, but it seems probable that in addition to the narrower duties of a chaplain he was used to make contacts with the Protestants encountered as the many coaches transporting the embassy trundled across Europe. An experience which he mentioned in a later sermon was witnessing the devout Catholicism of Ferdinand, now Holy Roman Emperor, when the embassy was at last given an audience, in October. He recalled this sight: 'the greatest Christian Prince (in Style and Title) . . . at the sound of a Bell kneele downe in our presence and pray; and God forbid, he should be blamed for doing so' (9:325). But both Doncaster and Donne were far more impressed by the danger facing the Protestants than by the devotion shown by the Catholics, and Donne was specially glad to be able to preach before Frederick and his wife Elizabeth; he had written the happiest and best of his 'marriage songs' to celebrate their wedding in 1613. These were memorable experiences. The difficulty, however, was that neither Ferdinand nor Frederick had any intention of reaching a solution by compromise – and in the background King James had no intention of trying to impose a solution by sending an army. Doncaster's mission therefore had no bargaining power and essentially it was wasting everyone's time.

A further test of Donne's ability as a diplomat came in December 1619, when he was called upon to preach in The Hague when the embassy was on its way back home. With no results to show, the diplomats had to do what they could to reassure the disappointed and frightened Dutch Protestants. Donne preached from notes a sermon which must have been even longer than usual, for when he came to write it out he divided it into two (2:269–310). It is not known who was in the audience, but whether the sermon was heard by the Dutch or merely reported to them it was a masterpiece of tact without abandoning the Gospel.

Tact was needed because the Synod of Dort, defining Calvinist orthodoxy and therefore the official religion of the Dutch, had recently concluded its business and the consequences were being felt very sharply. Donne must have welcomed the synod's decision that God had not predestined particular individuals to hell 'from eternity' before the Fall of Adam had begun the story of human sin, but he would have been far less happy about another decision: that Christ's death had been intended to save from hell no one except those (few?) whom God chose to save as his 'elect' when they had come into existence. And still less could he be happy about the per-secution of the Arminians whose belief that Christ had died in order to save 'all' had been rejected: hundreds of clergy who preached what Donne himself believed were being deprived of their pulpits by the Calvinist equivalent of the Inquisition. One reason for this persecution was that Arminian theology was linked with a political movement, advocating a policy of peaceful and profitable commerce instead of war alongside the Protestants of central Europe – precisely the policy which Donne's own royal master favoured in practice. In the Netherlands the leader of the peace party was executed.

In his sermon Donne was neither undiplomatic nor unfaithful. He preached about the call of Jesus to fishermen in Galilee, a Scriptural text generally acceptable in a religious and seafaring nation. He pointed out that the apostles were not told to disobey the authorities – and that was a signal from a royal chaplain which would satisfy the party now in power in the Netherlands. He also pointed out that fishermen earned good rewards – and that was a signal from a citizen of London of sympathy with the party which wanted to trade and make money in peace. And he stressed that the fishermen were not told to fish in the murky waters of theological controversy – a clear signal from a man who in many ways always thought as a layman and who now agreed with those of the Dutch who had not been fascinated by the agenda of the Synod of Dort. But he was also positive as a preacher of the Gospel, using (with good precedent) a parable as a teaching instrument. He said that the fish caught by the apostolic fishermen ended up in the banquet where God was the host because of that host's invitation – a message which endorsed the emphasis of all the Calvinists on the priority of God's gracious mercy. But he added that the fish missing from the banquet were absent not because they had never been invited but because by their own decisions they had swum away. It had been within their God-given power to reach their proper destination.

By that last twist in the parable Donne hinted at his own belief. But by his tact he had avoided offence to the victors at the Synod of Dort and was presented with one of the gold medals which had been struck in proud commemoration of that event. This was to be his only big taste of diplomatic work and he must have realized that a pompous mission to spread good will in Europe had achieved nothing over five months except polite but hollow exchanges.

He was to have no further cause to envy his friend Henry Wotton, a consummate diplomat who became disillusioned with that profession. While ambassador in Venice Wotton had discovered that the Venetians preferred a compromise with the papacy to an alliance with faraway England. He also found that his royal master preferred sending ambassadors to paying them. In 1611 he had returned to England, only to find that he was out of favour: his financial petitions irritated, his more cynical witticisms became known and gave offence (but did he actually say that an ambassador is an honest man sent to lie abroad for the good of his country?), he was given a nickname which suggested that he had become Italian. Eventually he was again employed as a diplomat but again there were problems over salary and expenses. When rewarded by appointment as the ill-paid Provost of Eton College his debts remained (once he was arrested) and his energies did not: he spoke of writing a history of England, a biography of Luther, a memoir of Donne, but little got written. He was ordained as a deacon and hoped for a Deanery but only a pension was granted. In his will he left pictures to King Charles, for whom he had acted in the choice and collection of Italian art – together with one last reminder that the Crown owed him money.

Wotton had spiritual depth (his poetry showed that) and a large circle of friends and admirers, but his career was not the complete fulfilment of the confident hopes of the days when he and Donne had begun their friendship in Oxford. The one who had been unemployed while his friend was in Venice was the one who died without a complaint; he had become an 'ambassador for God' and as Sir Frank Kermode wrote in 1971 'there is no possible doubt that the sermon suited Donne's talents perfectly'. Whatever we may think about the truth of what Donne preached, we ought to agree that he believed it well enough to perform convincingly and that in so doing he at last fulfilled himself.

A fine miniature portrait of Donne has survived, dated 1616. The work of the well-known artist Isaac Oliver, it depicts the new royal chaplain who will also be available as a diplomat. His hair is neatly trimmed, his face is smooth, his starched ruff is immaculate. But four years pass and almost another man is shown in a portrait (by an unknown artist) which has remained in the Deanery of St Paul's Cathedral. The smartness has gone; there are bags under the eyes; the clothes are vague, with no ruff or collar. At the age of 49 here is a man well acquainted with grief, for in 1617 his wife had died; and familiar also with hard work, for his sermons and his other activities as a priest have needed the habit of constant self-discipline. But he stares straight at us; he knows where he stands and he knows what he must say. It seems excessive to claim that the difference between these two portraits has been caused by a conversion after ordination or bereavement, but certainly his religious message has been deepened. The darkness of Anne's death has compelled him to be more deeply attentive to 'a light that shines' and to be more urgent about what he could say to others in the dark.

All but one of the bishops appointed by James I to be his assistants in governing the Church of England had enough learning to be doctors of 'divinity' and most were energetic preachers – which was to be expected, since the king was himself an author and poet who could handle religious subjects and he liked to have bishops who would be a credit to their Supreme Governor. He made his courtiers attend many sermons (some by Donne), although he was, it seems, not often in the congregation himself. In many districts the clergy formed 'combinations' which delivered sermons to each other, and to a surprising number of the laity gathered in the church of the market town, and then discussed them over dinner. 'Godly' laymen appointed special 'lecturers' to preach regularly in churches which could be crowded for the occasion. The Puritans who formed the strongest spiritual movement in the Church of England thought that nothing was more important than Bible-based preaching and were indignant when parish priests were 'dumb'. The House of Commons petitioned for more sermons throughout the country when the king allowed it to meet, and corporately attended long sermons in St Margaret's church in Westminster.

By the end of the changeful sixteenth century the English people seem to have become in the main Protestant, chiefly perhaps because it seemed treasonable to be a Roman Catholic, but if the Protestantism was to be heartfelt, filling the emotional vacuum left by the disappearance of the great Church of the Middle Ages, it must be preached. Protestantism based itself on the Bible and 'the Bible only' but actually the Bible needed to be interpreted if its complexity was not to seem too confusing, and its message needed to be earthed in the realities of daily life if its moral standards were not to seem impossibly high. In the near future great attempts were to be made to use the power of the government to impose an Anglican system of worship as ordered by king and clergy, and then to impose a Puritan system of faith and godliness after a triumphant revolution, but in Donne's time the answer to the religious needs of the nation seemed to lie mainly in preaching which would arrest, inform and convince, and there was no great gulf between the 'Anglicans' (a term not yet used) and the 'Puritans' (a nickname used by scornful Elizabethans). A sign of this was that although Elizabeth had removed from Edmund Grindal the authority to function as Archbishop of Canterbury because he was not tough enough on the Puritans, James chose as his archbishop (1611–31) George Abbot, who had a strong sympathy with them. 'High' Church men stressed the sacraments of the Church more than did the Puritans, but what united these two movements was far larger than any division. All accepted the Church of England as the nation's Church, and the king as its Supreme Governor on earth; all accepted the Bible as the supreme and infallible revelation of

God; and all accepted preaching the Bible's message as the Church's main responsibility. Moreover, all agreed that preaching ought to be reasonable, not hysterical, and that scholars were needed. Preaching in 1624, Donne's friend Joseph Hall claimed that the scholars among the Church of England's clergy were *stupor mundi*, the wonder of the world. We should not exaggerate the theological unity of the Church which King James governed: one of the ablest of its theologians, William Ames, had to live in a Puritan nonconformist's exile from 1610. But the clergy were more united than they were to be in the next reign.

The message which united most of them was confidently authoritative, for the Church of England was not in the business of encouraging a do-it-yourself religion. (After the Gunpowder Plot executions of traitors were conducted with the usual barbarity outside St Paul's Cathedral and in 1612 two Protestants accused of gross heresy were burned, the last in English history to suffer this fate.) Any atheists, or people indifferent to religion, must be told firmly that nature proved the existence of God; Roman Catholics must be shown that the Bible proved that their Church had not been faithful to God's self-revelation, particularly in the matter of the royal supremacy; and individualists in religion must be appropriately rebuked. Unlike the poet Donne, Dr Donne the preacher repeatedly denounced 'singularity' and we find him saying that 'the generall opinion . . . is for the most part good evidence' (4:155). He believed that he had been authorized by Church and State to teach the people to walk in 'a way that the Fathers and the Church have walked before'; his mission was not to advertise 'a discovery made by our curiosity or our confidence' (7:267). Reason was, he was sure, on the side of Revelation although not necessarily a supporter of an individual's emotions. 'Let us therefore looke first to that which is best in us naturally, that is, Reason; For if we lose that . . . and strike into an incapable and barren stupidity, there is no footing, no subsistence for grace' from God (10:46). 'It is not true in any sense . . . that there is faith, where there is nothing but faith' (7:228–9). So Donne was one of those who trusted that 'the sincere preaching of the Gospel in our settled and well disciplined Church shall prevaile against those four pestilent opposites, Atheists and Papists and Sectaries and Carnal, indifferent men' (10:60).

Many sermons have survived from that period and scholars who have had the patience to work through considerable numbers of them assure us that most of the preachers were not major poets, deep thinkers or magnificent orators. For better or for worse, their material was often far simpler than what Donne felt he could offer in the royal court and in the cathedral and churches of London. He complained about some fellow preachers in his day who 'make the emergent affairs of the time their Text, and the humours of the hearers their Bible' (4:276), but it is clear that such a complaint would not be fair if made about most of the preachers, most of whom fell more or less into the category now called 'Puritan'. We know, from their great impact on England and New England in the years to come, that Puritan preachers were less nervous than Donne was when handling politics or 'emergent affairs'. But we also know that their main thrusts were severely biblical and austerely moral, and that when they had the opportunity they were going to do what they could to impose their beliefs and morals on people who, in Shakespeare's famous phrase, preferred 'cakes and ale'. A younger Donne had set himself a 'probleme': 'Why do Puritans make long sermons?' His answer had been 'It is their duty to Preach on till their Auditory awake'. But the Puritans had the last laugh – until they awakened a violent reaction.

A Puritan preacher whom Donne may have heard lecturing in Cambridge in the 1580s, William Perkins, had a wide influence before his death in 1602. His *Arte of Prophecying* was the manifesto of the 'plain' style, breaking away from the medieval tradition. That had been sharply divided into the academic and the popular, but whether the preacher had made his points by logical arguments based on Scripture and the Fathers of the Church, or by anecdotes, the message had always been essentially the same: believe the Bible, believe the Church, use the Church's sacraments. Now Perkins affirmed that 'to prophesie signifieth to teach the Word of God to the people of God by applying the same to the consciences for their edification'. Only thus could the art of preaching end in 'the science of living blessedly for ever'. 'Believe the Bible' was still the main point but it was the task of the preacher to state plainly the 'sense of Scripture' without reliance either on the Fathers or on anecdotes, and to apply Scripture to the conscience without much dependence on what could be done by the sacraments. Like Donne, Perkins preached without a script but with notes for reference in the pulpit; younger Puritans revived the popular medieval style of preaching from the heart, without notes; and with or without notes in the pulpit all were in earnest. A Puritan who succeeded Donne in the pulpit of Lincoln's Inn, John Preston, combined that pulpit with the headship of a Cambridge college and the duties of a royal chaplain, but he died, worn out by too much preaching, in 1628. Had he lived he might have been influential in reducing the tension which was to grow into a great rift between these 'plain' preachers and the monarchy.

It seems that in his lifetime Donne was himself attacked by some Puritans, not so much because of his theology as because of the complexity of his language. After his death one of his admirers, 'R. B.', wrote a poetic tribute which recalled that he had been 'humm'd against' because his 'fine words' made him a 'bad edifier' – and also because some fellow preachers 'envy'd' him while he was 'magnifi'd' by the congregations who welcomed the fact that he did not preach like his critics. It seems that many of those who gathered to hear Donne in the pulpit had a number of reasons to prefer his style. Without an entirely medieval insistence on the authority of the Church, Donne was impressive through his quotations from the teachers of the Church over many generations.

Without a naïve over-simplification of the authority of the Bible, he loved every word of it and relished the exploration of the significance of every word. Without being as simple as the Puritans were, his interpretation was a heartfelt reaction to what the Bible said. And without either ascending to airborne perfectionism or descending to earthy anecdotes, he applied the Bible's message to daily life.

By 1660 it could be seen that the rigour of Calvinist theology was discredited and that the enthusiastic crusade to purify the nation's morals by compulsion was over. Yet the 'plain style' of the Puritans survived – with a different message. What seemed to be needed now was a simple presentation of reasonable piety and everyday morality, in reaction against the wars which in the name of religion had done great damage both in England and in central Europe. The first master of this style was John Tillotson, the Archbishop of Canterbury who had been another of Donne's successors in the pulpit of Lincoln's Inn. Donne anticipated the tone of Tillotson's preaching when he remarked that 'rectified Reason is religion' (2:293). Despite the differences in his style from the simplicity advocated by Perkins, Preston and other Puritans, despite the humming against his love and use of language with a scholarly poet's sophistication, he at least told himself that he ought to be 'plain', helpfully pastoral and moral, a sinner speaking to sinners. And at least he was plainer than Lancelot Andrewes, approximately his equal as the leading non-Puritan preacher – and he gave a higher priority to preaching. After the death of Andrewes in 1626 he stood alone and no equal arose for many years after his own death. He was far from being the only preacher in the style which was to be called 'metaphysical' because full of 'conceits' but he and Andrewes were its acknowledged masters.

When he was in the pulpit Andrewes impressed, for his personality was unified and beautiful in its holiness and his learning seemed to be inexhaustible. King James appears to have felt awed in his presence and summoned him to preach at court on the greatest occasions, celebrating festivals of the Church's year with sermons which were feasts in themselves. But Andrewes had spent 34 years learning or teaching in Cambridge University and at heart he always remained the academic theologian who studied much and prayed much but, if he could, saved up speaking for lectures or sermons. The strangest of all the king's favourites, he was honoured by membership of the Privy Council but is reported to have said little during its deliberations. Although he became the bishop of a succession of dioceses including Winchester it seems that he could be content to spend only two months in the year in his diocese and only two hours of the day on doing business and receiving visitors (after his midday dinner). The preparation of the sermons which were later printed must have involved a great deal of work but he does not seem to have preached frequently. Certainly he did not share the Puritans' emphasis on preaching in the parishes: he thought that most of the clergy would talk nonsense if they preached too often. They would be wiser to read the Bible itself to their people and to concentrate on private prayer, public worship and pastoral care. He valued the sacraments very highly, as the principal means of God's grace to sinners. In his own chapel he maintained a dignity in ceremonial and ornament which was by the standards of his time High Church, and on his knees he wrote and used a book of private prayers which when printed was to be a treasure of Anglican spirituality; the handwritten copy was stained by his tears.

In contrast with Andrewes the sacramentalist, Donne could claim that 'to take away preaching were to disarm God' (4:195) and that a word preached was 'a portion of the bloud of thy Saviour' (3:364). He compared the sermon with a trumpet sounding various calls in a military camp: the alarm, the call to battle, the summons to a meeting, the order to retreat for 'a safe repairing of our souls' (2:169–70). His first sermon in St Paul's Cathedral was about the mission of St John the Baptist to be a 'witness to the Light' and more than once he returned to that text and, as he hoped, 'not to a light which is His, but a light which is He'. In his poem 'To Mr Tilman' he called the privilege of preaching a 'Coronation' and asked:

> Why doth the foolish world scorne that profession,
> Whose joyes passe speech? . . .
> What function is so noble, as to bee
> Embassadour to God and destinie?
> To open life, to give kingdomes to more
> Than kings give dignities; to keep heaven's doore?

But of course Donne was not always God's noble ambassador. We can find some unedifying evidence that he was human in some surviving documents which give us bits of the story of his relationship with his daughter Constance.

In 1617 his wife died (and much more will be said about Anne Donne in Chapter 9). After that bereavement which affected him far more deeply than has always been acknowledged Constance kept house for him: a situation which meant that men of her own age who might marry her did not appear in the Deanery and that her father was not very active in arranging a marriage. Eventually a husband did appear who was well-off but considerably older than Constance: he was Edward Alleyn, once a mere actor but now a theatre manager and large-scale dealer in properties. At the time Donne was pleased for her sake but the atmosphere soon soured. Alleyn asked Donne for a loan; Constance asked him for a horse and a promised diamond ring; her father refused the loan, sent the horse to Constance's brother in Oxford and kept the ring, perhaps feeling that Alleyn who had now secured a good housekeeper ought to be old and rich enough to manage his own financial affairs and buy his wife a horse and a ring. An indignant letter from Alleyn survives in a much-revised draft, saying that he had been shocked by the dean's behaviour and language. But he did not live long, Constance inherited a small fortune from him and married again, and during his long, last illness Donne was looked after in her home.

Having observed a man who had still not managed to become a saint, we can now make a brief study of this scholarly poet who did manage to become a preacher.

His mature style was dignified, learned and spiritually authoritative, but also self-involving for preacher and congregation alike. Donne had to make his own convictions clear and public, as he had not done when writing either poems using many voices or books which were tangled in language and argument. Now congregations knew that he was in earnest about the content of his message and about its urgency. 'To call upon the Congregation to heare what God hath done for my soule is a blessed preaching of my selfe' (9:279), but at last he felt no need to talk all the time about his own emotions: he had a message to deliver. The skills which he had developed in order to impress (or imagine?) a mistress (or a wife?) must now be redirected, for 'True Instruction is making love to the Congregation, and to every soule in it' (9:350). One cannot imagine either a Puritan or Bishop Andrewes saying that. But this self-involvement by the preacher must be matched by the listener. If a listener 'heares but the Logique, or the Rhetorique or the Ethique, or the poetry of the Sermon', he does not hear what matters most, for 'the Sermon of the Sermon he hears not' (7:512).

'A man', he warned, 'may thread Sermons by half dozens a day, and place his merit in the number, a man may have been all day in the perfume and incense of preaching' without really hearing a single sermon (6:149). By the same token, a man may preach eloquently without making any real impression. 'Twenty of our Sermons edifie not so much, as if the Congregation might see one man converted by us. Any one of you might out-preach us. That one man would leave his beloved sinne, that one man would restore ill-gotten goods, had made a better Sermon than ever I shall, and should gain more soules by his act than all our words (as they are ours) can doe' (2:275–6).

He insisted that 'a Sermon intends Exhortation principally and Edification, and a holy stirring of religious affections, and then matters Doctrine, and points of Divinity, occasionally, secondarily, as the words of the text may invite them' (8:95). A preacher must not offer 'a Pye of Plums without meat' or an 'Oration of Floweres and Figures, and Phrases without Strength' (7:329). 'It is not the depth, not the wit, not the eloquence of the Preacher that pierces us, but his nearnesse' (3:295). A preacher of the Gospel must be 'acceptable to God's people, and available for their Edification' by speaking 'plainly, sincerely, inelegantly, inartificially' (4:91).

Of course Dr Donne the preacher had Jack Donne the poet inside him and he could not stop being witty. One of his little jokes was that he had heard 'men preach against witty preaching, and doe it with as much wit as they have; and against learned preaching with as much learning as they could compasse' (10:148) – but some who heard that joke no doubt felt that Donne ought to have been laughing at himself (as perhaps he was). He had been called to preach the Gospel but he pointed out that when the holy apostles had been called to stop being fishermen, 'they did but leave their nets, they did not burne them' (2:285). All his surviving sermons, even those where he is obviously trying to be as simple and as pastoral as possible, are the work of a man who enjoyed displaying both his scholarship and his skill with words including both memorable epigrams and purple passages of prose-poetry. But Donne well understood what the best teachers of 'rhetoric' in the Renaissance recommended. This was not only 'elocution' with the Latin masters as models, whether Ciceronian (stately) or Senecan (pithy). The art of rhetoric included also 'invention' and 'disposition', finding the theme and arranging the material; and after that preparatory work, it involved 'memory' and 'pronunciation' as no less essential if the material assembled around the theme was to be retained in the mind and delivered without a script. And Donne showed that he did not shirk any of these professional labours.

He was not absolutely tied to London. His zeal diminished after preaching every Sunday during term to the friendly but limited congregation in the chapel of Lincoln's Inn, and in the early 1620s he hoped to be made Dean of Salisbury, or failing that Dean of Gloucester. In the event he was appointed to a Deanery within London but had he lived he might have accepted a bishopric in the early 1630s. (His name appeared in a small list of senior clergy being considered in this connection, before his last illness.) However, London was what he knew and in it he had audiences which he could not have found anywhere else: the royal court to which he preached regularly over fifteen years as a royal chaplain (and it seems that about 1,700 people, whether courtiers, clerks or servants, were to be found in Whitehall Palace); exceptionally intelligent and active people making a success of a business or a profession; people who might have less money but who were willing to spend it on going to a new play by Shakespeare; and clergy and others who became eager fans or critics of the leading preachers, often taking notes. In a sermon to the Lord Mayor and Aldermen of London which must have taken two and a half hours if it was preached as it was written out, Donne boasted that 'this City hath the ablest preaching Clergy of any City in Christendom' (4:113). He could say that a businessman who had failed to be charitable to the poor might be reminded on the Last Day that while on earth it had been his habit to hear two sermons on a Sunday and go to 'lectures' by preachers on weekdays (10:62). Congregations were so interested that Donne could complain about 'the murmurings and noises which you make when the Preacher concludeth any point'. Whether these noises expressed enthusiasm or disapproval, they were 'impertinent Interjections' which could 'swallow up one quarter of his houre' while the preacher still had much to say. And some of the noise could come from 'many who were not within the distance of hearing the Sermon' but remained standing in the cathedral and trying to hear it amid the noise (10:133).

Donne was fortunate in that he was able to develop his preaching in the encouraging atmosphere which surrounded him while he was 'Reader in Divinity' in Lincoln's Inn, 1616–21. His main task there was to prepare and deliver a lecture-like sermon for every Sunday during term. He must have preached at least two hundred such sermons although only about a tenth of that number survives.

With his past, the new role might have been difficult. The Benchers (senior lawyers) might have objected that they did not wish to entrust this prestigious pulpit to a man whose history was scandalous and whose ordination was recent, and they might have grumbled even if the nomination came from the king. The students might have been interested in him only as a man who in his own student days had written erotic and anti-Establishment poems which could now be passed from hand to hand. Many of the sermons which we can read from this period when Donne was back in that haunted scene refer with some passion to sin, its power, its persistence and its guilt. 'We labour to break hedges', he said, 'and to steale wood, and gather up a stick out of one sin and a stick out of another, and make a fagot to load us in this life and burne us in the next.' Changing the metaphor, he said that while drowning in a sea of sin a man can find himself held up 'by the chin' – yet God will withdraw that helping hand if the sinner so relies on it that he goes on sinning (2:124). However, it seems clear that the seniors grew to respect Donne: he, like them, had laboured to study his subject and had prepared carefully what he said in public; he, like them, could be charming in private; and he seemed sincere in his religion. For their part, the students saw that he was both sincere and human. He had known what it is to want money, to want a woman, to want a job, and he was not so hypocritical as to deny it – but he had also wanted God.

He was able to persuade Lincoln's Inn to do something after saying for years that the chapel needed to be rebuilt. His friend Christopher Brooke seems to have been in charge of the fund-raising and Donne was invited back to preach when the new chapel was consecrated in 1623. He then prayed: 'In these walles to them that love Profit and Gaine, manifest thy selfe as a Treasure and fill them so; To them that love Pleasure, manifest thy selfe as Marrow and Fatnesse, and fill them so; And to them that love Preferment, manifest thy selfe as a Kingdome, and fill them so' (4:363). He knew his congregation so well that he knew how to offer heaven in terms which lawyers would immediately understand: it is 'where all Clients shall retain but one Counsellor, our Advocate Christ Jesus, nor present him any other fee but his own blood, and yet every Client have a judgment on his side' (2:244). And he could tease them about their excuses for absence from the chapel: 'Beloved, it is not always colder upon Sunday than upon Satterday; nor any colder in the Chapell than in Westminster Hall' where judges and barristers went to work (4:377). He could even tease them about their sex lives: 'Chastity is not chastity in an old man, but a disability to be unchast' (2:244).

In 1621 he was installed as a Dean of St Paul's and that cathedral in whose shadow he had been born (almost literally) became the centre of his life until his death in 1631. In the year before his appointment King James had visited St Paul's in state, in order to launch an appeal for the necessary restoration of its medieval fabric. The response had been disappointing but the king must have known that although he had played a leading role in the building of the new chapel for Lincoln's Inn Donne would not be likely to put the very much larger cathedral's physical needs at the top of his agenda. Letters of petition or gratitude addressed very humbly to the king's current favourite, George Villiers Duke of Buckingham, are among the evidence which shows how anxious this 'poor worm' had been to get the job, once again crawling with a complaint about his 'narrow and penurious' finances. Having left no stone unturned in his efforts to secure his move to St Paul's, Donne had no intention of devoting his life to fund-raising and the repair of the cathedral's stonework. When some material already collected to begin the cathedral's restoration found its way to the Duke of Buckingham's mansion (this was York House, being repaired and extended) its movement suited the dean as well as the duke.

When Donne was dead the project to restore the physical appearance of the cathedral was relaunched. William Laud was then Bishop of London on his way to Canterbury and the scheme was the centre-piece of his strategy which was to bring back the dignity of the Church of England's churches. The 'high' (main) altar was made visibly holy and separate from the people. The little houses close to the walls of the cathedral were demolished. The outside pulpit from which preachers had delivered sermons which were more or less the equivalent of modern broadcasts was also pulled down, and preachers were told that they must submit their sermons to the bishop before reading them out. These special sermons were transferred to the nave, from which Laud excluded the noise and disorder of daily use by the public. If they wanted merely to gossip or do business, Londoners must use the large portico which Inigo Jones constructed in a Palladian (classical) style out of keeping with the main fabric, which was patched up but remained dirty. Some thirty years later, it was all wrecked by fire.

That lay in the future. Under his own patron, King James, Donne was free to concentrate on the construction of sermons.

He was not now under any obligation to preach every Sunday but Walton says that he usually did, 'if not oftener', apart from the time which he spent in his two country parishes each summer. When in London his life could be called a 'continued study' since he worked at meditation, reading and writing throughout many a week unless he had to attend to business, before taking Saturday off to relax with friends and refresh himself for Sunday's performance. A sermon made heavy demands on his memory of what he had planned to say as well as on his energy as an orator and the routine of long preparation for the pulpit cannot have been easy to maintain, but it helped that since student days he had been accustomed to rise at four in the morning. More work would be required in writing out and polishing a fuller version of the sermon, if this was required; again both memory and energy were needed, since only notes remained as the basis. Donne made versions which could be published of 80 of these sermons while taking refuge in Chelsea for five months during the plague of 1625. He mentioned in a letter that it normally took him eight hours to do this job. He did more work on old sermons during his long and last illness in the winter of 1630–31.

No manuscript written out by this painstaking preacher has survived but one has been discovered which, although the work of a professional copyist, included corrections in style and substance made in Donne's own handwriting. It seems clear that the text which was eventually printed differed considerably from what had been preached. However, the modern convention of writing that he 'said' this or that which reaches us in print would probably not have displeased Donne. He always regarded a sermon as essentially something to be spoken and included in his own written version some tricks of a preacher's trade, as when he moved the climax of a sermon to its beginning, in case he or anyone else died before the urgent message was finished (3:226). On another occasion he went on preaching when the sand in his hour-glass told him that his hour was up, saying that the eternal destiny of his hearers, who were the king and his courtiers, might depend on their allowing him a few more minutes (7:368).

He did not ignore the sacraments in his enthusiasm for sermons. 'Christ', he said, 'preached the Christian Doctrine long before he instituted the Sacraments', which are 'subsidiary things' – but he went on to compare the sacraments with the miracles of Christ, for both are 'visible signs of invisible grace' (10:69). We know from sermons preached at 'Christenings' that he could be eloquent about Baptism as a new birth, a regeneration. 'We know no ordinary means of sowing grace for a child but Baptisme; neither are we to doubt of the fulnesse of salvation in them that have received it' (9:105). Baptism 'washes away' the 'Originall sin' inherited from the sin of Adam and Eve – but alas, Baptism cannot halt the piling up of 'actuall and habitual sins' committed by the baptized and destroying the prospect of their salvation unless there is 'reconciliation to God' (9:272).

About the Eucharist, he told the congregation in the cathedral on Christmas Day 1626: 'Beloved, in the blessed, and glorious, and mysterious Sacrament of the Body and Blood of Christ Jesus, thou seest the Lord's Salvation and thy Salvation' (7:294). He accepted a High Church theology about that sacrament, one of the many survivals from his Roman Catholic upbringing. He taught firmly that 'the Communion Table is an Altar; and in the Sacrament there is a Sacrifice. Not onely a Sacrifice of Thanksgiving, common to all the Congregation, but a Sacrifice peculiar to the Priest, though for the People. There he offers up to God the Father (that is, to the remembrance, to the contemplation of God the Father) the whole body of the merits of Christ Jesus, and begges of him, that in contemplation of the Sacrifice so offered, of that Body of his merits, he would vouchsafe to return, and to apply those merits to that Congregation' (7:429). He believed that in principle 'it is no Church that hath no Priest' with 'a spiritual power received from them, who have the same power in themselves' – preferably by 'such a Succession and Ordination, we have had, from the hands of men such as were made Bishops' according to the canon law of the Roman Catholic Church. Reformed Churches were, however, entitled to dispensation from this law 'in cases of necessity' (9:128–30).

In keeping with the belief that the Communion was holy but 'subsidiary' – a means of 'sealing' the faith of the faithful, not of adding to their number – it was held in St Paul's infrequently, on the great festivals in the Church's calendar and otherwise only once a month. In contrast, the services of Mattins and Evensong were sung by the choir every weekday and included lessons from the Old and New Testaments, and two long sermons were preached every Sunday, with at least two additional sermons in the course of the week. Shortly before Donne's arrival the clergy had agreed that the laity should be admitted to seats near the pulpit – although the new dean complained that some laymen were still unwilling to take off their hats or kneel.

In the Middle Ages the cathedral would have been colourfully full of pictures in glass, statues in wood and stone, and other ornaments which were the 'Bible of the poor' who could not read. Donne collected pictures when he could afford them for enjoyment in his Deanery, but had little interest in seeing such images in a church. 'We should wonder to see a Mother in the midst of many sweet Children passing her time in making babies and puppets for her own delight. We should wonder to see a man, whose Chambers and galleries were full of curious master-peeces, thrust in a Village Fair to looke upon sixpenny pictures and three farthing prints' (9:80). Now English Protestants could be assured that they had direct access to the 'Image of God' in their own souls and to the 'Word of God' in the Scriptures – and if they needed further images and words, they needed sermons.

Three years after his arrival in St Paul's he was glad to accept an invitation from his admirer the Earl of Dorset to become also the vicar of the nearby church of St Dunstan-in-the-West, where the earl had the right of appointment. In the first of his sermons to that congregation he spoke at length about the relationship of pastor and parish as being like the marriage of husband and wife, and it seems clear that St Dunstan's was to some extent therapy for his continuing sense of loss after Anne's death and as his children left home. It brought him extra work and he did not need the extra money, which was not much, but it also brought him into pastoral and social relationships which were harder to form in the vast, gloomy, cold and decaying cathedral. His predecessor had been vicar for almost half a century but seems not to have been very active in this particular post among those which he held. In contrast, Donne preached there often, attended the committee meetings and dinners of the 'vestry', and had such personal relationships that the parishioners gave him a substantial present of wine each Christmas. After the middle of 1628 this involvement was reduced, but in 1630 Donne told a friend that he still intended to preach there 'as often as my condition of body will permit'. He gave or bequeathed money to the poor of this parish, as well as to the poor in the two rural parishes which were also his and where he spent time each summer.

In order to supplement his income he had been granted the rectory of Keyston in Huntingdonshire in 1616, soon followed by the rectory of Sevenoaks in Kent, but he had resigned from Keyston shortly before his installation as Dean of St Paul's and in 1622 he was instituted as rector of Blunham in Bedfordshire, keeping Sevenoaks. A rather wicked poem by C. H. Sisson tries to imagine what this outspoken preacher might say to the modern parishioners in Sevenoaks, but another question is what parishioners might say nowadays to a rector who spent almost all his time outside the parish.

Naturally, to modern eyes it is something of a scandal that Donne accepted income from these three parishes as well as from St Paul's. However, it was the custom (inherited from the Middle Ages) that clergymen who were specially studious, or specially favoured, should be encouraged by being allowed to be 'pluralists', and few consciences objected, provided that the regular services and the pastoral duties were in the hands of a curate for whom the absentee rector paid. The deeply respected Bishop Andrewes had refused to be a bishop on the financial terms offered by Queen Elizabeth but had seen nothing wrong in drawing a range of incomes while Dean of Westminster Abbey.

Although after ordination Donne was primarily a preacher, part of his message in the pulpit was the importance of conversation outside it. 'Men onely can speake', he pointed out; 'therefore speech is the Glue, the Cyment, the soul of Conversation, and of Religion too' (8:338). We cannot know much about this talk in private and not many personal letters can be used as evidence about this period, partly because he was much busier than in the years of unemployment, partly because in London he had more opportunities to talk with friends, and partly because the considerable quantity of correspondence found in his study after his death has not survived. Izaak Walton appears to have looked through these papers. They included notes about 'all businesses that past of any publick consequence, either in this, or any of our neighbour-nations': notes written 'either in Latine, or in the Language of that Nation'. But the papers also included 'Copies of divers Letters and cases of Conscience that had concerned his friends, with his observations and solutions of them' – copies which, if preserved, would have transformed the task of Walton's successors as biographers and commentators. They would have been compelled to take seriously the fact that those who knew Donne best consulted him about their troubles and their moral problems. However, we have some glimpses of the dean being friendly with colleagues and staff in the cathedral. When making his will he remembered many names. He performed his duty to be hospitable and preached that by his presence at parties Christ justified 'Feasting, somewhat more than was merely necessary for society and chearful conversation' (7:143).

These easy relationships were no doubt helped by an unwillingness to spend time on trying to reform the Church. He accepted the practices of appointing friends and relations to positions at the disposal of the senior clergy, and of leasing out the cathedral's estates to favoured laymen who paid rents far below the rate of inflation but also 'fines' which went to the senior clergy when a lease was renewed. Walton was told that the dean had a reputation for being honest (and he passed on an anecdote about how this strange dean had refused to profit from one suggestion about how his income could be increased) but this could not be said about everyone else. Donne seems to have thought that a blind eye had to be turned towards some situations if he was to be able to devote himself to what he regarded as his vocation, preaching.

In the winter of 1623–24 he had occasion to preach to himself, when he and the doctors who were summoned in a panic had good reason to believe that he might well be very near death. The illness seems to have been a 'relapsing' fever, which in those days was often fatal. Naturally Donne, who at the best of times was extremely interested in himself, felt and thought about his illness and about its possible end, and was both emotional and clever with an agitated intensity; and since he could not move from his bed to a pulpit, and was forbidden to read, naturally he kept a kind of diary. This diary seems to have been polished and completed when the crisis was over. It was published as *Devotions upon Emergent Occasions*, a little book which provides a large amount of the evidence about his psychology as he prayed: 'O Eternall and most gracious God, who considered in thy selfe art a circle, first and last and altogether; but considered in thy working upon us art a direct line and leadest us from our beginning, through all our wayes, to our end . . .'

The *Devotions* are certainly not a get-well card to himself: they are gloomy thoughts about sickness as typical of the human condition, resulting in 'Debatements with God' which combine a devout humility with a continuing insistence on argument. They begin with this response to a sudden illness: 'We study Health, and deliberate upon our meats, and drink, and Ayre, and exercises' but 'in a minute a Cannon batters all'. Donne expects a 'torment of sicknes' – earthquakes, lightning, thunders, eclipses, blazing stars and rivers of blood, all within his body – and tries to persuade himself that this, not God's 'musique', is what he needs. He is in his bed but that is no comfort: he remembers it was a 'bed of wantonesse' in past years. Strangely, 'the Physician' is sent for only on the fourth day of this crisis; less strangely in view of seventeenth-century medical expertise, Dr Fox is 'afraid'. So the king sends his own physician and the assembled doctors 'use Cordialls', they 'apply Pidgeons' (dead) to draw 'vapours' out of the feet, and they tell Donne to cheer up – advice which gets this indignant response: 'Did I drinke in Melancolly into myselfe? It is my thoughtfulnesse. Was I not made to thinke? It is my Study; doth not my Calling call for that?' The patient turns to thoughts about eternity ('Eternity had bin the same, as it is, though time never had beene') and about his sinful use of time ('I have sinned . . . in my ostentation and the mingling of a respect of my selfe, in preaching thy Word'). Already, on the fourth day of this illness, he has decided that if a man is a little world then 'selfe' is no bigger than the size of the land while 'misery' is as large as the oceans. But on the sixteenth day he hears the 'passing' bell which announces that a neighbour is approaching death, and the sound summons him to think about other people and about the positive use which God makes of the afflictions which everyone suffers. Donne recovers. He returns to the Scriptures more attentively and the use which he makes of his experience is to write up and publish these thoughts in order to help other people in their afflictions. But he never addresses the reader directly: he is preaching to himself.

By permission he dedicated the little book to Charles, Prince of Wales, for he did not underestimate the importance of an occasion when a Dean of St Paul's bared his heart. In his sermons a reference to 'I' is not always meant to be autobiographical, but here as Donne addresses himself or his Maker he exposes himself in self-pity and, ultimately, in self-sacrifice – with, as Sir Thomas Browne put it, 'Strange Fire'. His sickness has brought him closer to his God: 'how fully O my abundant God, how gently O my sweet and easy God, doest thou entangle me'!

The *Devotions* include a meditation which is as beautiful as anything in his sermons and which is a reminder of other features to be found also in them: a vision of human unity in life and death, a pride in the Catholic Church of Christ, a love of learning in an international fellowship. That was why, three centuries later, Ernest Hemingway could call his greatest novel *For Whom the Bell Tolls*: it was about the Spanish civil war as a warning that the whole of Europe was about to suffer in war. Donne wrote:

> The Church is Catholike, universall, so are all her Actions; All that she does, belongs to All. When she baptizes a child, that action concerns mee; for that child is thereby connected to that Head which is my Head too, and engrafted into that body, whereof I am a member. And when she buries a Man, that action concernes me; All mankinde is of one Author, and is one volume; when one Man dies, one Chapter is not torne out of the booke, but translated into a better language; and every Chapter must be so translated; God emploies several translators; some peeces are translated by Age, some by sicknesse, some by warre, some by justice; but God's hand is in every translation; and his hand shall bind up all our scattered leaves againe, for that Library where every booke shall lie open to one another . . .

> No Man is an Iland, intire of it selfe, every man is a peece of the Continent, a part of the maine; if a Clod be washed away by the Sea, Europe is the lesse, as well as if a Promonterie were, as well as if a Mannor of thy friend's, or of thine own were; Any Man's death diminishes me, because I am involved in Mankinde; And therefore never send to know for whom the bell tolls; It tolls for thee.

During the winter of 1630–31 Donne astonished his friends twice. That autumn he had gone to his daughter Constance's home in Essex; he wanted her to care for him during an illness which was almost certainly cancer. He took his mind off the pain and debility by writing out old sermons for which he had kept his notes, but he did not return to London to preach. Then, feeling that the end was near, he accepted the usual invitation to preach to the royal court in Whitehall Palace on the first Friday in Lent, which in 1631 fell on 25 February. When he returned to the Deanery his friends were so shocked by his appearance that they begged him to cancel the engagement, but he persevered and his farewell to the king and to the pulpit took the form of a passionate meditation on the inescapable destination of death, all human life being a progress to that and to the resurrection (described at less length).

> We celebrate our own funeralls with cryes, even at our birth . . . That which we call life is . . . our life spent in dying . . . Our youth is worse than our infancy and our age worse than our youth. Our youth is hungry and thirsty after those sinnes which our infancy knew not; And our age is sorry and angry that it cannot pursue those sinnes which our youth did. And besides, at the way, so many deaths, that is to say so many deadly calamities, accompany

> every condition, and every period of this life, as that death it selfe would bee an ease to them that suffer them.

He had handled this theme before, but the sermon which was published as *Death's Duell* was his own sermon for his funeral and like flowers on a coffin it clothed the suffering and total decay of death with the beauty of the English language in which he had become a master. Perhaps for the first time in his life, he read out a fully prepared script.

To him the unreliability of his memory would be a sign of senile weakness but the sermon was not totally morbid. 'The humble soule (and onely the humble soule is the religious soule) rests himselfe upon God's purposes and decrees; but then it is upon those purposes and decrees of God which he hath declared and manifested; not such as are conceived and imagined in our selves . . .' He reminded his hearers of what Christ had suffered in order to fulfil the purposes of the Father: 'a sadnes even in his soule to death, and an agony even to a bloody sweate in his body, and expostulations with God, and exclamations upon the crosse'. 'God doth not say, Live well and thou shalt dye well, that is an easie and a quiet death; But live well here and thou shalt live for ever.' 'Whether the gate of my prison be opened with an oyld key (by a gentle and preparing sicknes), or the gate be hewen downe by a violent death, or the gate be burnt downe by a raging and frantique feaver, a gate into heaven I shall have . . .' His trust was, he said, in 'God's care that the soule be safe, what agonies so ever the body suffers in the hour of death'. He ended on the same note as in the *Devotions* (discussed on pp. 172–4).

He was exhausted but obstinate: he attended a business meeting on the next day and dealt with the affairs of the cathedral until 21 March, although he had written out his long will on 13 December (on St Lucy's Day). One piece of business was to prepare his monument. Walton records that his doctor suggested this;

presumably he thought it a kind way of warning the dean that the end was near. Donne threw himself into the project, which is easier to understand if we remember that coffins were not yet fashionable. He had fires lit in his study, stripped naked, was clothed in a shroud as for burial, left his emaciated face visible, and had a sketch made. This astonishing portrait he then kept in the bedroom to which he retired, taking leave of his friends but concentrating on his prayers, in the end simply repeating the Lord's Prayer. He died on 31 March 1631, and those who were near him at the time reported that he died in peace, closing his own eyes as he composed himself for the experience of what he had so often imagined.

As had been intended, the sketch was used not only when *Death's Duell* was printed but also by the sculptor Nicholas Stone, who had made Anne's monument back in 1617. Donne's intention to be buried with her had been cancelled: now he belonged to his cathedral and to London. Thirty-five years later St Paul's was to be reduced to a ruin by the Great Fire but this monument survived and was placed in the crypt of Wren's cathedral. Late in the Victorian age it was brought upstairs, to the south choir aisle. In that position, however, the face of the statue is no longer turned to the east, as was the final point of the epitaph which Donne composed. What remains from his plan is that he is standing, not sleeping, and although the eyes are not yet open the expression on the face, no longer cancer-ridden, is one of delight at the approaching resurrection. But he is not dressed as a clergyman: in his shroud, he is simply a human being who needs resurrection. In his present position he confronts a Bishop of London in bronze, robed in all the pomp of the Established Church before 1914.

The Latin epitaph which he wrote as a miniature autobiography is now placed high above this strange statue, and at the time it was carved in quite small letters as a piece of prose, so that it is hard to read even if the Latin can be understood. But it is as interesting for its silences as much as for what it says. It stresses the labours of the scholar but ignores all the poetry. It recalls the ordination but does not mention anything from the earlier life except the education. It gives thanks for the influence of the Holy Spirit but hints that this might not have been decisive without King James. It remembers when he became Dean of St Paul's but gets the date slightly wrong; presumably he had been too ill to look it up. (But he did not make a mistake about the year in which he became a priest: according to the calendar then in use January 1615 was still within 1614.) It preaches that no earthly honour lasts for ever but over the grave it proclaims a Christian's one hope, 'his Jesus'. It makes it difficult to remember the sensuality and the cynicism of his early manhood, or the unemployment with the depressions and confusions which had brought temptations to despair, even to suicide.

John Donne

Doctor of Divinity,

after varied studies, pursued from early years
with perseverance and not without success,
entered into Holy Orders
under the influence and pressure of the Holy Spirit
and by the advice and exhortation of King James,
in the year of his Jesus 1614 and of his age 42.
Having been invested with the Deanery of this church
on 27 November 1621,
he was stripped of it by death on the last day of March 1631.
He lies here in the dust but beholds Him
whose name is Rising.

PART TWO

About Donne

5 Thou hast not done

When thou hast done, thou hast not done,
For I have more.
'A Hymne to God the Father'

The surviving evidence about the life of Donne is, as we have seen, quite substantial, and in much of it he seems to be exhibiting himself, right up to the days of the dying and the burial. But the literature of opinions about him is much larger and it proves that the evidence can be interpreted in very different ways, by biographers and commentators who vary from the over-awed to those who think themselves superior. All these interpretations cannot be equally correct; so it has to be said that not everyone who has written about Donne has done an equally good job.

In the twentieth century some scholars, mainly in the USA, offered a solution to the problem of the connection between Jack Donne and Dr Donne by claiming that even in the young poet the great preacher could already be heard, solemnly and impressively. Thus in the 1990s published work by commentators with academic credentials suggested that when the speaker in a poem by Donne was ordering a mistress to undress he was seeking a spiritual revelation; that when he said that he was fascinated by the 'centrique part' of a woman he meant that he wanted to find the centre of All; that when he composed a mock marriage song for the entertainment of other students he was celebrating the triumph of life over death; that when flirting wittily he was exercising skills in the branch of theology known as 'casuistry' because it pondered difficult cases in ethics; and that when he was trying to seduce a girl (in 'The Flea') his arguments are best interpreted as theology about the Eucharist. And in each case it proved possible to make such a surprising suggestion by interpreting some evidence in the poem with considerable ingenuity. But the difficulty is, of course, that the suggestion becomes extremely improbable for most of us when we reflect on what we know about Donne as a young man. A collection of essays on *John Donne's Religious Imagination* in 1995 included a number of such suggestions which were too religious, and therefore too imaginative, in comparison with the evidence.

In a different approach taken by less devoted commentators, the emphasis has been on a Donne who was more or less sick in mind. An American scholar, Stanley Fish, has already been mentioned (on pp. 10–11). In *John Donne, Undone* (1986) Thomas Docherty, a lecturer in Trinity College, Dublin, swept aside the work of other writers and the facts about which they had written. He suggested that since the facts are 'deliberately obscure and secretive' what helps most is 'an attempt to release Donne's texts into their full obscurity, so to speak: to make them *difficult*'. With this aim he released himself from any need to consider strictly 'what the text says' and to argue with earlier opinions about what it means. Unfortunately for him, the evidence which we have does not support his bold suggestions that Donne was intensely troubled by the discovery of the earth's true relationship with the sun and that his whole way of relating to things on the earth was transformed by the invention of the telescope. Nor does the evidence demonstrate that Donne's erotic poetry resulted from a long struggle against *female* promiscuity, or that 'the priestly hand of Donne converts sexual foreplay into the activity of blessing', or that the speaker of a poem can change sex during it. Nor does the evidence show that for Donne the male and female roles in sex and society became interchangeable, or that for him the moment of death could not be distinguished from the moment of the present.

Nor does it present us with a Donne who, 'striving towards Godhead in an untrammelled ambition', equated himself with the Son of God or dressed himself in the form of the Mother of God in order to bring forth the Word of God. In fact the evidence is clearly against each and all of these suggestions.

The truth seems to be that Donne was neither a saint nor a madman. Yet it needs to be admitted that modern commentators who have suggested that he was either the one or the other have not been the first to exaggerate.

Donne's first biographer, Izaak Walton, was a fan. In a poem dated four days after the funeral he said it: 'he lov'd me . . . I am his Convert'. This became one of the tributes printed in the first edition of Donne's collected poems. Seven years later he paid a longer tribute in prose, inviting his readers to meet his hero.

> He was of Stature moderately tall, of a strait and equally-proportioned body, to which all his words and actions gave an inexpressible addition of Comeliness. The melancholy and pleasant humours were in him so contempered, that each gave advantage to the other, and made his Company one of the delights of Mankind. His fancy was unimitably high, equalled only by his great wit . . . His aspect was chearful and such as gave a silent testimony of a clear knowing soul and of a Conscience at peace with itself. His melting eye shewed that he had a soft heart, full of noble compassion . . . He was by nature highly passionate, but more apt to reluct at the excesses of it . . . He was earnest and unwearied in the search of knowledge . . .

Meeting Donne changed Walton's life. In the 1620s he was in his thirties and kept a shop in London. He attended the nearby church of St Dunstan-in-the-West and was impressed by the vicar – so impressed that he was delighted to be allowed to get to know him outside his pulpit, to enjoy the delight of his company and, although a social inferior, to be introduced to some in his circle of grand friends. After Donne's death one of these, Sir Henry Wotton, asked him to supply notes about Donne's life. David Novarr, who included the most thorough study of Walton's connection with Donne in his book on *The Making of Walton's Lives* (1958), argued persuasively that the connection cannot have been intimate; in particular, it is very unlikely that Donne told him the whole story of his life with him taking notes. Unfortunately Wotton died before this material supplied by a parishioner could be used in a memoir and the project seemed to die with him. But in 1639 Donne's son announced a plan to print some of his father's sermons, over which he had gained control. There was, it seems, some anxiety about their reception: the publication of some of the sermons of Bishop Andrewes in 1629 had gone well but Donne's own recently published poems had not been reassuring about his preparation for the pulpit. It was therefore agreed that Walton should introduce the book with a brief but edifying 'Life and Death' of Donne, concentrating on the exemplary death.

First printed in 1640, this memoir was expanded, and made still more dignified by small changes, in successive editions until 1675, and thereafter its popularity continued. The shopkeeper had been launched as a biographer. He was encouraged to produce 'Lives' of other Anglican churchmen: Wotton the model layman, Robert Sanderson the learned and holy bishop, and two priests who were to become about as famous as Donne himself, Richard Hooker and George Herbert. And amid the hard times for Anglicans under Cromwell in the 1650s he wrote the most loved of all his writings, his *Compleat Angler*. Having lived to see the monarchy and the Church of England reinstated, he concentrated on his memories, his friendships and his fishing. He was buried in Winchester

Cathedral more than half a century after the death of John Donne, who is now commemorated in the window above his grave.

His was a portrait of a saint at a time when the Church of England, already threatened by the troubles which were to destroy its Supreme Governor, Charles I, wanted to be assured that it could produce saints. Yet this was an Englishman's portrait of a very English saint, charmingly casual and homely in its presentation, with a subject which (as he treated it) made no great spiritual or intellectual demands. For about 250 years it was enjoyed while Donne's own works in prose, his sermons and even his poems were given less attention. It did not seem to matter that Walton had attempted only a few sentences about what Donne wrote; nor was the appeal of his 'Life' much reduced when between 1796 and 1825 Thomas Zouch made some corrections and additions. If defects were noticed, it could be thought that Walton had already made a sufficiently disarming apology: in view of his 'education and mean abilities' it was a wonder that he had written anything, but his 'artless Pensil' had produced a 'plain Picture'.

In fact his portrait was not nearly so artless as he pretended, for he knew what to stress or omit if this was to be an icon of an Anglican saint. There were many subtle touches, gathered in the final version. The first paragraph began the snobbery: 'the Reader may be pleased to know, that his Father was masculinely and lineally descended from a very antient family in Wales' and that 'he had his first breeding in his Father's house'. This claim that Donne was connected with the Dwyns seems more plausible than some modern scholars have allowed, for Donne used that family's crest on the ring with which he sealed letters and it reappeared on his monument in St Paul's. We have no record of anyone having mocked or disputed the claim, which was repeated by his son John. But it is also the case that no evidence has survived which proves that the father was so descended, or which shows Donne using such a family connection to his own advantage (although Sir David

Dun, for example, was a prominent lawyer and as the 'Dean of the Arches' the senior judge in the legal machinery of the Church, a man characterized succinctly by the Archbishop of Canterbury as 'corrupt'). Anyway, the family tree on the father's side mattered far less in Donne's life than did his link through his mother with Sir Thomas More and other Roman Catholic martyrs, on whom Walton would be less keen.

Another touch was to postpone the travel through Catholic Italy and Spain to the end of the 1590s, when Donne had demonstrated his manly patriotism by joining the two naval expeditions against the Spaniards. The 'Picture of him at the age of eighteen' which (as we have seen) was the portrait of an aggressively Roman Catholic crusader was also handled tactfully. It was postponed until after a description of the monument in the cathedral, and the motto around the picture was mistranslated so as to suggest that it was a prediction that the young man would be transformed into an Anglican dignitary:

> How much shall I be chang'd
> Before I am chang'd . . .

The tragic death of Donne's brother was not mentioned. Donne's early activity as a lover and poet was left in an almost equal obscurity, although Walton had to admit that something had taken place. He did this by recording that his hero had expressed great regret about 'some irregularities of my life' and about the writing of poems 'made only to exercise his sharp wit, and high fancy'. Some of these poems had been 'facetiously composed and carelessly scattered' although Donne had wisely destroyed others.

Donne's marriage was 'the remarkable error of his life' which he would 'occasionally condemn', as Walton finally decided to say, having written in the 1640 edition that the husband 'never seemed to justifie' marrying his wife. In the 1658 edition he took the opportunity to preach a pompous layman's sermon about love, as 'a passion! that carries us to commit errors with as much ease as whirlwinds remove feathers'. In defiance of the law courts he added his opinion that because this marriage was without the 'approbation' of 'friends', it was not even 'lawful'. Then he admitted that Anne had been 'curiously and plentifully educated' – presumably because her proud husband had said so – but he never gave her name. His reference to her father included several mistakes. He also got the date of her death wrong although it was recorded on her tomb in a church not far from where he was writing. The death did move him to write about 'that abundant affection which once was betwixt him and her, who had long been the delight of his eyes, and the Companion of his youth', but now the focus was on the survivor's grief and his problems as 'the careful father of seven children then living'. In the end, the most positive thing which Walton could bring himself to say about the marriage was that their 'mutual and cordial affections' meant that his hero's repentance for his error was not 'heavy'.

Although Walton printed extracts from some of Donne's letters in his middle period, the bitterness of this time was greatly reduced. The religious poetry was almost all dated to the years when he was a priest and, although not much of it was quoted, it was used to show an edifying Christian humility in this distinguished and popular priest. It was not used to show spiritual struggles before ordination; these were 'high, holy and harmonious composures'. Mitcham, which Donne called a prison when writing to his friends, became for Walton (almost as if he was selling a house in it) 'a place noted for good air, and choice company'. There his hero was so happy, reading and writing, that he would have been glad to remain 'during his life'. His lodgings in London were said to be rather grander than the reality: they were 'near to White-Hall' and this proximity to the royal palace would make high-level contacts convenient. He was 'often visited by many of the Nobility' and consulted by 'most Ambassadours of forraign Nations'. The king himself was 'much pleas'd when Mr Donne attended him' for 'deep discourses'. After one of these conversations *Pseudo-Martyr* was written 'within six weeks' as the king had urged. In the (wisely unpublished) book about suicide 'all the Laws violated by that Act were diligently surveyed and judiciously censured'. In Walton's pages Donne moves through the years of unemployment as if in control; in reality, he became a high-class beggar.

The time which Donne reluctantly spent in France because he needed the money from the Drurys who were tourists was presented by Walton as being participation in a 'glorious Embassie' to King Henri IV – who at the time was dead. And three anecdotes were told about this middle period which cannot be accurate. One was a vividly detailed ghost story about the anxious husband's vision during that trip with the Drurys in 1612; he saw his wife with a dead baby in her arms on the very day of the baby's death, shortly before a messenger brought the news from London. But we know that Donne was still ignorant about his family's tragedy two months after the event; so the 'Person of Honour' who told the tale must have got something wrong. Another story, also detailed, was of conversation in 1607 about the highly profitable parish which was offered to him. But this long story was sent to Walton by a bishop (Morton) then in his nineties, recalling an event some fifty years before. A third, shorter, anecdote was of Donne being summoned by 'the Earl of Somerset when at his greatest height of favour', and told to 'Stay in this Garden' while the earl fixed his appointment to fill a vacancy as one of the secretaries of the Privy Council. The king, however, persisted in his wish that Donne should be ordained. But there was no such vacancy on the council's staff at this time.

The theme of Walton's tribute to his vicar was that Donne was a second St Augustine, resembling the great Bishop of Hippo in a youth to be regretted ('he accounted the former part of his life to be lost'), in a conversion to be celebrated, and in 'learning and holiness' very seldom equalled. The change made by conversion and ordination seemed so obvious that when Donne was 'made Doctor in Divinity' by Cambridge University it was with 'exprest gladness' (in fact it was with great reluctance, but the king was obeyed). The impression had been made on Walton by his knowledge of this delightful saint as his parish priest. He cannot have known much about Donne's life as Reader in Divinity in Lincoln's Inn, for he mistakenly thought that his hero was given that post after his wife's death, as a consolation; he was vague about the activities as Dean of St Paul's and royal chaplain; he thought that Donne was vicar of St Dunstan's for longer than was true; he did not venture to analyse the theology preached; but he did remember the man speaking like an angel and becoming his friend. He was proud to have been among the friends with whom Donne wanted to talk during his last days (and he passed on the memory of the dean's refusal to drink all the milk ordered by the doctor). He knew that Donne's flesh had by now been reduced to dust but he ended his tribute by saying that he was sure that on the day of resurrection he would see the dust 'reanimated'. He himself breathed life into our thinking about Donne by his little book; it preserved facts and impressions which otherwise would have been lost, and it did so in style.

Some two hundred years later Augustus Jessopp resembled Walton in his devotion to this poet turned preacher. As a Cambridge undergraduate he became fascinated. In 1855 he edited the *Essayes in Divinity* for Victorian readers with elaborate notes. They remained uninterested, however, and when he published a short study of *John Donne, Sometime Dean of St Paul's* in a series on 'Leaders of Religion' 42 years later, he introduced it by confessing that 'I have never been able to feel much enthusiasm for Donne as a poet'. His verdict was that 'if we except some few exquisite passages . . . it is difficult to believe that these earlier poems were not loved for the poet's sake'. Some poems were not such as Donne himself 'would wish to be read and dwelt on by the pure and innocent'.

Jessopp's enthusiasm was reserved for the man who despite a lack of innocence was going to become a pure churchman. 'The wits and the courtiers, the nobility and the luminaries of the law courts' all, he thought, agreed in their admiration of the young Donne, and his own admiration was not shaken by the book about suicide: the idea that Donne was tempted to commit this sin 'must always appear incredible to any who have learned to know the man, and to appreciate the true nobility of his character'.

In the end Jessopp paid Donne a tribute more impressive than all this sentimentality. Research into Donne's life had been his hobby during many years as a country clergyman and the results were published in his substantial article in the *Dictionary of National Biography* (together with a tribute to Walton's less laborious work, which 'stands, and must remain for ever, the materpiece of English biography'), but he knew that he could not understand the erotic or spiritually disturbed poetry; so he withdrew from a plan to write a big biography jointly with Edmund Gosse. Sending him a copy of his own little book in 1897, he promised to follow this gift with all the material which his industry had produced over the years.

Gosse had fewer inhibitions and only two years passed before the two volumes of his *Life and Letters* were on sale. Until 1970 this was the standard biography but it depended on Jessopp's work and on the copying of manuscripts by a research assistant who was less reliable – and it was not only in details that Gosse's own contributions were defective. When he tackled the secular poetry, it was with a Victorian disapproval as firm as Jessopp's. He saw no alternative to treating the most striking of the poems as records of actual affairs with mistresses including at least one married woman (a 'great criminal liaison'). Donne, he reckoned, 'was above all things sincere', so that it had to be said that 'his writings, like his actions, were faulty, violent, a little morbid even, and abnormal'. And so Gosse was quick to denounce.

Various poems were condemned as 'most frankly sensual', 'with no evidence of soul' but with 'the symptoms of a malady of the mind'. Some were read as a series of outbursts of a passionate lover when rejected by a mistress – a bitterness which lasted until the exhausted writing of the 'Nocturnall'. The fourth 'elegie' was Donne's account of his behaviour while courting Anne: 'that it is a recital of facts I do not for a moment doubt' and the facts were, Gosse thought, greatly to Donne's discredit. Poems with more tenderness and beauty in them cannot have come from the developing love, since 'at this moment of his life his poetical talent seems to have almost entirely deserted him'. Donne's chief talent, it appears, was for behaving badly.

Gosse was convinced that 'penitence and a genuine sorrow for faults of instinct' took a long time to develop after the marriage. When Donne attempted poems on religious subjects, these amounted to no more than 'extremely ingenious exercises in metrical theology', corrupted by the influence of 'Spanish ingenuities'. When he began to write poems more deeply religious, 'nothing could be more odious' than the poem on Good Friday 1613; the 'Anniversaries' were 'positively preposterous' and 'it is difficult to understand how the desire to please and the intoxication of his ingenuity have so blinded Donne to the claims of self-respect'; the lament for Prince Henry was 'not animated by one touch of sincere emotion'. The prose was also condemned; even the *Essayes in Divinity* were an intellectual exercise where 'nothing is for edification'.

Although Donne was ordained in January 1615, and was chosen in October 1616 as Reader in Divinity by the Benchers (senior lawyers) in Lincoln's Inn many of whom were Puritans, Gosse was strangely sure that 'there is abundant evidence to show' that he did not experience a Christian conversion before the winter of 1617, after Anne's death in August. Even then the convert was still capable of gross flattery in order to secure his appointment as Dean of St Paul's, and his *Devotions* of 1624 were full of 'diseased vivacity' and 'painful ingenuity'. As a layman Gosse shied away from any close examination of the sermons, which might have modified some of these verdicts. It is therefore not surprising to read at the end of the *Life and Letters* that 'we are tempted to declare that of all great men he is the one of whom least is essentially known. Is not this, perhaps, the secret of his perennial fascination?' Readers were warned not to accept him solely as a 'prophet of the intricacies of fleshly feeling', or as a 'crafty courtier' or as a 'crystal-hearted saint', for 'he was none of these, or all of these, or more'.

But Donne's modern readers have had some reasons to be grateful for Gosse's two fat Victorian volumes. Although he himself owed much to Jessopp, the air in his book was free of incense. He was the first to print the letters which illuminate the drama of the marriage and the three poems in the Westmoreland manuscript which throw light on the religious development. Gosse corrected some of Walton's errors and did much (not all) of the editorial work which Donne's son ought to have done when publishing some of the correspondence.

Not before the twentieth century did scholars emerge who applied themselves to a thorough study of the texts of Donne's surviving writings and painstaking research into what remained of evidence about his life. The best editors of his poetry made possible an understanding of his personality at a level different from the hero-worship of Walton and Jessopp and from the Victorian morality of Sir Edmund Gosse. These came from Scotland (Sir Herbert Grierson, 1912), England (Dame Helen Gardner, 1952 and 1965) and the USA (Professor John Shawcross, 1967). And then Australia and the USA jointly produced a scholar, R. C. Bald, who gathered together research already done in England, added his own labours although he had no English base, and wrote a biography which when published in 1970 at last placed the study of Donne on a foundation of recorded facts.

Herbert Grierson's edition of the poems in 1912 was the most careful yet seen, but his achievement was to make the subsequent debate possible, not to prevent it. He included as authentically by Donne some poems which either he or later editors later found unconvincing and his text did not take into account all the manuscripts which later editors were to consult. And like Gosse he found it difficult to understand the personality behind the poems. In his introduction to a revised edition published in 1933 he still thought it was not possible to do much more than 'make explicit these contradictions'. He found it comparatively easy to contrast Donne's boyhood in the devout and strict atmosphere of the 'Catholic revival' with the young man's 'sensuality, naturalism and cynicism', and he saw the break as occurring during his time in Italy and Spain when 'the blood was flowing passionately in his veins', producing 'an intense susceptibility to the fascination of sex'. But Grierson found it harder to connect the 'manifold contradictions' of the later years, when ambition for a career was combined with the plan to end *Metempsychosis* with an all-out attack on his queen and poems and letters with a high moral tone were combined with 'excesses of flattery' to Donne's patrons including 'protestations of devotion to James's abominable favourites'. These 'ambitious compliances' were for Grierson much harder to forgive than the passions of early manhood.

If Donne's middle period remained a puzzle to Grierson, so did the period after ordination. He found it easy to praise the religious poems (ascribed to this period) which recaptured the strong passions of the love poetry, and also to admire the sermons where 'the talk is poetry'. But he thought that the poems showed that the heart of the preacher was 'never at rest'. In particular he found evidence of continuing unease in the sonnet which begins 'Show me, deare Christ, thy Spouse'. He interpreted this poem as meaning that Donne was still not at all sure that he had been shown that the Church of England truly was a part of the Bride of Christ.

Helen Gardner made important advances on Grierson's edition. She did more work on the manuscripts and thought with more determination about the poems as evidence on the personality. She was subtle and wise about the idea that what Donne wrote was straightforward autobiography: to her it was clearly not that, yet poems can be used with discretion as evidence about the life, somewhat as the work of an artist can be used to build up a portrait of the painter. 'The truths of Donne's love poetry', she wrote, 'are truths of the imagination, which freely transmutes personal experience.' Thus she agreed with Grierson that this poetry reflects the influence of Italy and Spain, although for her the influence came mainly through books, not through the passionate pulsating of Donne's young blood when under the even hotter Mediterranean sun. She also agreed in principle that the poetry can be used to show a transition from promiscuity to married 'union', although unlike Grierson she was careful not to say that particular poems must be about the marriage. And she made a breakthrough in the understanding of the religious poetry.

Gardner examined it more closely and gave reasons for her conclusion that most of it was written before, not after, ordination: it was troubled, but these were not the secret doubts of a preacher. And she convincingly explained why the religious poetry differs from the erotic in being not the celebration of a conquest but a struggle to surrender. 'The Divine Poems', she wrote, are 'records of struggles to appropriate a truth which has been revealed.' Donne did not invent the Christianity; he inherited it from the Bible and the Fathers of the Church, and from more recent teachers both Catholic and Protestant, but he made this heritage his own in a style of his own. The sonnet to which Grierson had drawn particular attention was one of the few poems dated by Gardner after the ordination, but she did not find it to be either disturbed or disturbing. On the contrary, she thought that it demonstrated that Donne had become a convinced Anglican. He looked round at other Churches and gave thanks for the Church of England, in itself both Catholic and Protestant. The poem 'could hardly have been written by anyone but an Anglican'. (It will be discussed on pp. 242–3.)

In 1967 John Shawcross published what he rightly claimed was the first 'complete annotated edition' of Donne's poetry. He was highly critical of Gardner's work on the text, basing his own attempt to come 'close to what Donne intended' on three times the number of manuscripts and including a long list of his disagreements. (In a volume published in 1995 to honour Shawcross, Ted-Larry Pebworth said that he would not give his own list since 'the shortcomings in Gardner's approach and practice are too numerous'.) He also thought that Gardner's cautious proposal that some of the poems were influenced by the marriage was 'most unconvincing' and his own position was that 'dating is and must be very tentative'. However, in order to 'elicit new discussion' he supplied a 'Chronological Schedule' suggesting dates for many of the poems including one for the 'Elegies' (1593–96) and another for the 'Songs and Sonets' (1593–1601?). Later discussion of this chronology has sometimes been critical, as he no doubt expected, but his work on the manuscripts was one of the inspirations behind the launch in 1995 of the *Variorum Edition* comparing printed and handwritten texts after study by many scholars aided by computers. Until this project is completed, the Shawcross edition is almost always cited by Americans writing about Donne.

In 1984 another American professor, C. A. Patrides, published another annotated edition of the poems. He differed from Shawcross in relying on the printed editions of the 1630s except 'where they are self-evidently inadequate' and in refusing to 'theorize on dates of composition'. But this apparent dismissal of manuscripts and dates did not prevent him from listing the most important disagreements between printed and handwritten sources. He also discussed dates, although without constructing another new chronology. So far from ignoring other scholars, he supplied a long bibliography of their contributions. This attention to detail explains why his edition, so far from being an unresearched attack on Shawcross, took nine years to prepare. After widespread use, his work was updated by Robin Hamilton in 1994. One generalization which Patrides commended to readers willing to be as careful as he was affirmed that 'Donne's skill is of the highest technical expertness in English poetry', contradicting the impression which the middle-aged Donne often tried to convey: that his poems had been tossed off in an idle and probably foolish hour.

It is surely understandable that there have been these differences of expert opinion about the text of Donne's poems. However, very seldom, if ever, does any difficult decision which is significant for a biography depend on a decision between textual variants. One interesting decision seems easy if one relies on common sense: when the 'Epistle' introducing *Metempsychosis* was first printed in 1633, the 'soule' that was in 'that apple which Eve ate' was called 'she' because it was the custom to treat every soul as feminine. But there was a reference to this soul of evil ending up in 'hee, whose life you shall finde in the end of this booke'. Two years later the printer changed that final 'hee' to 'shee' and the change, which was probably careless, has been quoted in support of the suggestion that the poem was to have ended with a massive insult to Queen Elizabeth as the embodiment of evil. But the reason why it seems probable that the printer made a mistake in 1635 is that it is very improbable that Donne made the mistake of treason.

John Donne: A Life by R. C. Bald (1970) has never been equalled as a biography based on research. It was almost entirely the work of an Australian scholar (for much of his career a professor in the

University of Chicago) and on his death it was completed by another, Wesley Milgate. Its claims about its six hundred pages, full of facts old or new, were just: 'In the scholarly enthusiasm for Donne of the last fifty years a good many fresh details have come to light and have been published here and there in the learned periodicals; these must be incorporated in any complete account. Other facts appear here for the first time, and it is hoped that the archival resources of the Anglo-Saxon world will have relatively little still to yield.' It may have been uncharacteristically naughty for Bald to hope that other researchers would be disappointed but the next thirty years did not produce much information both new and important. At present it seems unlikely that the work will ever need to be done again. It included some treatment of what Donne wrote and preached, and as was to be expected Bald was always sensible, but the space allocated to literary criticism was smaller than that devoted to historical facts. The result is that we close this invaluable book having learned more about Donne's activities than about his feelings.

Recently the centre of Donnean studies has shifted decisively to North America. An Englishman may be allowed to make in this connection some points which to him seem obvious. Here is a text which although remote in geography springs from English roots, as does much else in North American life. It is in a language which, although now unfamiliar in the form used by Donne, is not totally foreign, and there is a special interest in the fact that he used this language as the great English migration to New England was beginning. And here is a text which is full of human interest; as Professor Shawcross noted, in the twentieth century as in the seventeenth 'readers' interest lay in the wittiness of Jack Donne's love themes'. But to these points may be added two suggestions which are perhaps less obvious.

When viewed from across the Atlantic, the island which is partially occupied by the English appears to belong to Europe; and when work has been needed to investigate the sources behind Donne's poetry and prose, most of the hard work has been done by North American academics who have not been content to confine their researches to English sources. These scholars have greatly refined the meaning of the labels traditionally attached to Donne, 'Renaissance', 'metaphysical' and 'original'. Especially in his preaching, Donne was a mixture of the medieval and the modern, and it has been shown in detail how that was true of the whole of the Renaissance, although the fusion in Donne was his own. Especially in his poetry, Donne used 'conceits' which made surprising connections between things apparently very dissimilar, and a knowledge of the European literature of his time has been used to show how extensive was this 'metaphysical wit' although the electrifying power in Donne's hands came from his brain. And in religion Donne was vigorously original, not by being 'singular' (a word which he more or less equated with 'arrogant' or 'ignorant') but by drawing on a vast heritage both Catholic and Protestant, both ancient and modern – and making it his own living faith, a European faith.

North American scholars have also been well-equipped and motivated to study Donne's religion, in a time when in Europe, including Britain for this purpose, the surrounding society has become if not more secular then certainly far less church-related. Many North American academics have a respect for traditional Christianity as small as any European's but in general the contrast between North American and European attitudes has been striking. Religion has boomed in the USA, and to a lesser extent in Canada, and inevitably it has influenced the academic world. It is not surprising that there have been some suggestions which to a European seem to arise from an unreasonable belief that even when writing erotic poetry the young Donne was being moral and even theological. Nor is it surprising that an attempt has been made to overthrow the usual account of his early formation.

Dennis Flynn's *John Donne and the Ancient Catholic Nobility* (1995) was one of a series of studies in which this respected scholar explored the influence of the Roman Catholic heritage. The question is not whether there was a large influence; clearly there was. But it has to be asked whether Flynn was right in his suggestions about the way in which the young man had experienced this influence.

He suggested that John Donne was withdrawn from Oxford after only one term because his family feared that even at the age of thirteen he might be required to take an oath accepting the Church of England. Flynn then argued that he was the 'Mr John Donnes' whose name appears near the bottom of the list of 'noble men knightes and Esquires and Gentlemene giving their Attendance one the Righte Honorable the Earle of Derby' who was sent on a specially grand mission to Paris in order to invest the French king with the insignia of the Order of the Garter: the earl was classified by Flynn as a member of the ancient Catholic nobility. The name of 'Mr John Downes' also appears among the 'Gentlemen Waiters' in a list of the earl's 'Householde Servants' in 1587. Flynn also suggested that John Donne was present in the Spanish army at the siege of Antwerp in the spring of 1585, since in 1652 epigrams said to have been originally written in Latin by him, but now translated by Jasper Mayne, were published along with material since agreed to be authentically Donnean, and some of these English verses seem to refer to that siege.

That is an interesting reconstruction of Donne's life between the two dates which are certain: his two enrolments, in Hart Hall, Oxford, in 1584 and in Lincoln's Inn in 1592 after a preparatory year in Thavies Inn. However, Flynn's theory is open to a number of objections.

While it is plainly true that in the early 1580s the Elizabethan government was in a panic about the possibility of an invasion by French Catholics in order to place Mary Queen of Scots on the throne, it is unlikely that this reaction was much of a threat to John Donne while he was well below the age at which Oxford University would demand his acceptance of the Church of England if he was to proceed to a degree. If this lad had been required to swear his loyalty to Queen and Church, probably he would have done so in company with many others whose real faith was Roman Catholic, and without disagreement with his stepfather, the London doctor who also kept out of trouble with the authorities. If as a Catholic he was in real danger in Oxford, it seems very unlikely that he would have been taken into the service of the Earl of Derby, who like most of the aristocracy was no Protestant but who at this time was in the government's good books, to the extent that he represented it in an embassy designed to put an end to the threat from France.

Had the young Donne been included in this delicate mission to Paris it seems improbable that he would have been taken to join the siege of Antwerp. If a mature Donne did write Latin poetry about that siege, the poetry did not depend very obviously on the experiences of a boy of thirteen on his first trip abroad: its English version is in the voice of a soldier familiar with war and also a sophisticated wit. But did Donne actually write such a poem? Jasper Mayne, who claimed to be its translator, was a clergyman fairly well known as a poet, dramatist and practical joker; in his will he left a legacy to a servant – a red herring. Most scholars have been very sceptical.

However, the strongest argument against Flynn's claim that the famous John Donne was in domestic service from 1584 to 1587 is that we know that only five years later he was flourishing as an extraordinarily clever and accomplished poet, as a man-about-town who had money to spend among friends of high social status, and as a rising star who rapidly acquired enough legal knowledge and ease in society to be suitable as a member of the small staff of Egerton, a man widely admired and trusted as a leading judge and a minister frequently consulted and used by the queen in confidential matters (for example, in dealing with the Earl of Essex). And many modern scholars think that at this stage Donne was already familiar both with the Latin classics and with the poetry of the Italian Renaissance, while being so confident of his own powers that he was ready to stand alone in the style of his poetry and to walk away from the opportunity to become a lawyer. A 'gentleman waiter' in an earl's household may well have had opportunities to develop skills in addition to those expected in his domestic duties, but there needs to be stronger evidence than any which is provided by Professor Flynn against Izaak Walton's report that Donne was well educated in Oxford and Cambridge, and kept up friendships begun in those years as a student. In particular Walton stressed that Donne and Wotton became friends in Oxford: 'the friendship . . . was generously elemented: And it was begun in their Youth, and in a University, and there maintained by correspondent Inclinations and Studies, so it lasted till Age and Death forced a Separation'. Walton made mistakes, but this does not appear to have been one of them: he was recording what these two men, both heroes to him, had told him about their shared youth.

6 Deare honestie

If our Soules have stain'd their first white, yet wee
May cloth them with faith and deare honestie . . .
'To Mr Rowland Woodward'

In this chapter I shall discuss two recent books by English scholars which claim to present an honest account of Donne, in particular of his religion. My objection is not to honesty: it is to unfairness.

Professor John Carey's book on *John Donne: Life, Mind and Art*, first published in 1981, has been widely used. It incorporates many of the researches assembled in Professor Bald's biography but is shorter and more lively, and it offers a fuller treatment of Donne's psychology as seen in his writings. Another reason for the welcome given to the book is that it is, on the whole, hostile to Donne: an approach which can be thought to make for realism and also for readability, exposing without any cover-up a Great Poet who is compulsory in courses on English Literature. However, I hope to demonstrate that while making many true observations Carey does not relate himself sufficiently to the evidence. In particular he despises Donne's religion so emphatically that he avoids the trouble involved in trying to understand it.

He is convinced that 'every theological issue hinges ultimately on imagination' (p. 158) and his central aim in his book is to demonstrate that 'Donne's opinions upon such furiously controverted issues as original sin, election, resurrection and the state of the soul after death, were generated by recognizably the same imagination as the poems about love and women' (p. xiv). Such theological opinions were, it is argued, not vitally important to the preacher, a cool customer who as a young man 'doesn't even seem to feel sexually excited' (p. x). What did excite Donne is, Carey thinks, shown in words which are repeated in the titles of the chapters in the first half of his book: 'apostasy' and 'ambition'. The book begins by telling the reader to remember that Donne was a Catholic who 'betrayed his Faith'. It continues by claiming that 'he chose hell' because he abandoned Catholicism while knowing that it 'must be right'. 'No church would ever be the same to him again', we are told (p. 16); indeed, he 'relinquished his religion' (p. 199), being motivated by ambition.

These are strange words to use about a man who gave many years of his life to his labours as a preacher in the Church of England, 1615–31. He certainly was ambitious – with such talents and industry, who would not be? – but it seems unfair to say that ambition was the emotion which dominated his life. Before being ordained he had spent almost as many years without a regular job and with a large family, and he had refused to draw an income from the Church of England although offers were made. He had lost his first job, when he had seemed well placed for a distinguished and profitable career, because he had secretly married, being sexually excited. Carey thinks that he married a girl believing that her rich father, when told, would produce a blessing and a large sum of money, but this suggestion does not stand up to examination (as I shall try to show on pp. 254–9).

Certainly he was an 'apostate' in the sense that he ceased to be a Roman Catholic, but it seems wrong to say that he 'chose hell'. What he chose was conformity to the Church of England and for many years this seems to have amounted to no more than occasional attendance at Anglican services and a willingness to swear an oath that he did not accept the deposition of Elizabeth I and James I by the pope. However, in the reigns of Elizabeth and James this was the practice of most of the English who in their hearts remained faithful to the 'old religion' and hoped for its restoration. Many Roman Catholic priests, including some who accepted martyrdom for themselves, tolerated this degree of conformity to the government and its Church, and they did not refuse Communion to those who saw no alternative to it. In particular they allowed it in cases where influence on society would have been lost by total honesty: thus some aristocrats who would have welcomed a restoration of the old Church but who were large landowners conformed, as did some courtiers and men in government. Moreover, English people who were really Roman Catholic in religion could think themselves entitled to add 'mental reservations' to any answers which they made in self-defence against their persecutors. This practice was not condemned by the papacy before 1679. So if Donne chose to conform superficially to the Church of England it is unlikely that he felt that he was going to hell. But the question remains: in his heart, did he feel ashamed?

In his third 'satyre', probably written in the 1590s, he asks himself with 'feare' whether 'thy father's spirit' will 'heare thee damn'd' –

> Thee, whom hee taught so easie wayes, and neare,
> To follow . . .

And he tells himself to 'aske thy father' which is the true religion. He does not explain clearly what he means: was he referring to his natural father the prosperous ironmonger who died when he was not yet aged four, or to his stepfather the prosperous doctor who (as Professor Flynn has shown) was 'easie' rather than enthusiastic in his old-style Catholicism? He does not refer to his mother who was the religious enthusiast and martyr in the family, in the new style of the Catholic Reformation. What he does say is that his father should ask his grandfather, for 'truth' is 'a little elder' than any falsehood in religion – and what matters is not the decision whether 'to adore or scorne an image'. Truth, he says, is what matters. It lived in Rome 'a thousand yeares agoe' but has now disappeared from that city apart from some 'ragges' of it. He announces that he will not now take instruction from image-adoring Pope Gregory, any more than he will obey King Philip of Spain or any of the image-breaking Protestant authorities. Instead,

> To stand inquiring right, is not to stray;
> To sleepe, or run wrong, is: on a huge hill,
> Cragg'd and steep, Truth stands, and hee that will
> Reach her, about must, and about must goe . . .

The comment by Helen Gardner is discerning. 'The poem shows that if Donne rejected the Roman obedience, he had derived from his upbringing an unquestioning acceptance of the claim of religion. The argument rests on two assumptions: that the search for "true Religion" is the primary duty of a moral being, and that truth exists and can be known.' For Donne this search was to be different from the 'easie wayes' which would have been 'neare' an Englishman who without any fuss had fitted into the society which had functioned around the medieval Church. The medieval civilization and its 'old religion' having ended, the search was now to be through great uncertainty, as if a traveller were to climb a mountain in a mist – but it was to be a pilgrimage upwards towards Truth, not a journey downward to eternal damnation.

The eighth of Donne's 'Holy Sonnets' was written while he was still trying to find his way up that mountain, guided by 'my minde's white truth'. His heart was still full of 'griefe', but at least he thought he knew this:

> If faithfull soules be alike glorifi'd
> As Angels, then my father's soul doth see,
> And adds this even to full felicitie,
> That valiantly I hel's wide mouth o'rstride . . .

And already in his third 'satyre' he showed that he was in earnest about religion. He must 'not laugh, nor weepe' about this subject. In other poems he has celebrated or attacked a long line of human mistresses, but to be serious 'Is not our Mistresse fair Religion'? Is not the thought of 'heaven's joyes' the only cure for earthly lusts? And does not the search for 'true religion' call for 'great courage', more than does either war or the exploration of the world? What matters supremely in this heartfelt third 'satyre' is the prospect of 'the last day' when some souls will 'perish'. They are doomed if they have trusted not in God himself but in mortals who have wrongly claimed 'Power from God'. Evidently Donne has rejected the power claimed by the papacy, but he also rejects both 'sullen' Calvinism and the 'vile ambitious' preachers of the new Church of England under royal supremacy. He condemns equally both the arrogant Puritans who 'abhorre all, because all cannot be good' and the Erastians who think that because all the faiths are of 'one kinde' the ruler is entitled to choose which faith will be made compulsory as the religion of the people. As he sees it, the road to Truth is not crowded.

There is, however, no evidence to support Carey's idea that 'the love poems are a veil for religious perturbations', where he 'rids himself of disloyalty by transferring it to women' (p. 24). It seems more likely that in real life women of the kind glimpsed in the poems of the 1590s, whether girlfriends, married women or prostitutes, would see no reason to be loyal for life to a young man whose financial prospects were uncertain, and whose favourite subject was his own cleverness. Not knowing that they had been in contact with one of the greatest poets in the English language, his women either got bored and dumped him, or else forgot him after taking his money. It also seems likely that Donne had not begun these relationships because he was feeling exceptionally religious.

It was an age when most educated people were interested in religious controversies which asked what was the truth about the God in whose existence almost everyone believed. These disputes were about eternity and about who would spend it in heaven, purgatory or hell. Meanwhile, before death, religious questions were morally, socially and politically important – and they could bring death, imprisonment, exile or poverty. It is not at all surprising that Donne was seriously interested. Nor is it surprising to find him telling us that from early years he thought seriously about suicide: he was as sensitive as any young person who has ever dreamed of that escape from a troublesome life. But like most young people Donne decided to go on living and to try to enjoy himself in the process. His poems show that he became fond of using 'dye' as slang for an orgasm and 'rise' as slang for a man's sexual arousal. And he could be happy to make a flippant use of other religious language.

In 'Change' the speaker says that 'much, much I feare thee'. But this is not the fear of God. He is worried that he will lose a mistress who has in the past proved her 'faith' by her 'good workes' in sex. He fears that her 'apostasie' will consist of a willingness to 'fall back' – and her Fall will consist of lying down to have sex with another man. But then the speaker reflects that another man is entitled to 'catch the same bird' if he can: 'these things bee' and 'change' (not religion) is the nursery 'of musicke, joy, life, and eternity'.

When Donne was looking for startling images to use in erotic poetry he could fall back on memories of Catholicism. In 'The Funerall' a rejected lover is 'Love's martyr'. In 'The Canonization' he imagines lovers who make each other's body a 'hermitage' and are then 'canoniz'd' like the Church's saints. In 'The Relique' he pictures two skeletons of lovers being venerated as the relics of saints, so that

All women shall adore us, and some men . . .

What these pious fools will not know is that when alive the two did not have sex, that in reality their restraint was the 'miracles wee did'. They will be adored as 'a Mary Magdalen' (believed to be an ex-prostitute) and, in his case, as 'a something else' – which may refer with a wink to the speculation that Jesus had a sexual relationship with that Mary.

'The Bracelet' is an early poem, as Carey agrees, and being immature it goes on too long. It concerns a very expensive 'seaven fold chaine' of gold which the speaker has somehow 'lost' and which needs to be replaced at 'the bitter cost' of twelve gold coins called 'angels': these must now be melted down. The word 'angels' sets him off on a lengthy pun which can be met in other Elizabethan poetry but is not to be expected from a poem from a man deeply perturbed by the prospect of hell. He pictures these angels being 'burnt and tyed in chains' by the command of his mistress, a 'dread judge'. He tells her that he accepts her demand for a new chain, but he uses the Lord's Prayer and the image of the Virgin Mary on the first Good Friday with a striking lack of religious sensitivity:

Thy will be done;
Yet with such anguish, as her onely sonne
The Mother in the hungry grave doth lay,
Unto the fire these Martyrs I betray.

In Donne's sixth 'elegie' there are references to Protestants who reject the pope's religious authority, to recusants who reject the queen's authority in obedience to the pope, and to sinners who are excommunicated. But the references are all really about the double prospect that his present lover will reject him and that he will get over it:

I shall
As nations do from Rome, from thy love fall.
My hate shall outgrow thine, and utterly,
I will renounce thy dalliance; and when I
Am the Recusant, in that absolute state,
What hurts it mee to be excommunicate?

Carey is able to underplay Donne's youthful delight in enjoying, or imagining, promiscuity because he thinks it probable that all the 'Songs and Sonets' where this is a frequent theme were written considerably later than the poet's traumatic 'apostasy' and later than his marriage. In his critical edition of the major works published in 1990 page 88 is reached before any of the 'Songs and Sonets' is printed, and we are told that there is no evidence for dating any of them before 1602. But there is strong evidence, for in the 1600s Donne was married to a wife for whom he had sacrificed his career and they produced children, about as often as was physically possible. Did he have a series of adulterous relationships, or a lot of vivid dreams about them? If so, why did he send poems celebrating serial adultery to his men friends, along with solemn thoughts about morality and religion? Carey himself believes that after his marriage Donne's fidelity to Anne was absolute: 'when he had her, he wanted no other woman' (p. 59). That seems to be true although it cannot be proved, and the only dating of the 'Songs and Sonets' which is consistent with Donne's fidelity after marriage is that those of them which celebrate promiscuity were written before he was married. If that is the case, it follows that the flippant use of religious language shows a young man who was not much troubled by the fear of hell.

It is also clear that he never regarded himself as an 'apostate' from the Catholic Faith. As much that he wrote proves, for him the central issue was not whether the Faith was true. It was one of jurisdiction: who had the supreme power, the pope or the national sovereign?

Once he had rejected the authority of the pope over the English monarchy, other rejections of Roman Catholicism followed but it seems clear that for him (as for many others in England from Henry VIII onwards) the decisive question was about papal jurisdiction: the popes had abused their authority by adding objectionable doctrines and practices to the Faith as defined by the Bible and the early Christian centuries. In his ironic but light-hearted poem 'The Will' he left legacies to people who 'had too much' already: so 'my faith I give to Roman Catholiques'. And the developments which he now attacked were not only doctrinal. During the 1620s he devoted two sermons preached in Whitehall Palace to a defence of the English Reformation (10:140–77). He took as his text the denunciation by the prophet Ezekiel of the bad shepherds who had made the Lord's own flock eat and drink 'that which yee have fouled with your feet'. He interpreted this text as a criticism of pastors who had muddied the waters of religion, motivated by 'covetousness and love of money' (10:172).

His attack was on legends, superstitions and complicated ceremonies all of which were designed to strengthen the power of the clergy over the minds of the people when the emphasis ought to have been on what the Bible said about simple prayer and good behaviour. While his preaching showed that he valued the practice of confessing sins to a priest (e.g. 9:310), he protested against making this compulsory. He denounced the wealth which the senior clergy and the monks had derived from this system and concentrated his heaviest fire on the Vatican, where popes surrounded themselves with splendour as they tried to control not only the clergy and laity but also the kings of the earth. And almost four hundred years after these protests, many Roman Catholics are known to agree very largely with Donne's line that such medieval developments are no part of permanent and essential Catholicism.

Certainly he never cut himself off from Roman Catholics as individuals, despite his growing disagreement with much of what was taught in their Church. The best – but not the only – example is his attitude to his mother. After being widowed for a second time, she married Richard Rainsford and went into exile with him in 1595 in order that they might both be free to practise their ardent Catholicism. After their return to England eleven years later he was twice imprisoned, in 1611 and 1613. Then she was widowed again, but her son gave her a home in his Deanery. (She died two months before him.) Earlier Donne had assured her that as the only one of her children 'left now', he would make up for the fact that her first husband's legacy to her had melted away over the years and would 'provide for your relief, as for my own wife and children'.

And certainly Donne never cut himself off from the Catholic spiritual tradition. It would be truer to use about him the nickname of people who tried to be both old and new in their religion, 'Church Papists'. Modern scholars have shown how his poems reveal a continuing use of Catholic forms of devotion, for example the form of reciting the rosary made popular by the Dominicans and used by Donne in 'La Corona' in 1607 (see pp. 224–6). It is also a fact that twenty years later he observed with great feeling the midwinter festival of St Lucy, which was not in the Anglican calendar (see pp. 272–5). As Professor Martz has demonstrated, he also made intensive use of the Jesuit method of meditation. In his prose works he cited a vast array of Catholic writers. His farewell gift to the senior lawyers of Lincoln's Inn, many of whom were stout Puritans, was a recently reprinted Latin Bible in six volumes with a commentary dating from the fourteenth century. This included many references to the Fathers of the Church, as did the books of a Jesuit contemporary of Donne's, Cornelius à Lapide, often consulted as he prepared sermons. The biblical quotations in these sermons show that he instinctively quoted first the Latin

Bible in the pre-1592 Vulgate version – and often quoted from memory, sometimes making a small slip. The last word in the epitaph which he wrote for his own grave, referring to Christ as *Oriens* ('Rising' in the east), is from the Vulgate Bible, which mistranslated Zechariah 6:12.

Writing to the Duke of Buckingham in 1623, Donne did not criticize the highly unpopular mission which that minister was undertaking as the companion of Prince Charles in his attempt to arrange marriage with the Catholic daughter of the King of Spain. Instead, he told the duke that in his own library Spanish authors were represented better than those of any other nation. He reflected that 'their autors in Divinity, though they do not show us the best way to heaven, yet thinke they doe. And so, though they say not true, yet they do not ly, because they speak their Conscience.'

In a poem congratulating Prince Charles on this plan, he called the Roman Catholic, Lutheran and Calvinist versions of Christianity 'beames' coming from the single 'sunne'. On another occasion he wrote that the Roman and English Churches were 'sister teats of his graces, yet both diseased and infected'. In one sermon he exhorted his hearers to 'love those universall and fundamentall doctrines which in all Christian ages, and in all Christian Churches, have been agreed by all to be necessary to salvation; and then thou art a true Catholique' (2:280). In another he said that if God asked him what his religion was, 'shall I not be able to say, It is that which thy word and thy Catholique Church hath imprinted in me?' (7:61). A little later he told Sir Robert Ker that 'my Tenets are always for the Religion I was born in, and the peace of the State, and the rectifying of the Conscience'. Presumably he had not forgotten that he had been born as a Roman Catholic, but now as an Anglican dean he claimed that he had never changed his religion. He expected his friend to know what he meant. In his *Essayes in Divinity* he declared that 'through all my thanksgivings to God I ever humbly acknowledge as one of his greatest Mercies to me that he gave me my Pasture in this Park and my milk from the breasts of this Church' – by which he meant, of course, the Church of his family and early years. But he wrote that book as a test of his fitness to become an Anglican preacher and what he preached in that capacity was what he had come to believe: that 'in another Church the Additonall things exceed the Fundamentall . . . and the Traditions of Men, the Commandments of God' (5:295). As a Roman Catholic boy he had imbibed the fundamental commandments and as an Anglican adult he was prepared to teach them.

He may have startled some of his hearers when he preached from an Anglican pulpit: 'I am a Papist, that is, I will fast and pray as much as any Papist and enable my selfe for the service of my God, as seriously, as sedulously, as laboriously as an Papist' (9:166). Admittedly he went on to say 'I am a Puritan, that is, I will endeavour to be pure as my Father in heaven is pure, as far as any Puritan' – but he had made his point in a time of English hysteria against Popery. Donne had to defend himself 'when we acknowledge the Church of Rome to be truly a Church'. He did it by calling that Church a 'Pest-house', where people with infectious diseases ought to be isolated – but 'the Pest-house is a house' (9:344).

Thus Catholic elements could be retained, both while Donne regarded himself as a 'Christian' without any other label and later when he became an Anglican priest and preacher. Carey reckons that 'restless desire for work and worldly success' (p. 46) explains why he joined 'the Anglican propaganda machine' (p. 37). There is some truth in these severe words, for Donne did write some less than reasonable propaganda against the teachings and behaviour of popes and Jesuits, and his motives in writing these books, and later in being ordained, included a desire to escape from long-term unemployment. But when he had been ordained, his eloquence about what he had found in the Church of England was so passionate that there appears to be no need to dismiss it as insincere.

He now identified the ultimate Truth with the living Christ and out of his experience he answered the question 'Where are we likeliest to find him?' His answer was that everyone must undertake the search personally, for 'thou must not so think him in heaven, as that thou canst not have immediate accesse to him without intercession of others'. There was no need to look for Christ 'beyond the Sea' – either in Rome where 'the Church is but an Antiquaries' Cabinet, full of rags and fragments of antiquity', or in Geneva where the Church of the Calvinists is 'so new a built house with bare walls, that it is yet unfurnished of such Ceremonies as should make it comly and reverend'. No, Christ is accessible to everyone who seeks, for 'Christ is at home with thee, he is at home within thee, and there is the nearest way to find him' (1:246).

In a later sermon he said that 'the aire is not so full of Moats, of Atomes, as the Church is full of Mercies; and as we can suck in no part of aire, but we take in these Moats, these Atomes; so here in the Congregation we cannot suck in a word from the preacher, we cannot speak, we cannot sigh a prayer to God, but that that whole breath and aire is made of mercy' (6:170–1).

Donne also seems to have been speaking out of experience – this time, of his years when he had been a churchless Christian – when he contrasted this discovery of mercy with the confusion and distress which could spoil private prayers. 'I locke my doore to my selfe, and I throw my selfe downe in the presence of my God, I devest my selfe of all worldly thoughts, and I bend all my powers and faculties upon God, as I think, and suddenly I find my selfe scattered, melted, fallen into vaine thoughts, into no thoughts; I am upon my knees, and I talke, and think nothing; I deprehend my selfe in it, and I goe about to mend it. I gather new forces, new purposes to try againe, and I doe the same thing againe. I beleeve in the Holy Ghost, but do not finde him, if I seeke him onely in private prayer; But when I go to meet him in Church, when I seeke him where he hath promised to bee found . . . I have . . . incorruption in the midst of my dunghill, spirit in the midst of my flesh, heaven upon earth' (5:249–50).

When preaching about the need for a better chapel in Lincoln's Inn he admitted that many saints of the Old Testament had found God outside a temple: Job on a dunghill, Hezekiah in a bed, Jeremiah in a dungeon, Jonah in a whale, Daniel in a den of lions, others in a fiery furnace. But he maintained that God could be found most easily in a church, which in his case was now Anglican (2:213–18). Preaching in St Paul's Cathedral one Whit Sunday he looked back: 'Of those who do professe Christ Jesus, some grovell still in the superstitions they were fallen into, and some are raised, by God's grace, out of them; and I am one of these . . . We are in the favour, and care of God; We, our Nation, we, our Church; There I am at home.' And so he gave thanks for 'what God hath done for me, and my soule; There is the Ego, the particular, the individual, I' (5:70–1). He now saw no great gap between the Church of England and God: indeed, 'nearer to him, and to the institutions of his Christ, can no Church, no not of the Reformation, be said to have come closer than ours does' (7:409). But he never ceased to feel that he was a Catholic, for he saw no great gap between the Church of England and the essentials of the Catholic Faith as held in the Church of his baptism and boyhood.

Carey tells us that 'to be moralistic about Donne would be foolish (p. 81) and that 'belittling him as a human being' is not his aim (p. 85). However he finds it 'hard to suppress a shudder' when Donne remarks in the pulpit that 'he that travails weary, and late towards a great City, is glad when he comes to a place of execution, because he knows that is neer the town' (p. 81). But the preacher uses this shudder-making idea in order to assure his congregation that someone dying is near a resurrection into glory, 'but one stop to thy Jerusalem' (2:266).

Carey does shudder (on p. 48) when he reads in Donne's *Devotions upon Emergent Occasions* the much-quoted words 'any man's death diminishes *me . . . never send to know* for whom the bell tolls, it tolls for thee' (the ironic italics are Carey's). But here Donne is not thinking only of himself, nor is he being so lazy that he sends someone to ask instead of satisfying his curiosity himself. In the *Devotions* the context is clear. Donne is confined to bed with a fever which may end in his death; he is troubled by the noise of bell-ringing which invades his bedroom from the nearby parish church of St Gregory, and he complains; then he hears the 'passing bell' tolling in order to call neighbours to prayer for someone who is dying. Donne does pray, now and after the death, and he meditates at considerable length on the solemn facts that this person is not only a neighbour but also a fellow member of the Church which is the Body of Christ, and that another soul is now going to judgement by Christ. In a later sermon he asks: 'is there any man, that in his chamber hears a bell toll for another man, and does not kneel down to pray for that dying man?' (8:174).

Unsurprisingly, Carey reckons that in Donne 'there is no thought about the man for whom the bell might be tolling', for 'the tone and the advice are entirely self-regarding' (p. 48) – and to be sure, Donne is as usual fascinated to observe his own reactions. Previously he has grumbled about the noise from the church ('that steeple which never ceases'), as it invades the room where he is a 'Prisoner' in a 'sicke bed' feeling very sorry for himself. He cannot sleep 'and oh, if I be entering now into Eternitie, where there shall be no distinction of houres, why is it al my businesse now to tell Clocks?' But the bell which invites him to pray for a fellow Christian who actually is 'entering now into Eternitie' is heard as a new sound. It is received as an invitation to escape from the prison created by his self-centredness.

His earlier concentration on his own woes is not amazing. He has felt that 'a sicke bed is a grave' and has complained that 'we doe not onely die, but die upon a Rack, die by a torment of sicknesse'. Being anxious to make his own diagnosis, he has 'cut up mine Anatomy, dissected my selfe' and in his anxiety he has watched the equally puzzled 'Phisician with the same diligence as hee the disease'. Then he has watched himself getting weaker even when his own doctor has called in colleagues to consult about the emergency. He has felt that if 'before hee had a beeing' he could have expected 'this miserie' he would not have chosen to be born, and he has moaned that even if a man 'tastes happinesse' he 'drinkes misery'. He has been forbidden to read and has often been left alone, complaining that 'the greatest misery of sicknes is solitude' and that 'Solitude is a torment which is not threatened in hell it selfe'. He has told himself that other people may be worse off: the paupers who cannot afford a doctor so that 'the first that takes knowledge is the Sexten that buries them', and the destitute who die not in a bed but on 'the flint of the street'. But until he hears this church bell, he is not fully moved by that vision of people who deserve pity even more than he does. It is only now that he is carried away by a flood of emotion. Because his own death may be very near he must make 'my recourse to my God' and if he survives he will be very fortunate. This bell is what teaches him to feel sharply that others may be 'farre more miserable, and farre more worthy to be less miserable than I'.

While we are on this point we may note that Carey is not alone in being unfair to the Donne of the *Devotions.*

When he usefully included many extracts in the Penguin edition of *John Donne: Selected Prose* (1987), Neil Rhodes called these meditations 'predominantly secular' because 'they do not resemble anything in the Christian meditative tradition, either Catholic or Protestant', adding that the 'expostulations' which are 'anguished' protests to God have a 'hectoring quality'. And to be sure, the style in which Donne meditates and prays is uniquely his own. But the position in which he finds himself is not unique. Believing that he may be about to die, he turns to God without formality about his faith and without pretence about his despair. He is not being secular. Roughly the same mixture of disturbed emotions may be found in the psalms of the Bible, and what is said in the gospels about Christ in Gethsemane and on the cross is not altogether different. As a Christian in distress Donne claims the right to make his protest with these precedents to 'my God, my God'. He knows that he must speak to God as a sinner who is 'the dust and the ashes of the Temple of the Holy Ghost' but he can ask 'what Marble is so precious?' because 'I am my best part, I am my soule'. This soul is 'the breath of God' in him and so 'I may breathe back these pious expostulations to my God'. That is not a man who is 'predominantly secular' or, when he prays, 'hectoring'. He belongs to a long tradition of prayer to God *de profundis*: 'Out of the deep . . .'. The self-pity in the *Devotions* is characteristic of humanity, and the self-exhibition involved in the publishing of these intimate thoughts is characteristic of Donne, but what he reveals in this strange little book is a double exposure. The tolling of a bell exposes him to a fellow Christian who is dying – and his fear that he too is about to die exposes him to 'my God' like a swimmer who is stripped on the edge of the cold sea.

Carey is obviously right to condemn as 'callousness' Donne's warning that family or friends ought not to shorten the suffering of people being hanged by tugging at their legs, on the ground that the law has 'appointed a painfull death to deterre others' and should not be 'defrauded'. Our indignation against the cold heart of this moralist is increased when we know that some of the people being choked to death by the hangman within reach of those who loved them were already so miserable that they had attempted to commit suicide and, when they had failed in that attempt, had made themselves criminals who had earned the death penalty and the confiscation of their goods under the law of that age. They were now being executed before burial in unconsecrated ground although they might have welcomed a fresh chance to rebuild their lives and support their families. But the passage which is quoted comes not from a sermon but from *Biathanatos*, where the thoroughly confused Donne is taking to this extreme the platitude that suicide ought to be discouraged although he expresses a bold sympathy with people tempted by this 'sickely inclination' and, also bravely, confesses that he himself has been so tempted. It is unfair to claim that this error of judgement was not only serious but also typical of 'Donne's relative immunity to the suffering of others' which is to be found 'throughout his work, in poetry and prose' (p. 192).

Carey is shocked when he hears Donne 'rhapsodizing' about the 'inexpressible comfort' which the passengers on Noah's ark 'must have felt when they saw everyone else drown' (p. 81). But we find that here the preacher is not gloating over the fate of sinners. He is trying to reduce their numbers and is talking about 'the joy in his safety' which 'a Christian is to take, even in this, that God hath taken him into his Church' (5:106). Certainly Donne accepted the belief that in the end humankind will be divided into the saved and the damned, but what is far more unusual in his sermons is his persistence in hoping for the best as he ponders the destiny of the majority of his fellow humans. Carey is far less charitable towards Donne, who is left to drown in a sea of false accusations.

Carey is also shocked to find Donne expressing a 'violent dislike' for beggars and 'denouncing the destitute' (pp. 81–2). And certainly in his early years Donne could be heartless about beggars, as in this disgusting epigram:

> I am unable, yonder beggar cries,
> To stand or move; if hee say true, he *lies*.

And even when his heart had been softened by life's knocks he could say something foolish about men who refused to work, as in this sermon: 'It will scarcely admit doubt, but that the incorrigible vagabond is farther from all the wayes of goodnesse than the corruptest rich man' (6:304). 'Thinkest thou to eat bread', he once asked a workshy beggar (who, however, was not in the congregation to hear him), 'and not sweat?' (1:207). He once warned the man who refuses to work that 'he kills himself' (1:209), for 'he that undertakes no course, no vocation, is no part, no member, no limbe of the body of this world' (4:160). He was specially indignant that in London 'street-beggary has become a calling, for Parents bring up their children to it, nay they doe almost take prentises to it, some expert beggars teach others about what they shall say, how shall they looke, how they shall lie, how they shall cry'. These were the beggars 'whom our lawes call Incorrigible' and whom Donne called 'vermin' because they 'devoure that which belongs to them who are truly poore' (6:304).

But about the neglect of 'them who are truly poore', Donne could be alarmingly eloquent. In an early sermon he said bluntly: 'The poore are He, He is the poore. And so he that oppreseth the poore, reproaches God' (1:287). He told the lawyers of Lincoln's Inn: 'Thou seest a needy person, and thou turnest away thine eye; but it is the Prince of Darknesse that casts this mist upon thee; Thou stoppest thy nose at his sores, but they are thine owne incompassionate bowels that stinke within thee' (3:137). He told a congregation in St Paul's Cathedral: 'He that makes himselfe insensible to the cries and curses of the poor here in this world doth but prepare himselfe for the howlings, and gnashings of the teeth, in the world to come' (8:280). 'Rich and poor are Images, Pictures of God', he explained; 'but (as Clement of Alexandria says wittily and strongly) the poor is *Nuda Imago*, a naked picture without any drapery, any clothes about it. And it is a much harder thing, and there is much more art showed in making a naked picture, than in all the rich attire that can be put upon it. And howsoever the rich man, that is invested in Power and Greatnesse, be made a better picture of God, of God considered in himself who is all Greatnesse, all Power, yet of God considered in Christ (which is the contemplation that concerns us most), the poor man is the better picture.' This is because the poor man 'most resembles Christ who liv'd in continual poverty' (8:285). And Bald's biography shows that Donne was not a hypocrite when he preached about the Christian's obligation to give to the poor, for in his own charitable giving he was generous and systematic.

Carey tells us that Donne was a hypocrite when he preached about the Christian's humble hope of heaven: he 'does speak of heavenly harmony and the joy of reunion with the dead, but these are side-shows compared with his personal advancement' (p. 212). In 1990 Carey wrote an introduction to a new edition of Donne's major works, ending with an allegation that Donne believed that in heaven he would not lose 'his style, or his aspiration, or his wish to attract and deceive spectators'. 'So Donne thinks', says Carey. 'Or says he thinks.'

The evidence produced for this astonishingly harsh conclusion is a quotation from a sermon, where Donne hopes that 'I shall be so like God, as the Devil himself shall not know me from God'. But the quotation is not completed by Carey. What Donne actually hopes for is that in heaven he will be like God himself, free of any temptation to sin. He says: 'the Devil himselfe shall not know me from God, so far as to find any more place to fasten a tentation upon me, than upon God'. Donne hopes to be in the kingdom of heaven and to find that Satan will not be able 'to conceive any more hope of my falling from that Kingdome, than of God's being driven out of it'. He hopes to be 'as immortal as God' not because he will be divine but because he will receive immortality as the gift of God, as 'the Sunne by shining upon the Moone makes the

Moone a Planet, a Star'. He hopes that 'those beames of Glory which shall issue from my God' will 'fall upon me, shall make me . . . an Angell of Light, a Star of Glory, a something that I cannot name now, not imagine now, nor tomorrow, nor next yeare'. But without God's mercy he is 'a clod of earth, and worse, a dark Soule, a Spirit of darknesse' (9:89).

We are told by Carey that Donne found 'in God, and in his own position as God's spokesman, a final and fully adequate expression of his power lust . . . for he had found something far more corrosive than satire with which to attack mankind, namely Christianity . . . Terror afforded him a histrionic triumph' (pp. 108, 110, 120). In later chapters I shall quote some passages in the sermons which to me, as well as to Carey, would seem to be bullying. But it is right that we should listen to Donne explaining what he thought was his duty. 'The Preacher makes a holy noise in the conscience of the Congregation, and when hee hath awakened them by stirring the nest, hee casts some claps of thunder, some intimidations, in denouncing the judgements of God, and he flings open the gates of Heaven, that they may heare, and look up, and see a man sent from God, with power to infuse his feare into them.' But Donne's motive in 'denouncing' (we should say 'announcing') judgements was, he said, that his hearers should find God's mercy. He continued: 'The Preacher doth so infuse the feare of God into his Auditory, that they shall feare nothing but God, and then they shall feare God, but so as he is God; and God is Mercy; God is Love. Then he shews them Heaven, and God in Heaven, sanctifying all their crosses in this World, inanimating all their worldly blessings, rayning downe his blood into their emptinesse, and his balme into their wounds, making their bed in all their sicknesse . . .' (8:43–4).

As Donne reflected on his experience as a pastor, he said that he had found seven 'dejected' people to one who was over-confident. He added that when he had given some comfort to someone depressed, 'that man hath given me a Sacrament . . . I go away

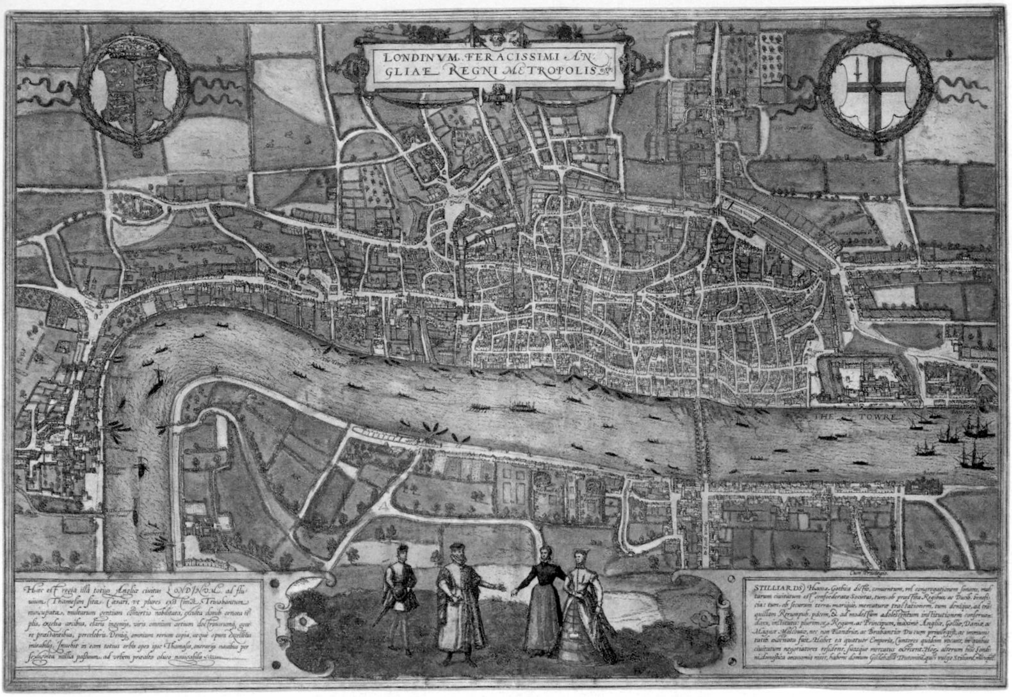

1. The London Donne knew

2. Donne in 1591

3. Donne in 1616

4. Donne in 1620

153

Sr

I send yow back by this bearer the letter wch I borrowed of yow. If yow wyll now to ease my imprisonmt spare me some of the French negotiations, yow shall have them as faythfully kept and as orderly returnd as these. And when I ame worth yor commanding I ame wholy yors. From my prison in my Chamber. 20 Febru: 1601

Yor lowest assured frend

J. Donne.

5. Donne asks for a book while under arrest

6° Julij 1602

Receved the Day and year abovewritten, of the
right ho: Sr Thomas Egerton knight L: Keeper of
the great Seale of England, my ho: L: and Master
by the hands of hys Servant Mr John Panton the
sum of one hundred pounds of lawfull Money
of England: wch sayd hundred pounds was given by
the right ho: the Lady Egerton late wyfe to the
sayd L: Keeper, to her Neece, Anne the Daughter
of Sr George More, now my wyfe, and ys now her
here received by me

J Donne

6. Donne's receipt for a legacy authorized by Egerton

7. Preaching at Paul's Cross in Donne's time

8. An engraving of Donne in his shroud used as a frontispiece for *Death's Duell*, 1632

9. Donne's effigy

comforted in my selfe, that Christ Jesus hath made me an instrument of the dispensation of his mercy' (8:249). His advice to one and all was: 'never consider the judgment of God for sin alone, but in the company of the mercies of Christ' (8:207). And forty years after Donne's death Richard Gibson wrote to Samuel Pepys, remembering one of the great dean's sermons. What had stuck in his mind was that 'ye Goodnes of God was not so much seene in our Creation as Redemption, nor soe much that wee are his, as that nothing can take us out of his hands'.

We are also told by Carey that although he dared not criticize the 'impossibilities that Christianity required him to believe' (p. 157) because of his position in the Church, yet 'we can be sure that Donne's scepticism lasted throughout his life' (p. 222). He assures us that 'it was precisely the impossibility of having true ideas about God which agitated Donne in his religious writing, and it is this above all which accounts for the sense of strain and confusion in the sermons when we compare them with the great love poems' (pp. 239–40). Is that so? The sermons can be felt to be too dogmatic when we compare them with many modern sermons, but when they do admit that no ideas or images referring to God can be completely accurate they do no more than repeat what has often been taught by the Scriptures and by the mystics and theologians: that the essence of God is beyond human sight, understanding or expression. That is the theme of the 'apophatic' theology in the tradition of Eastern Orthodoxy, and of the *via negativa* in the theology and spirituality of Western Catholicism.

It can be suggested that the 'new Philosophy' had thrown educated people including Donne into scepticism about the fundamental claims of Christianity but there is no evidence that this was the case. A thorough denial of the existence of God (atheism) seems to have been very rare and although disbelief in actions by God after the creation (Deism) was beginning to grow it does not appear to have been numerically significant in Donne's lifetime. As we shall see, he preached eloquently against these ideas. Here we may note that the most spectacular feat in the new 'natural philosophy' or science was the bold theory of Copernicus that the earth moves around the sun (published in 1543). This contradicted the Old Testament but Donne seems to have shared the general belief of educated Englishmen in his time that it did not destroy belief in the Creator and the Saviour: England was not responsible for the foolish persecution of Galileo, who proved the theory right, by the authorities of the Church in Italy.

Donne was of course interested. He mentioned to the Countess of Bedford that

> As new Philosophy arrests the Sunne,
>   And bids the passive earth about it runne,
> So wee have dull'd our minde, it hath no ends . . .

And in his 'First Anniversarie' he mentioned that

> . . . new Philosophy cals all in doubt,
> The Element of fire is quite put out;
> The Sun is lost, and th'earth, and no man's wit
> Can well direct him, where to look for it.

But Donne could write or preach without bothering with the 'new Philosophy', when the old idea that the sun runs around the sky seemed more suitable for a poem or a sermon. As Carey notes (on p. 271), in 'The Sunne Rising' even before his invitation to the sun to circle around the lovers' bed he rebukes it for moving in such a way that it disturbs their sex-exhausted sleep:

> Busie old foole, unruly Sunne, . . .
> Must to thy motions lovers' seasons run?

Probably more than twenty years later, on Christmas Day in 1624, he compared the Church's expansion across the Atlantic with the sun's daily journey round the earth. The sun, he reminded the congregation, moves 'circularly'. Similarly, 'this Church . . . moves . . . circularly; It began in the East, it came to us, and is passing now, shining out now, in the farthest West' (6:173). In his *Devotions* there was a rare touch of flippancy: when he feels giddy he remembers that he is on a planet which is not stable. But on Easter Day in 1627 he told the congregation that 'the standing still of the Sun for Joshua's use' in the Old Testament was a miracle, but a greater miracle was the fact that 'so vast and immense a body as the Sun should run so many miles in a minute' (7:374). And in *Ignatius his Conclave* Donne sent Copernicus to join the Jesuits in hell, as another troublesome innovator – but put into the mouth of Ignatius a greeting which showed a lack of profound interest, with the cool words that the new theory 'may well be right'.

So was Donne permanently sceptical about Christianity despite his eloquence in the pulpit? As we shall see when we look at his sermons in Chapter 10, he was aware of some questions which may be called modern and his answers could suggest that a particular part of the Bible or of the Church's tradition needs to be treated in a way which begins to be modern. But Carey cannot produce a shred of evidence to support his accusation of basic hypocrisy, for every word that has survived is consistent with what can be expected reasonably: Donne was neither a fundamentalist nor an unbeliever. Whereas in his earlier years he could express politically conformist loyalties in public while being in private quite cynical about the regime, neither before ordination nor after it did he ever leave on record any question about the truth of what he regarded as the essentials of Christianity. His private letters were as full of piety as were his sermons: they confessed to depression but never to unbelief. Like a considerable number of other seventeenth-century Englishmen who put their thoughts on paper, quite often he found difficulty – even agony – in relating Christianity to himself and to the world around him, but like almost all of them he attributed that to his sin or his blindness, not to the falsehood of his religion; or to God being infinite, not to God being unreal. Carey's suggestion that Donne was at heart a sceptic arises from twentieth-century secular feelings, not from seventeenth-century facts. We may prefer the verdict given by another great poet, W. B. Yeats, who wrote in 1912 to Sir Herbert Grierson, congratulating him on his edition of Donne's poetry: 'the more precise and learned the thought the greater the beauty, the passion; the intricacy and subtleties of his imagination are the length and depth of the furrow made by his passion'. Yeats thought that 'his pedantry and his obscenity . . . make me more certain that one who is but a man like us all has seen God'.

What kind of God did Donne worship?

Carey notes that Donne 'quotes St Augustine approvingly: "Never propose to thy self such a God, as thou wert not bound to imitate"' (p. 226), but it seems that he thinks that Donne decided to imitate an extremely cruel God. His God is 'the most hideous that Christianity had yet evolved', a 'Calvinist monster in the sky who creates large numbers of men for the express purpose of torturing them for all eternity' (p. 225). What makes Donne's religion even worse in Carey's eyes is that (as he thinks) he came to believe that God had arbitrarily decided to create him with a destination in heaven: he quotes the preacher as saying 'God did elect mee, before he did actually create mee' (8:282). But Carey's interpretation of the position which Donne reached is demonstrably a misinterpretation.

Like many other sensitive Christians, Donne became full of wonder that such a sinner as he was could be loved by the all-holy God and he could draw no conclusion other than the belief that God had freely chosen to love or 'elect' him as he had freely chosen to 'elect' everyone except those who persistently rebelled against his good purpose for them. (This was the version of predestination which appealed to the greatest modern theologian in the Calvinist or 'Reformed' tradition, Karl Barth.) But Donne knew that for many years he had resisted the call of God and had been left free to do so. He also knew, from experience both as a convert and as a pastor, that any man 'can answer the inspiration of God, when his grace comes, and exhibit acceptable service to him, and co-operate with him' (1:271–2), for 'even naturall man may, out of the use of that free will, come to Church, heare the Word preached, and believe it to be true' (3:36). Therefore he insisted that there is freedom on both sides: God is free to say yes, the sinner is free to say no. As he put it in an age when men could be recruited for an army or navy by force: 'Christ beats his Drum, but he does not Press men; Christ is served by Voluntaries' (5:156).

To put it in more theological terms, Donne believed in 'election', the choice by God of whom to 'save' among sinners, but had no sympathy with the belief that before anyone was created God had already decided exactly who was to be a 'reprobate', perpetually incapable of hearing and obeying him. Donne was very far from teaching that God 'hated some of his creatures so virulently as to damn them even before they have come into being' (Carey, p. 277). He stated what he did believe by quoting St Augustine: 'There is no predestination in God, but to good.' 'Our destruction', he added, 'is from our owne sinne, and the Devill that infuses it; not from God, or from any ill purpose in him that enforces us' (5:53–4).

He maintained that 'he is our God; and God is love; and therefore to conceive a cruell God, a God that hated us, even to damnation, before we were . . . or to conceive a God so cruell, as that at our death, or in our way, he will afford us no assurance that hee is ours and we are his . . . this is not to professe God to be terrible in his works; For . . . God hath never done, or said anything to induce so terrible an opinion of him' (8:125). To say that God could 'peremptorily hate' anyone who was not guilty 'as a manifold sinner, and as an obdurate sinner' – to say that God could 'mean to make him, that he might damne him' – is 'to impute to God, a sowrer and worse affected nature, than falls to any man . . . Doth any man beget a sonne therefore, that he might dis-inherit him? Doth God hate any man therefore, because he will hate him?' (9:390). His teaching was unambiguous: 'God does not Reward or Condemn out of his decrees but out of our actions' (7:17).

We have already glanced at the Synod of Dort which defined Calvinist orthodoxy (on pp. 105–6). It is clear that Donne's own beliefs were those which the synod condemned as Arminian heresy. But even the victorious orthodox did not dare to say at Dort that God condemns the innocent. They taught that 'God has decreed to leave certain people in the common misery into which they have plunged themselves by their own fault'. Nowadays almost everyone would agree that this formula left God guilty of almost the greatest cruelty imaginable, but it is different from the further step of saying that God is the 'Calvinist monster in the sky' who has no mercy on faultless people, the divine sadist who creates people because he knows for sure that they will spend eternity in his torture chamber. And in his sermon in The Hague in 1619 Donne showed some of his impatience with this whole fierce debate. He did not deny that people are sinners; he was one. But he believed that God wishes to save sinners; that, too, had been his experience, which he wanted to share. People, he said, were weary of hearing from pulpits nothing but talk of 'Election and Reprobation, and whom, and when, and how, and why God hath chosen, or cast away'. It was enough 'to know enough for the salvation of your soules; If you will search farther into God's eternall Decrees and unrevealed Councels, you should not cast your nets into that Sea, for you are not fishers there' (2:279). On another occasion he was even more homely: 'I enquire not what God did in his bed-chamber' (2:323). When back in England he was unabashed in claiming that the synod had shown the same restraint: ignoring its discussions of predestination, he simply reported that 'in the last forraine Synod which our divines assisted, with what blessed sobriety they delivered their sentence: That all men are truly and in earnest called to eternall life by God's Minister' (7:127). When making his will he bequeathed to Henry King his gold medal commemorating the synod – and accompanied it by two portraits of Roman Catholic theologians which he had displayed more prominently in the Deanery.

In an exceptionally public and controversial sermon preached at St Paul's Cross in 1629, he mocked 'the over-pure despisers of others; Men that will abridge and contract the large mercies of God in Christ, and elude and frustrate, in a great part, the generall promises of God. Men that are loth that God should speak out so loud as to say, *He would have all men saved*, And loth that Christ should spread his armes, or shed his blood in such a compasse as might fall upon all. Men that think no sinne can hurt them, because they are elect, and that every sin makes every other man a Reprobate. But with the Lord there is . . . plentifull redemption, and *an overflowing cup of mercy*' (9:119).

The faith which Donne proclaimed was thus a faith that God's will is that all can be saved, and that Christ has died for the benefit of all, declaring the divine love for all, but that sinners can resist God's will, even to the end. Those who are being saved by God are those who respond both by faith and by life to the gracious goodness of God, for 'as his mercy is new every morning, so his grace is renewed in me every minute, . . . the eye of God is upon me, though I winke at his light, and watches over me, though I sleep' (8:368). There can be no human goodness without this grace of God inspiring it, but it is also true that 'Grace could not worke upon man to Salvation, if man had not a faculty of will to worke upon . . . God saves no man without, or against, his will' (5:317). Everything does not depend on God's 'election' of his favourites without regard to behaviour. Donne recalled how Christ had replied to the rich young man who asked how he could enter eternal life among the saved: he had told him first to obey the commandments about behaviour and then to get rid of his wealth. He had not told him 'you must look into the eternal decree of Election first, and see whether that stand for you or no' (6:229).

A result of this vision of God as good was a sharp decline in the estimate of the population of hell. While many Christians were eager to send most people, including many fellow Christians, to hell, Donne maintained that because he is Love 'God hath made all mankinde of one blood and all Christians of one calling' (1:122) and he could go so far as to say that 'whosoever lives according to rectified Reason, which is the Law of nature, he is a Christian' (4:119). 'There are an infinite number of Stars, more than we can distinguish', Donne said, 'and so by God's grace, there may be an infinite number of soules saved, more than those of whose salvation we discern the ways and meanes' (6:161).

He claimed that this generous belief could be found in the teaching of the Fathers of the Church in the days when the Church was surrounded by a pagan world. 'Those blessed Fathers of tender bowells' saw God's mercy extending to 'the Pagans that had no knowledge of Christ in any established Church'. 'Partly', he explained, 'they goe upon that rule, which goes through so many of the Fathers, . . . That to that man who does so much as he can, by the light of nature, God never denies grace; and then, say they, why should not these good men be saved? . . . I know God can be as mercifull as those tender Fathers present him to be; and I would be as charitable as they are; and therefore, humbly imbracing that manifestation of his Son which he hath afforded me, I leave God to his unsearchable waies of working upon others, without further inquisition' (4:78–9).

In 1990 a second edition of Carey's *John Donne: Life, Mind and Art* was published, without revision but with the addition of an 'afterword' which was a highly critical examination of two books of 1986, Thomas Docherty's *John Donne, Undone* and Arthur Marotti's *John Donne, Coterie Poet.* He complained that Docherty's 'reading practice is guided largely by ingenuity and whim' rather than by 'historical criteria' and that much of Marotti's study of possible influences on the poetry by the limited readership expected for it is 'undeniably sited in a wilderness of unsatisfactory conjecture'. I do not have the space in which to discuss these criticisms, which are far less justified about Marotti than about Docherty. But I have to ask whether Carey is in a position to make them.

In his study of *Donne's Religious Writing* (1997) Paul Oliver tells us that 'John Carey's work on Donne was the initial stimulus to my own'. The sub-title of his book is 'A Discourse of Feigned Devotion', which seems to promise a demonstration that everything Donne said or wrote about religion was 'feigned'. As we have seen, he was a tough self-critic, but in sermons already quoted (pp. 20, 170) Donne explained clearly enough what he meant by 'feigned devotion': he suffered – as who does not? – from wandering thoughts while trying to pray.

Oliver has found some good points in Donne's prose. He admires the letters, where the voice is 'frank, humble, pliant, frequently self-mocking (or something very close to it)' (p. 239). He even admires the 'very different' voice of Donne the preacher – sometimes. In the sermons he praises their 'creation and sustained utilization of an extraordinarily forceful style whose main features are a capacity for surprise which guarantees attention, a rich sense of humour and irony, a propensity for vivid, often homely imagery and a tendency to apparent self-exposure' (p. 265). But he has no respect for the message of the sermons or for the personality to which the religious writing gives 'apparent self-exposure'.

The emphasis in his onslaught is on the preacher's hypocrisy. He rejects 'the assumption that the writing puts us in direct contact with Donne's own beliefs and piety' (p. 6). Before his ordination the preacher has been 'the professional propagandist who is capable of writing on either side in a given dispute and decides to work for the higher bidder' (p. 18). Now his sermons 'present this specially constructed self in a highly ostentatious manner' (p. 239), making of him 'something of a hypocrite' (p. 213). The preacher has written religious poems, but these showed 'a complete lack of interest in religious doctrines' (p. 58), since religion was to him 'merely a rich source of exploitable religious raw material' (p. 193). Prayers expressed as poems were 'melodramatic posturing' (p. 115) with 'no concern for morality' (p. 118). Petitions to the Trinity were 'a brusque demand' (p. 124), 'harshly imperative' (p. 226) and 'emotional blackmail' (p. 216). When Donne asks God the Father to 'find both Adams met in me' (the first Adam the Sinner and the second Adam the Saviour), it is claimed that he 'splits the Trinity' (p. 220). When his wife has died and he turns to God in a new intensity of prayer, it is claimed that he has 'lost much of his sense of purpose' (p. 45).

When making these crude attacks on Donne's sermons and prayers, Oliver appears to ignore the fact that phrases which he dislikes had already been used by innumerable Christians. And when assessing Donne's position in the religious life of his age he exposes himself to criticisms – not about his own sincerity, nor about his own beliefs and values, but about a repeated failure to understand the theology and spirituality of that age which has now vanished. For example, he is under the impression that Calvin taught that 'good works and the view of the sacraments as channels of grace' are 'abominable' (p. 188) – teaching which would have astonished those who in Calvin's Geneva lived under a famously strict code of moral discipline and knew how fervently congregations addressed by Calvin's spoken or written words were exhorted to take both Baptism and Holy Communion with the utmost seriousness. It is demonstrably and grossly untrue to say that the 'Anti-Calvinist model' is unique in that it alone 'leaves room for personal striving and prayer' (p. 232).

A writer such as John Carey or Paul Oliver is very ready to accuse Donne of a lack of honesty when he preaches or prays. But what should we say about a writer who claims to be expounding Donne's religious thought, when he gives almost no sign that he understands it? Certainly Donne ought to be criticized. As we have seen (and will see again in the next chapter), he attacked himself in an agony of penitence. But he invested his life in his belief that he was not being thoroughly dishonest when he held to God throughout all his moods, or when he was a priest and preacher in the Church of England. In a verse-letter he gracefully told Rowland Woodward that he was not willing to send him copies of his early poems, called by him 'love-song weeds' and 'Satyrique thornes'. His position now was 'there is no Vertue' except the virtue to be found in the practice of 'Religion'. In all honesty he admitted that 'our Soules have stain'd their first white' but he told his friend that this was not the end of the matter.

> Seeke wee then our selves in our selves; for as
> Men force the Sunne with much more force to passe,
> By gathering his beames with a christall glasse,
>
> So wee, If wee into our selves will turne,
> Blowing our sparkes of vertue, may outburne
> The straw, which doth about our hearts sojourne.

But we need to see at greater length what Donne says when he speaks up for himself. He says much in his poetry about sex which would shock Walton and Gosse – and he says much in his poetry and sermons about God which would displease Carey and Oliver. But he is also a poet about married love, which he regards as an education in love for God.

PART THREE

Donne Speaks

7 Let my body raigne

Till then, Love, let my body raigne, and let
Mee travell, sojourne, snatch, plot, have, forget . . .
'Love's Usury'

When no longer young and no longer arrogant Donne referred to his poetry dismissively and he appears to have been sincere in this attitude which astonishes us. Indeed, it seems that he destroyed many poems. When sending a poem to Magdalen Herbert he said that it had barely escaped being burned

With all those sonnes whom my braine did create

but he told the paper that it would have been wiser if it had remained

hid with mee, till thou returne
To rags againe, which is thy native state.

More than once he called his poems 'rags' (paper was then made from compacted cloth) and his verse-letters to friends and patrons could be 'salads and onions' (not meat). When Henry Wotton asked to see what had not been burned, Donne begged him not to allow anyone to copy the poems. 'To my satyres', he wrote, 'there belongs some feare and to some elegies . . . perhaps shame.' When Henry Goodyer advised him to approach the rich Countess of Huntingdon with a poem in her honour, he hesitated because he now wished to be thought of as pursuing 'a graver course than of a Poet, into which (that I may also keep my dignity) I would not seem to relapse. The Spanish proverb informes me that he is a fool which cannot mak one Sonnet, and is mad which makes two.' In the end he settled for being a clergyman – and in that capacity preached that 'if we be over-vehemently affected or transported with Poetry' it is a sin (4:143). He gave Ben Jonson the impression that having become a preacher 'he seeketh to destroy all his poems' and certainly he announced that he had buried his poetic Muse.

Only one poem in his handwriting has been discovered by modern researchers and it is not an important one. In 1614 Donne had to go to the trouble of asking friends to send him copies of his own poems, now needed for the (aborted) project to print a collection, and what he gathered then may have been the manuscript deposited with Ker when he went abroad on his diplomatic mission five years later. It may have been used in the preparation of the first printed edition but that is not certain and it can be argued that some of the surviving manuscripts reflect what the author wrote more reliably than the printed text does. It is surprising that Donne, who originally must have taken great trouble to write the poems, did not make more careful arrangements for their survival and publication, but the fact is that he did not. They were not mentioned in his long will, although he specified which of his friends were to receive which of the paintings in his possession. In contrast, contemporaries who were careful to collect and revise their poetry for publication included not only George Herbert and Ben Jonson but also lesser figures such as Samuel Daniel and Michael Drayton.

It does not seem to have troubled Donne that he died without putting his poems into any logical or chronological order, although during his painful last illness he wrote out sermons with a view to publication and during his last days the priest who ministered to him was himself a poet, Henry King, who was entrusted with the sermons but apparently not with the poems. It has been suggested that he planned for the poems to be left in disorder because he wanted them to be judged as literature and not as the records of his life, and perhaps also because he regarded them as literature about the very varied emotions which are stirred up by 'love', but so far as we know he never said so and a simple lack of attention seems a more probable explanation. It is unlikely that he would have welcomed what happened.

The first edition, put together by the bookseller John Marriot, included poems which were in fact by other men. It was introduced by the boring *Metempsychosis* and it was not a complete collection. The next edition tidied the poems up a bit and added 28 more, and it has been suggested that Izaak Walton was responsible for the improvement, but if he performed this service to his hero's memory (he certainly wrote the poem under the frontispiece) it is surprising that the first poem was now the most flippant, 'The Flea'. The lack of a clear order showing Donne's development as a man and as a poet may have been one of the reasons why within half a century of his death his life was known only through Walton's memoir – and Walton had expressed nothing but regret about the secular poetry while causing bewilderment by dating the religious poems, many of which were highly disturbed, as having been written in the period when Donne was in public an orthodox and fervent preacher. It was easy, and not totally unreasonable, to draw the conclusion that the poetry which Donne had left behind so casually was little more than a display of pointless wit when secular and of a shocking uncertainty when religious. Readers were not encouraged: there were seven editions of his poetry in 1633–69, when people still alive could remember the world which had been his background, but between 1669 and 1779 there was only one, published as a curiosity in 1719 and (as we have seen) regarded as a 'Heap of Riddles' in the Age of Reason.

It is now impossible to establish the precise order in which the poems were written. It is not even possible to be certain in every case about the periods in which they originated. However, by now the work of many scholars can be used if we want to make an effort to clear up the confusion to a certain extent. It seems reasonable to believe that the poems which advocated sexual promiscuity were written before his marriage, that the poems which reflected a great confusion and unhappiness in his feelings about religion were written before his ordination, and that the poems which sound as if they were inspired by a marriage were not written by a bachelor or an adulterer. That is what we should expect and evidence stronger than any which is known would be needed to prove that our natural expectation is wrong. Also, a few of the poems can be dated more precisely.

In her introduction to her edition of Donne's *Divine Poems* in 1952 Helen Gardner stressed that the development of a religious teacher out of the young poet is very surprising. 'In his early poetry', she wrote, 'there is nothing to suggest a latent spirituality. He is by nature arrogant, egotistical, and irreverent. His mind is naturally sceptical and curious, holding little sacred. In his love poetry he is only rarely tender and never humble . . . In his almost total blindness to the beauty of the natural world he reveals a lack of that receptivity, that capacity for disinterested joy which is one of the marks of a spiritual man . . . But . . . in spite of his temperament Donne was genuinely religious, if by a religious person we understand a person to whom the idea of God not only is self-evident, but brings with it a sense of absolute obligation.' It was out of this sense of obligation to God that the development came, but even in his religious poetry Donne is, Gardner thought, a 'religious person' largely in the sense which is true of most 'religious' people: 'for all his genius as a poet, his intellectual vivacity and his passionate and complex temperament, his religious experience seems . . . to have been largely a matter of faith and moral effort'.

However, it seems possible to say something more than Gardner did both about Donne's love poetry and about his religion. When introducing the love poetry in her 1965 edition she applauded 'the rapture of fulfilment and of the bliss of union in love', going beyond her earlier emphasis that he was 'only rarely tender'. She also pointed out that 'in his love poetry he is not concerned with what he ought or ought not to feel, but with the expression of feeling itself. Passion is there its own justification, and so is disgust, or hatred or grief.' But she added that 'gratitude for love bestowed, the sense of unworthiness in the face of the overwhelming worth of the beloved, self-forgetting worship of her as she is: these notes Donne does not strike' – and there she seems too cautious. She appears to underestimate the contrast between the poems about promiscuity which record 'disgust, or hatred or grief', and the poems, also passionate, about the 'bliss of union in love'. Some experience must have caused this contrast and it seems very unlikely that it was experience confined to the writing or reading of literature. If an actual union in love which lasted was the basic cause, we know of no one apart from his wife who could have transformed Donne in that way. It therefore seems sensible to ask whether there is any evidence that she did.

In Chapter 9 I shall produce evidence from the sermons to show what Donne thought and taught about marriage, but here I appeal to the evidence in the poems. As Alan Sinfield noted in *Literature in Protestant England* (1983), 'Donne's poems of reciprocated, fulfilling and enduring sexual love are generally his most popular and they are without precedent'. In his study of *The Reinvention of Love* (1993) Anthony Low demonstrated that in the literature of the seventeenth century there was a new, modern, emphasis on marriage as a richly emotional relationship which flourished in a private world, often in tension with the world outside – and he put John and Anne Donne at the centre of this profoundly important development. As books more in the sociological mode have reminded us, these changes in literature should be weighed alongside the probability that many marriages of which no literary evidence survives did not change: there had been marriages based on love before the revolution in literature and there would be marriages based on less romantic factors after it. But within the world of literature there was indeed a revolution and within that revolution Donne was indeed, as Low said, 'a chief actor and influence'. Many years before Low, Sir Herbert Grierson thought that one must believe that the poems 'in which ardour is combined with elevation and delicacy of feeling were addressed to Anne More before and after their marriage'. Subsequent discussion has made it clear that he ought not to have claimed that all such poems 'must have been addressed to Anne', for some may have been merely influenced by her and others may have been influenced by earlier relationships which softened and matured Donne in preparation for marriage. But the key point is that, whether or not a particular poem was addressed to Anne, it is not stupid to ask whether his marriage was decisive in the 'reinvention' of the poet and therefore of 'love' in English literature.

It is true that Donne had an arduous spiritual journey, amid confusion and depression: his prose shows that, and conclusive evidence is provided by his religious poems to be considered in the next chapter. It is also true that he never expressed the mystical assurance and identification with Christ which are recorded about some of the saints (Francis of Assisi, for example). Gardner was surely right about his need for 'faith and moral effort'. However, there seems to be more of an overlap than she allowed between some of the religious poems and the sermons (where some passages seem close to what Francis felt about Christ). The poet and the preacher were not different men: instead, some of the poems as well as all of the sermons testify that Donne came to believe in the depths of his personality that he had not been merely seeking what Gardner called 'the meditation's deliberate stimulation of the emotions'. That makes is sound as if he believed that he did all the work. He had been praying that God would act to reveal his love by his power. He had been genuinely and unwillingly disturbed, filled with anxiety and fear, brought face to face with death, made to picture himself being ultimately rejected by God as well as by employers on earth. He had been to hell and back – and by the end of that crisis, he believed that he had not always been talking to himself: in his spiritual journey as in his search for sexual fulfilment, love had been given to him and the seeker had been found.

Although they have done excellent work in this field, some scholars have been unconvincing when they have attempted to overturn Gardner's verdict that in the early poetry of Donne there is nothing to suggest even 'latent spirituality'.

In *John Donne, Conservative Revolutionary* (1967), Nancy Andreasen argued that he was advocating a conservative moral position even in the poems about sexual relationships outside marriage. She suggested that when he appears to be celebrating or lamenting his fortunes or misfortunes as a sexual predator in fact he is already a kind of preacher, exposing the 'wrong use of the things of the world; the lovers, overly committed to goods which are transient by nature, bring misery on themselves because the joys of transient goods are transient joys; the lovers sin by making the things of the world an end rather than a means, and they punish themselves by choosing to love something which cannot fulfil their inordinate love'. In *Doubting Conscience* (1975) Dwight Cathcart wrote in a similar vein about the arguments with girlfriends which occupy a great deal of the erotic poetry: 'Donne's speaker, wanting to be in harmony with order but stymied because that order is unclear and not reflected in the special situation, needs a particular instrument to clarify the law which he feels governs his actions and to apply that law to his particular case. That instrument is casuistry' (philosophy about ethics, in that period usually based on theology). And in *Kinde Pity and Brave Scorn* (1982) M. Thomas Hester argued that any scorn in Donne's 'satyres' was due to the earnestness with which the young 'religious devotee' advocated a 'process of active Christian reform'.

But these are, it seems, the charitable verdicts of Christian scholars who have been too kind to the future preacher, and it is far more likely that the truth about the young Donne is less abnormal. If he combined a high moral tone when attacking the vices of women, courtiers and lawyers with a private life which was a combination of hot sexuality with cold ambition, he was not unique. And he would not be the only young man who while attacking other people's faults did not display a truly Christian spirit. The opening lines of his third 'satyre' used by Professor Hester in the title of his generous book may be understood less charitably if we feel less generous. They may be interpreted as a display of self-satisfied and patronizing contempt for those whom he is about to denounce:

> Kinde pitty chokes my spleene; brave scorn forbids
> Those teares to issue which swell my eye-lids . . .

Donne told a friend that the bitterness with which he poured 'skorne' on his seniors during and after 1593 was due in part to his grief that his brother had been the victim of laws which these seniors administered (we saw this on p. 46), but the mixture of scorn for older men with love for young women is not uncommon in young men, for the 1590s were not the last time in the history of the world when demonstrations of sincere idealism about the need for a new generation to strive for justice and peace in public life have been combined with a more indulgent attitude to youth's own sexual needs, resulting in a motto such as 'make love not war'. And the mixture is not incompatible with some uneasy self-questioning or self-criticism, as honesty breaks through. Donne's first 'satyre' seems to be an example of this. It has been interpreted as the acceptance of the duty of a Christian scholar to benefit others by being an evangelist or pastor in the wicked world (to be sure, the phrase 'lost sheep' occurs). It has also been understood as a debate between the body ('thou' or 'he') and the soul ('I'). But it seems more likely that this 'satyre' resulted from the introspection of a young man who is intelligent enough to see that emotionally he is two men.

A 'fondling motley humourist' (a foolish, changeable clown) comes to a scholar's study and suggests that he could have fun away from his books and his ideals. The scholar hesitates. He fears that if he comes on an expedition his companion will find him less attractive than someone 'more spruce' such as a soldier or a courtier, a magistrate clothed in velvet or a rich man handsome in silk and gold – or, alternatively, will prefer the company of a 'plumpe muddy whore or prostitute boy'. But after a brief conference 'with God and with the Muses' the scholar falls to the temptation: 'come, let's go'. In the street they do indeed come across more than one 'fine, silken, painted foole', and his red-blooded companion does indeed spot 'his Love in a windowe' – only to find that when he enters the brothel the place is overcrowded, a fight follows, and he is 'turn'd out of dore'. So the tempting companion returns to the boring scholar, 'hanging the head'. The last line of the poem reveals that the scholar's study is also the tempter's home. This is where the tempter 'must keepe his bed', waiting for the next time when the passions of youth may overcome ideals learned from books. Both of these men are Donne.

That first 'satyre' reminds us that Donne was a dramatist able to re-create street life, including low life, knowing something about it. Although his poems may not record his actual experiences they can show us what were the realities if a student in London in the 1590s felt that he needed a sexual relationship. He might have to visit a brothel and face dangers not only from venereal disease ('the Poxe') but also from other infections ('the Plague'). The alternative was to attempt to strike up a relationship with a woman who did not need to be paid – but who, if she was married, might have a furious husband and who, if single, might get bored.

Donne had at least one 'Sun' to brighten his life temporarily (as we saw on pp. 39–40), but whoever this sun was, she set. Perhaps she broke off their relationship because she sensed what was his normal attitude to women in this period. It was expressed in one of the witty 'paradoxes' which he wrote out for the entertainment of other young men, pretending to argue against a general opinion. The paradox which he advanced was that 'it is possible to find some vertue in some women' and his argument was that they overthrow valiant men and are patient when themselves overthrown. And despite the talk of some critics about the obscurity of his 'riddles', Donne could be very explicit about what he meant by women being overthrown. In *Metempsychosis* he gave this account of the reaction of the girl to the amorous ape:

> First she was silly and knew not what he ment . . .
> Succeeds an itchie warmth, that melts her quite;
> She knew not first, now cares not what he doth . . .

It would not be surprising if having been overthrown in this manner by an ape-like student, a woman were to recover her balance and escape as rapidly as possible. Then Donne would have to console himself by the kind of sour grapes which he set out in his paradox called 'A Defence of Women's Inconstancy':

'Women are like Flyes which feed amongst us at our Table, or Fleas sucking our verie blood, who leave not our most retired places free from their familiaritie.' A similar attitude was taken in another short piece of prose written somewhat later but also believed to be witty: women do not have souls any more than do apes, goats, foxes or serpents whose natures are similar to theirs and if men 'have given woemen soules' it is 'onely to make them capable of damnation'.

Usually the male speaker in the poems of the 1590s celebrates the release of his sexual urges in promiscuity. In 'Communitie' he begins as if he is in training to preach: 'Good wee must love, and must hate ill.' However, there are, he says, things which are neither good nor bad but simply natural, and among them is the law of 'wise Nature' that 'all may use' women. Women are themselves neither good nor evil,

> But they are ours as fruits are ours . . .
> Chang'd loves are but chang'd sorts of meat,
> And when he hath the kernell eate,
> Who doth not fling away the shell?

And in 'The Indifferent' (which means 'The Impartial') the speaker claims that he can love and discard not only blondes and brunettes but also the rich and the poor, the loners and the joiners, the country girls and the streetwise, the trusting and the sceptical, the sad and the happy:

> I can love her, and her, and you and you,
> I can love any, so she be not true.

So he practises promiscuity and preaches it:

Let mee, and doe you, twenty know.
Rob mee, but binde me not, and let me goe.

Several poems express this enthusiasm about the blessing bestowed by 'wise Nature' on promiscuity. In the seventeenth 'elegie' the speaker celebrates the bounty with which Nature pours out her gifts on one and all. In gratitude he announces that he will not confine his love to a dark lady – or to a blonde:

Let no man tell me such a one is faire,
And worthy all alone my love to share . . .
I love her well, and would, if need were, dye
To do her service. But followes it that I
Must serve her onely, when I may have choice?
The law is hard, and shall not have my voice.
The last I saw in all extreames is faire,
And holds me in the Sun-beames of her haire; . . .
Another's brown, I like her not the worse,
Her tongue is soft and takes me with discourse . . .
How happy were our Syres in ancient times
Who held plurality of loves no crime!

And in 'Confined Love' the speaker makes the witty suggestion that the law that a woman must 'know' only one man was invented – and the inventor was a man who was too 'false or weake' to enjoy what Nature has provided. 'Sunne, Moone, or Starres' are not forbidden to smile on all; birds and beasts are not rebuked when they choose new lovers; ships are built to 'seeke new lands'; and a man knows that to spread oneself is not only natural, it is good:

Good is not good, unlesse
A thousand it possesse . . .

In 'Love's Deitie' the speaker recalls that it is the work of Cupid to fit 'actives to passives' and to unite two hearts by one 'even flame', of course keeping the woman passive – but now this woman loves someone else and he is hurt. His first thought is that Cupid's law that two hearts must be united in love and loyalty must be forgotten now that she has left him. He must remember the good old days, before Cupid got to work, when everyone was free and 'lov'd most' without any law about the need for loyal love. So

> I long to talke with some old lover's ghost,
> Who died before the god of Love was borne . . .

But he is still irritated by the fact that she, not he, made the decision to leave. Then on second thoughts he sees that even now people have freedom – and that includes women. If his ex-mistress were to pretend to love him, that would be 'falsehood'. So she must be free of him – and he must be free of her. And in 'Love's Diet' the speaker rejoices that he need not waste many tears because a mere woman has 'burnt my letters'. There are plenty of women left and the sport of sex is like starting up birds for hawks to chase:

> I spring a mistresse, sweare, write, sigh and weepe:
> And the game kill'd, or lost, goe talke, and sleepe.

Casualness when an affair ends is possible because 'love' is simply sex, as 'Love's Progress' declares. Men can claim that in their wives they admire virtue, beauty or money, but if 'we'

> Make love to woman; virtue is not she:
> As beauty is not, nor wealth . . .

Only 'one thing' in a woman matters to a man and it is 'the Centrique part'. To find it, a man should not begin with the hair, or with the feet although the feet are 'the first part that comes to bed'. A man should go straight for the centre, which is compared with an open purse. The message of 'The Prohibition' is that sex is not really about love, any more than it is about hate; it is about a man's need of the 'one thing'.

In 'Woman's Constancy' the speaker works through possible arguments which a woman will use when she has left him after loving him 'one whole day'. They are all bad arguments, he knows, and she uses them only in order to 'justifie' herself when she has already 'purpos'd change'. He could 'dispute and conquer' – but he will not bother to argue, partly because she is a 'lunatique' and partly because 'by to morrow I may thinke so too'. (Here the light-hearted bachelor is not yet the father of the Donnes' first daughter, named Constance.)

In other poems he is also very far from being the husband who through marriage has learned both loyalty and sensitivity. In 'The Curse' he exclaims at the start:

> Who ever guesses, thinks, or dreames he knows
> Who is my mistris, wither by this curse . . .

But at the end he shows that he is not worried that scandal may harm a woman's reputation. Let his curse, he says,

> Fall on that man; For if it be a shee
> Nature beforehand hath out-cursed mee.

And in 'The Triple Foole' he again treats women as raw material for his lusts and his poems. Clearly he does not intend his apology

> For loving, and for saying so
> In whining Poëtry

to be taken seriously, for he explains that for him – which is what matters – writing poetry can 'allay' the 'paines' of love. His only complaint is that when he has written a poem 'some man' can make a song of it, 'his art and voice to show'. Then the poet's pain can come back, which is irritating.

In some other poems he does seem to acknowledge that parting with a woman may bring 'anguish' to her, but that is still treated as a bit of a joke. It is the theme of 'The Message' but this poem is not totally heart-broken, for it is a song which was set to music, like the song which laments that finding a woman who is both 'true and faire' would be like catching 'a falling starre'. It is also the theme of 'The Apparition' but this poem is not totally about a man's defeat. A mistress has become the speaker's 'Murdresse' by scorning him, but he enjoys himself as he expects to return as a ghost. He will find her in bed with her new partner. She will pinch the new man when she wakes up in the middle of the night, needing comfort, but he is already 'tyr'd' of her and will pretend to sleep while he thinks 'thou calls't for more'. As a neglected wretch now bathed in a cold sweat, she will 'lye a veryer ghost than I'. And the speaker adds to his gloating pleasure by refusing to divulge what he will then say or do.

A man, he reckons, should not worry too much about the partings and other disappointments which occur in a life of promiscuity, but it is illuminating to notice what at this stage Donne thinks will worry a man. In 'Love's Alchymie' he looks back over his career as a lover, when 'I have lov'd, and got, and told', and finds 'Oh, 'tis imposture all'. Lovers dream of getting 'a rich and long delight' in a 'summer's night' – and find that the night is like winter, for an evening of love grows cold and then the darkness is long. There is nothing substantial or lasting in sex; it is a mere 'Buble's shadow'. For men, the lesson is 'hope not for minde in women' – and hope not for lasting physical satisfaction either, for when 'possest' at the end of the excitement women feel like dead flesh, like 'Mummy', a powder made by grinding Egyptian mummies in order to make a medicine which was in this period recommended by some doctors. In 'Farewell to Love' the speaker regrets that after intercourse comes

> A kinde of sorrowing dulnesse to the minde.

But then he sees why Nature has made a man 'eager' only 'for a minute': sex is exhausting and shortens life, so the eagerness is not meant to satisfy for long, yet sex is necessary in order to beget children, so the eagerness must return. Sex is Nature's game too.

Twice the young Donne adopted the voice of a woman in order to write a poem about sex and each time he suggested that women are really interested only in the 'one thing' which all men possess. In 'Breake of Day' (a song) he imagined a mistress complaining that her man thinks it necessary to go to work just because the sun has risen. Surely, all we need is love? Love 'brought us hether', so why 'Must businesse thee from hence remove?' In 'Sapho to Philaenis' he wrote what has been welcomed as 'the first female homosexual love poem in English', as if he was a precursor of Katherine Philips in the celebration of 'female friendship'. But in his poem the relationship between the women is not, and never has been, unalterably lesbian. The weeping Sappho remembers her absent female lover, and their love 'brest to brest or thighs to thighs', but she weeps because Philaenis has abandoned her in favour of 'some soft boy' or 'harsh rough man'. At an earlier stage she had herself been dropped by a male lover, here called Phao. In the end she manages to express best wishes for a heterosexual future:

> So may thy mighty, amazing beauty move
> Envy in all women and in all men love.

This poem which appears to be liberal about homosexuality has more aptly been called (by Ronald Corthell) a 'heterosexual male fantasy' since in the end it repeats a familiar message to women: every woman needs a man, they are made to fit together. It is a bold poem: it depicts Sappho touching her body in front of a mirror while thinking about her female lover and it took courage to do this in an age when the possibility of a lesbian relationship was unmentionable in polite society. (Even Ovid, normally very relaxed in all matters to do with sex, wrote his poem about Sappho's grief when her male lover deserted her.) But all Donne's references to homosexual relationships between men are hostile and there is no good reason to think that he made an exception for such relationships between women. The explanation of this poem seems to need to take account of the almost certain fact that it was written for the amusement and encouragement of randy young men, to remind them that it takes a man to satisfy a woman.

The most famous of the poems about sex could not be published before 1669 (during the merry Restoration over which Charles II presided) because it is so explicitly lustful, being then entitled 'To his Mistress Going to Bed'. She is imagined as a wealthy woman and (presumably) as someone else's wife: she wears a 'glittering' girdle, a star-spangled 'breast plate', a chiming watch and a coronet. Or at least she wears all this until instructed by the speaker to strip. The most relevant part of him is already 'standing' but he becomes further excited as her gown comes off. Theological terms are now used with a touch of blasphemy: women are 'mystick books' when their bodies are 'reveal'd' and like the Saviour they have merits which can be 'imputed' as 'grace' to men who are sinners. Geography is also used with a touch of humour which partly conceals the brutality of the comparison between colonization and the conquest of a woman's body:

Licence my roaving hands, and let them go
Before, behind, between, above, below.
O my America! my new-found-land,
My kingdome, safeliest with one man man'd . . .

But there is no ambiguity about what is going to happen:

Full nakedness! All joyes are due to thee . . .

And we are told where he locates this woman's self: 'as to a Midwife shew thy self'.

'Full nakedness' is what we are invited to praise in other 'elegies'. One tells a mistress not to worry about her husband's jealousy when in reality she would be delighted to see him dead. The second recommends a friend to marry Flavia, a woman who is exceptionally 'foule': because of her age and looks, she will have no alternative to being faithful. The third proclaims that 'women are made for men, not him, not mee' and a jilted lover must take the consequences of that law of nature. The fourth denounces the protective family of a mistress. The father threatens to deprive her of the money which is the 'food of our love'; the mother suspects that she is pregnant as the fruit of that love; the little brothers are bribed to tell tales of what is going on in 'our chamber'. Now the speaker is really fed up; he has taught his silk clothes to stay silent as he makes his way to 'our chamber' but he has been betrayed by his loud perfume. The seventh 'elegie' attacks a woman to whom he has taught the whole art of love including the 'Alphabet of flowers': now she is making love to another (her husband?). The eighth is a merciless portrait of someone else's mistress. The tenth announces that a dream is better than any real mistress, since 'all our joyes' are 'fantasticall'. And other 'elegies' which may or may not be by Donne have the same character.

Clearly not all these celebrations of promiscuity can be autobiographical. He seems to have been guarding himself against all his poems being read as such when he said in a much later sermon that he had written some poems in order to impress young men who 'thought it wit to make Sonnets of their own sins'. In real life he 'had no means to doe some sins, whereby I might be equal to my fellow', but he would 'say I had done that which I never did'. What had been genuine, he claimed, had been 'the pride I had to write feelingly about it' (2:107–8). But even if many or all of the details were imagined in order to titillate his fellow students, it still says a lot about the young Donne that he could imagine so vividly a life so promiscuous and so contemptuous. We have before us evidence of what he thought would impress men who impressed him, even if it was not what he often practised – and of what tempted him, even if he stuck to his books for most of the time.

The erotic poems of the 1590s were no doubt influenced by Donne's reading of Ovid, the Roman poet who was highly fashionable among the sophisticated English of the Elizabethan Renaissance, but Donne added to this influence something which made his own celebration of love distinctively his own. There was in his poetry a disquiet, a dramatic intensity, an anxious tenseness, a brutality, not to be found in the other Elizabethan Ovidians – or in Ovid himself. And Donne could write poetry in a tradition which was similar to the Ovidian fashion only in that it, too, was imported from Italy. He could write in the 'Petrarchan' style begun by Boccaccio, Petrarch and their followers in the Italian Renaissance. This was poetry about love-without-physical-sex. There could be drama in it but it was the drama of frustrated suffering – and there could be anxiety, the anxiety of being perpetually unable either to get, or to forget, the woman who was desired. But about this Petrarchan tradition there was also an air of unreality and when Donne wrote poems in this tradition the unreality became their most striking feature. These are the places at which the attacks on 'conceits' without foundations in facts ought to have been directed.

A good example is 'Twicknam Garden', so named after one of the residences of Lucy, the sparkling young Countess of Bedford; she took it over in 1607. It is most unlikely that Donne, who was then unemployed, was in a sexual relationship with a countess who was one of the richest, most fashionable and most influential women in England and the queen's closest friend. But Donne adopts the Petrarchan stance in order to flatter and tease her:

> Blasted with sighs, and surrounded with teares,
> Hither I come to seek the spring . . .

The speaker now wishes, however, that it was still winter, so that the budding trees might not 'laugh' at his misery. He would like to remain in the garden like 'a stone fountain weeping', so that lovers could 'take my teares' and by a test see that in comparison with his sorrow the tears of the lady who says good-bye are 'false' because she does not really love him, surprising as this is. 'None is true but shee'; the countess persists in being faithful to her husband, to whom she had been married at the age of thirteen and to whom she was to remain faithful when he had been paralysed by a fall from a horse; so 'her truth kills me'.

Another example of Petrarchan flirtation which seems artificial may also have been written for the enjoyment of the unattainable Countess of Bedford. 'The Blossome' is placed in a garden and again the time is spring. During a visit for 'sixe or seaven dayes' the speaker has watched the birth and growth of a blossom which now 'dost laugh and triumph on this bough' – but tonight there will be a frost and tomorrow this blossom will lie fallen on the ground. The speaker now addresses his heart: it, too, must fall from the 'forbidden tree' in the Garden of Eden, the tree of 'knowledge' which is slang for sex, since the lady of the garden will not respond sexually. To this the heart replies that its charm will prove irresistible if the speaker removes his body from the scene. So it is allowed to stay behind for 'twenty dayes', without the body. But it is warned:

> A naked thinking heart, that makes no show,
> Is to a woman but a kinde of Ghost.

Meanwhile the speaker is off to London, where he will become 'more fat by being with men' and then, rejoined by the heart, will give himself to a 'friend' who will be 'as glad to have my body as my minde'. Here is another poem of flirtation which ends with a reaffirmation of marriage for the lady and for the visiting poet, in different marriages – and both poems may well have been written as thank-you letters at the end of visits to the countess in Twickenham.

It does not seem merely sentimental if we guess that the reference to growing fatter 'by being with men' points to the eating, drinking and men's talk in one of the clubs to which Donne belonged in London, before he went back to Mitcham to offer heart, mind and body to his long-suffering wife. But Anne would have reason to be suspicious or jealous of her husband's connection with this rich and glamorous Lucy, specially when the countess condescended to be a godmother of the Donnes' second daughter, to attend the baptism in Mitcham when the baby was named Lucy, and to visit their cottage. Donne had cosy suppers with this patroness in London while his wife was left at home with their children. He told her in a letter that 'my best depth of understanding is to be governed by you' and promised to write poems only for her, explaining to a friend that she 'only hath power to cast the fetters of verse upon my free meditations'. She asked for copies of his poems and in return showed him some of her own. There was mutual admiration.

One of his new poems was addressed to her with a flattery which would have amounted to blasphemy had it been meant – or taken – literally:

> Reason is our Soule's left hand, Faith her right,
> By these wee reach divinity, that's you . . .
> But soone the reasons why you are loved by all
> Grow infinite, and so passe reason's reach . . .

The poem went on to praise her 'birth and beauty', her 'learning and religion'. She was 'God's masterpeece' and

> The first good Angell, since the world's frame stood,
> That ever did in woman's shape appeare.

Another poem flattering the Countess of Bedford to the point of obvious unreality began 'You have refin'd me' but Donne was not too refined: he reused some of these ideas in his poem flattering the Countess of Huntingdon. He found that his anxiety was justified, for the first countess who had bestowed her favour on him was indeed mightily offended. She was not going to compete with other ladies for the attention of a poet; poets were meant to compete for her favour (and cash). She was even more put out when Donne wrote – and actually printed – long poems in fulsome praise of an obscure girl, Elizabeth Drury. While still in France with the Drurys the chastened poet began a verse-letter of apology and a draft survives, uncompleted. He wrote to Goodyer that 'I have been heretofore too immodest towards her, and I suffer this purgatory for it'. After a reconciliation she promised to settle all his debts. In the end she did not, pleading that she now had her own financial problems but also letting it be known that she did not think that the poet who had called her God's masterpiece would make an ideal priest. She fell ill and became both the patient and the convert of a doctor who was also a Puritan – and who definitely disapproved of Donne. A relationship which had once been overheated cooled permanently, no doubt to Anne's relief.

Not much heat was left to warm the heart of the Countess of Huntingdon, but Donne did his best. He began by teasing her:

> Man to God's image, Eve to man's was made.

But he continued by acclaiming her as a miraculous 'new starre' in the sky: 'that's heavenly things, that's you'. And he cleverly pretended he was not exaggerating:

> If you can thinke these flatteries they are,
> For then your judgement is below my praise.

Even less heat could be produced in honour of the Countess of Salisbury. His poem to her in August 1614 compared her with a summer's day:

> Faire, great and good, since seeing you we see
> What Heaven can doe, and what any Earth can be.

But this time the poet was not really in the Petrarchan mood. For reasons already set out in Chapter 3, Donne felt that he was lying 'in a dark Cave, yea in a Grave'.

A less fraught relationship developed with the widowed Magdalen Herbert, the calm and thoroughly good mother of Donne's friends Sir Edward and the poet George, and a poem somewhat like 'Twicknam Garden' seems to have resulted from a visit to Montgomery Castle in Wales, the Herberts' family seat.

The castle stood on Primrose Hill and the 1635 edition of the poems added a sub-title to 'The Primrose', saying that this location was why this poem was so named. In it the speaker declared that on this hill 'I walke to finde a true Love', but he has found that the lady must be 'more than woman' because 'shee would get above all thought of sexe' and would 'thinke to move my heart to study her, and not to love'. If this meeting was with Magdalen Herbert, it was part of a close friendship which continued when she married again. When she died Donne preached a passionate sermon about her life (7:61–93) which ended by saying that following her example could make anyone a saint.

Izaak Walton, who heard that sermon and saw him weep, linked Donne's poem 'The Autumnall' with Magdalen Herbert. There seems to be no way to prove that he was wrong, but if he was right the poem must have been a piece of teasing, not a serious description of reality. If this poem seriously referred to her, and was shown to her, it is a wonder that the friendship grew, for here is a struggle to find compliments for the beauty of an 'Autumnall face' complete with 'wrinkles', before old age brings a winter face with a 'slacke' skin, a 'worne out' mouth and missing teeth. The most that he can offer is the thought that her wrinkles are 'Love's graves' because as a 'trench' or 'tombe' each wrinkle records a past which has been spent loving – with this hope for the future:

> Since such love's motion natural is, may still
>   My love descend and journey down the hill,
> Not panting after growing beauties, so
>   I shall ebbe out with them who home-ward goe.

That offer to accompany the woman downhill all the way does not sound as if it was made to one with a husband already at her side, and if it was made to Magdalen Herbert before her second marriage (in 1608) it was made before she was aged 42. At that age she married a rich man who was twenty years younger and famously handsome (John Aubrey, who was his friend, says that people would go out in the street in order to admire); so it seems probable that she had not lost her looks or her charm. Almost twenty years later Donne could still praise her 'comeliness' as he preached about her life. He admitted that 'melancholy' had afflicted her in her declining years but he preached the hope that her beauty would be restored in her resurrection: 'That body at last shall have her last expectation satisfied, and dwell bodily with that Righteousnesse, in these new Heavens and new Earth, for ever, and ever, and ever, and infinite and super-infinite evers' (8:92). It seems very unlikely that such a woman would have received 'The Autumnall' as 'an exquisite compliment', which was Grierson's guess.

In 'The Undertaking' the speaker gives the advice to keep Platonic 'love' well hidden because no one will believe that in real life a man and a woman who are close friends can 'forget the Hee and Shee' and love only the 'loveliness within'. And in 'The Relique' he imagines the interpretation which will be put on the bones of friends who say about themselves that they knew 'no difference of sexe': people will dismiss the idea of a sexless partnership and the bones will be venerated as the relics of lovers. And it seems that Donne's own emotions could not be stirred deeply unless the difference between 'Hee and Shee' had in it the possibility of physical expression. Without that, what he writes about women sounds unreal.

The same atmosphere of unreality is found in verse-letters to men. Donne was a pioneer in using this medium which became fashionable suddenly in the 1590s. He tells Samuel Brooke 'I am harsh' – but he is not, for he flatters extravagantly. Thomas Woodward is told that he has produced 'wit and Art' better than anything 'before or after': Donne admits that he has helped his friend to be a poet, but 'I am thy Creator, thou my Saviour'. Samuel Brooke is praised for the 'bright sparkes' of his own poetry and Donne apologizes that there is 'noe fuell' in the poems which he sends. This tone is found in the tributes of homage and love paid to each other by many men of this period but its adoption by the arrogant Donne is notable.

The poems of mourning are also extravagant. Two were written at the request of the Countess of Bedford, to honour cousins of hers who had died in her home in Twickenham. Lady Marckham could be flattered like the countess herself:

> She sinn'd, but just enough to let us see
> That God's word must be true, *All sinners be.*

About Cecilia Boulstred he wrote that she had been 'proofe 'gainst sins of youth' although in an honest poem (which to his horror had been shown to her) Ben Jonson had called the living woman the resident prostitute in the royal court. After the death of Henry, Prince of Wales, in November 1612, Donne's sense of the nation's loss was probably genuine, but in the tribute which he added to those coming from other poets he wrote so obscurely that Jonson claimed that the lament had been composed solely in order 'to match Sir Ed: Herbert in obscurenesse'.

His two 'Anniversaries' were also a lament and also disregarded common sense; Edmund Gosse thought them 'preposterous'. Many readers have found them very obscure because of the difficulty of answering the question: what did Donne mean when he told Jonson that they had been written about 'the idea of a Woman' and not specifically about the life of young Elizabeth Drury? It has been suggested that he had Queen Elizabeth I in mind, partly because near the beginning of the 'First Anniversarie' he referred to the custom of a royal 'progress' through the houses of the nobility and richer gentry in a region of the countryside before returning to a palace well before winter:

> When that Queene ended here her progresse time,
> And as t'her standing house, to heaven did clymbe . . .

But that is the only comparison made between the two Elizabeths and it seems very improbable that Donne's motive was to write a long lament for the real queen so long after her death (as it is improbable that he had planned to attack her in *Metempsychosis* while she was alive). Equally far-fetched is the proposal that he was lamenting the suppression of the cult of the Virgin Mary, although the cult of England's Protestant queen had been more or less the official substitute for that Catholic devotion. Had Donne so wished, he could have crushed Jonson's criticism by saying that he had indeed paid a tribute to Mary, but instead he said repeatedly in his poem 'Shee's dead' – which no devotee would have said about the Blessed Virgin. And if he intended the 'Shee' to refer to the *anima mundi* ('soul of the world') in pagan thought, or to the Wisdom within the creation in the Old Testament (also feminine), or to the *logos* or divine Word within all that exists in the New Testament, he left no clear indication. It seems that we must accept what he did say: that he wrote about a woman. And we must accept that her name was Elizabeth Drury, because that was why her parents rewarded Donne for honouring her.

However, we must also accept that Donne did not mean to write about her 'as she was', as if he had been writing a school report about the girl's progress or lack of it. As he explained to a friend, 'when I had received so very good testimony of her worthinesse . . . it became me to say, not what I was sure was just truth, but the best that I could conceive'. It seems that he wrote about the Image of God in a woman's immortal soul. He had done so before. When flattering a great lady such as the Countess of Bedford he had claimed that he stopped short of idolatry, for he was praising 'that Deitie which dwells in you', in 'your vertuous Soule'. Similarly, when he called the Countess of Huntingdon a star or 'heavenly things', he could claim that his intention was 'God in you to praise'. Now he could not classify Elizabeth Drury as a great lady but he could celebrate her as a pure virgin – and did so, not only in the

'Anniversaries' but also in the epitaph for this 'Paradise without a serpent' which he composed for her tomb. And he could praise her as a model soul, as an unblemished Image of God, as

> Shee that was best, and first originall
> Of all fair copies . . .

Her death could then be used as a peg on which to hang a wide-ranging religious meditation.

Of course he exaggerated her merits, as he exaggerated the world's grief, decay and matching death. He told the world that it would have found it easier to spare 'the Sunne, or Man' than to lose her, for

> Her name defin'd thee, gave thee forme and frame.

He wrote that 'a fainte weake love of virtue and of good' remaining in the world was only 'her Ghost' walking in the 'twi-light'. He wrote that no health was left, lives were short, sizes were small. In the new society

> 'Tis all in pieces, all cohaerence gone . . .
> Prince, Subject, Father, Sonne, are things forgot . . .

He wrote that the world had no more beauty of proportion or colour, that the sky now dropped not rain but meteors – and he wrote much other nonsense. In her study of the impact of the new science Marjorie Hope Nicolson claimed that the 'Anniversaries' were 'an "epitome" of the intellectual universe in which Donne lived', of 'what the Elizabethans had made of the world and the universe' – but as other scholars have demonstrated, the Elizabethan world-picture could be pessimistic or optimistic according to one's mood. The compliment paid by Joseph Hall at the time was more accurate: what Donne created, he wrote, was a 'world of wit'. The poet himself denied that the 'Anniversaries' were intended to describe the world and the universe in the light of new knowledge. He asked

> What hope have we to know our selves, when wee
> Know not the least things, which for our own use bee?
> We see in Authors, to stiffe to recant,
> A hundred controversies of an Ant

– and he had no intention of wasting time on a close observation of ants. Nor did he propose to discuss questions about 'why grasse is greene' or 'why our blood is red' or 'what Caesar did' or what 'Cicero said'. Such 'matters of fact' were to him 'unconcerning'.

Donne was in debt and very depressed at this time. The world which the poem said had been devastated by Elizabeth Drury's death was, it seems, his own mental world, darkened by the problems in his own life – although no doubt he was also sensitive to the grief of the girl's parents. But as he had done before, in his depression he kept his wit. He also kept the faith which he had expressed in his 'Holy Sonnets' (to be discussed very shortly), that the cure for the sorrows of life is death. It is illuminating to compare the 'Anniversaries' with *Metempsychosis*. They are united by a sub-title: in 1601 the long poem was sub-titled 'The Progresse of the Soule' and in 1611 Donne put at the head of his second 'Anniversarie' the words 'Of the Progresse of the Soule'. They are also united by a depressed atmosphere: in 1601 the 'age of rusty iron' made a poet who was close to the fighting between individuals and factions think of the world as a battlefield without morality, while in 1611 the disappointment of his hopes made him view the world as a desert without life. But the intervening ten years have strengthened his beliefs that the 'soule' belongs to one individual person (he had long ago abandoned the 'conceit' that the soul of evil could transmigrate through many creatures) and that the person's only ultimate hope must lie in heaven. In that limited but supremely important sense, the soul can make 'progress'.

In the 'Second Anniversarie' he began with the most tasteless of all his 'conceits': the world is now like the head of a criminal who has just been beheaded. But he continued in a style which seems to be a sign of a far greater seriousness, for he moved to the 'essentiall joy' of heaven and this theme inspired snatches of poetry as fine as anything he ever wrote, for example:

> Thinke then, My soule, that death is but a Groome,
> Which brings a Taper to the outward roome,
> Whence thou spiest first a little glimmering light,
> And after brings it nearer to thy sight . . .

What seems to have happened at a deep level in Donne's personality is that he had been cut down. In the 'pride and lust' of his early manhood he had used women promiscuously, as objects which could briefly satisfy his strong sexuality. He had despised them, as in his moral-seeming arrogance he had despised men who for the time being ranked above him in society. Then the 'idea of a Woman' had taken flesh before his eyes, in the person of Anne More whom he married in a great act of self-sacrifice – to be followed by a miserable period in which he paid the price. Now he had to flatter courtiers, or great ladies, or the rich parents of a dead girl, in order to earn money to keep his own head above water and for the support of his family. He had been humbled and a part of the humiliation had been having to adopt what he had previously despised as the feminine position, at the receiving end. It was relevant that when he thought of his soul – the essential Donne – he thought of it in the manner of his age, as feminine. And so he learned to accept as an undeserved gift the salvation which does not seem to be available from any other source. At any rate, that is what his 'Divine Poems' said he was learning, step by step, and to them we now turn.

8 Batter my heart

Batter my heart, three person'd God: for you
As yet but knocke, breathe, shine,
and seeke to mend . . .

Holy Sonnets *XIV*

Donne's poem called 'The Crosse' was probably written when he was about 35. It is not a meditation on the Passion of Christ but it reuses ancient and medieval suggestions that cross-like images are widespread and, with this heritage, it is a defence of the Church of England's retention of the ceremony of 'signing with the cross' in Baptism. To Puritans the ceremony seemed unbiblical and Popish but to Donne it was a reminder that crosses are seen everywhere in daily life and particularly in the life of a Christian. He wrote

Swimme, and at every stroake thou art thy Crosse . . .

A bird in flight, or a mast with arms for the sails, also makes a cross. But more importantly, a Christian must find 'joy in crosses': 'the eye needs crossing', so does the heart and so does 'concupiscence of witt', the lust to be clever with words.

He seems to have yielded to that last temptation even while writing that poem, which was bookish: many books were available helping devotion to the cross of Christ and some offered pictures of the crosses to be met in daily life. His seven sonnets called 'La Corona' (because they are woven together somewhat like a crown) are of much the same character although they suggest a real effort to make the traditional images more relevant to him personally.

The effort was being urged in this period by many Catholic writers on spirituality and some Anglican Protestants such as Joseph Hall, who wrote on *The Arte of Divine Meditation* in 1607. (Hall supplied verses to commend the 'Anniversaries': he, too, owed much to the Drurys, and he ended up as Bishop of Norwich.) These seven sonnets seem to be the 'Hymns' sent with a verse-letter to Magdalen Herbert in 1607.

The first is a prayer of preparation. Donne's mood is 'low devout melancholie', but the closure is more hopeful than strict Calvinists would allow, for he asks

> that heart and voice be lifted high,
> *Salvation to all that will is nigh.*

A rejection of strict Calvinism is seen in the remaining sonnets, which adapt the Catholic tradition of 'saying the rosary', reciting a series of prayers in honour of the Blessed Virgin. Some adaptation is necessary because the centre must now be the Saviour, not his sorrowful or joyful mother, but the devotion expressed is more Catholic than Protestant. It is said of the Virgin that in her womb Christ 'can take no sinne' and an old form of praise is quoted:

> Thy Maker's maker, and thy Father's mother,
> Thou hast light in darke; and shutst in little roome,
> *Immensity cloystered in thy deare wombe.*

More striking still in this meditation on the Annunciation to Mary is Donne's reuse of three lines from *Metempsychosis.* There these lines had been a passing mention of the crucifixion, in the course of a reference to the story ('as devout and sharpe men may fittly guesse') that the cross stood on the very place where the forbidden tree had stood in the garden of Eden. Now the lines became a far more reverent contemplation of what had entered the Virgin's womb:

> That All which alwayes is All every where,
> Which cannot sin, and yet all sinnes must beare,
> Which cannot die, yet cannot chuse but die . . .

In accordance with the tradition of the rosary the poem then moves from the Nativity to the Crucifixion, stopping only to consider the visit to the Jerusalem temple in Christ's boyhood. It moves devoutly and these meditations employ praises which had been voiced by the devout in earlier generations: in the temple the Word which had been silent in infancy 'speakes wonders', on the cross evil men 'prescribe a Fate' to the Lord 'whose creature Fate is'. But when the poet finally addresses the crucified Christ directly, at the end of the fifth sonnet, it is with words which sound conventional rather than intense, and the remaining two sonnets maintain the same tone. The impression is left that Donne is doing his best to imagine salvation, but as yet it does not mean everything to him, so that his poetry – always essentially about his own feelings – remains frigid.

In 1608 the feast of the Annunciation (Lady Day) fell on the same day as Good Friday and this coincidence in the calendar inspired Donne to write a poem about his soul in contemplation of the Christ who is conceived in the womb and killed on the cross:

> Shee sees him nothing twice at once, who is all;
> Shee sees a Cedar plant it selfe, and fall,
> Her Maker put to making, and the head
> Of life, at once, not yet alive, yet dead . . .

But on this Good Friday did Christ mean 'all' to Donne? It seems from this poem that he was more preoccupied with thinking up 'conceits' which would rhyme. Yet poems which appear to have been written during the next twelve months are of a very different character, following a long period of depression and an illness which seems to have been neuritis.

Helen Gardner gained wide acceptance for her theory that early in 1609 Donne sent six sonnets about the 'Last Things' (death and its sequels) to Richard Sackville, who had just inherited the earldom of Dorset. Some facts appeared to support this theory. Six sonnets with this character have been included among the 'Divine Poems' in the printed editions, which have also included a verse-letter addressed 'To E. of D. with six holy Sonnets'. Also, this earl was the patron who appointed Donne as vicar of St Dunstan's in 1624, shortly before his own death. And three of the sonnets about death seem to have been written before the middle of 1609, for they express views which are contradicted by what Donne wrote after that date. However, there are problems about this suggestion.

One is that the verse-letter 'To E. of D.' pays tribute to the 'fatherly yet lusty Ryme' of the person addressed, and it is said that his poetry is related to Donne's own 'drossie Rymes' as a father is related to his son. This is puzzling because in 1609 Richard Sackville was seventeen years younger than Donne and although his grandfather was a good poet if the young man wrote poems none has survived. Another problem is that since the poems sent were about the fear of death and hell – although they were called 'songs' – they would have been a very strange present to send as the 'fruits' of his own poems to a young man who had just inherited a fortune and was resolved to spend it to the limit and beyond. John Aubrey mentioned in his *Brief Lives* that this earl 'lived in the greatest grandeur of any nobleman of his time in England'. However, having no son he left his estates to his brother heavily encumbered with debts. It therefore seems probable that Donne can be spared the charge that he bared his soul with thoughts about God, sin and hell in the hope of receiving some of the money which an immature aristocrat was about to spend on luxury with gusto.

Were the 'six holy Sonnets' sent to another patron? It seems probable that they were and a suggestion has been made, based on the fact that in the important Westmoreland manuscript which was copied out by Rowland Woodward, and in the first printed collection of the poetry, this verse-letter which submits the sonnets to a patron was included among other verse-letters which date from a period before 1609. To add slightly to the confusion, here in the title 'E. of D.' becomes 'L. of D.'.

In 1988 Dennis Flynn therefore proposed that the verse-letter was sent to the Earl of Derby ten years or so before 1609, but he still maintained that the poems enclosed were about the Last Things. This proposal was connected with Flynn's theory that the Earl of Derby was the member of the Catholic nobility who had acted as Donne's employer and patron. However, here fresh problems arise. These poems are not Catholic in doctrine about the Last Things and they are joined to other sonnets which find no solution for their religious anxiety in the Catholic reliance on the sacraments. And if Donne was so seriously troubled about his sins when confronting death in the early 1600s, it is indeed curious that he also wrote *Metempsychosis.* The only safe conclusion seems to be that we simply do not know who 'E. of D.' or 'L. of D.' was. 'E. of D.' was probably part of a title added many years after the writing of the poem. 'L. of D.' would imply a less formal reference to the same man; for example, the Earl of Dorset could be called 'My Lord of Dorset'.

If a reader is intrigued by this little puzzle, it may be worth mentioning my own guess about the identity of 'E. of D'. Henry Danvers was a brother of the John who married Magdalen Herbert in 1608. He was a soldier who at that time was one of the commanders in Ireland but he was to be given more agreeable positions by two kings, and was to be created Earl of Danby in

1622. Like the other earls who have been nominated as E. of D. he is not known to have written poetry, but if Donne did flatter his efforts in that hobby as 'fatherly' and 'lusty' it would not have been very extraordinary: the two men were of almost the same age and although in his hotblooded youth Henry Danvers had killed an enemy in the course of a family feud he had been pardoned and seems to have developed a character which was compatible with a feeling for poetry and poets. He may have been influenced by his years as a page in attendance on a soldier-poet, Sir Philip Sidney.

Years later he formed a close relationship with George Herbert. Walton wrote that he 'lov'd Mr Herbert so very much' that he had him to stay in his 'noble House' in Wiltshire so that he might regain health. While enjoying the sensitive hospitality the patient did indeed recover, so 'improv'd to a good degree of strength and chearfulness' that he resolved to marry a neighbour's daughter and to become a parish priest. In the same spirit Henry Danvers was a benefactor of Oxford University, paying for the creation of its beautiful Botanic Garden in the year when he was made an earl. John Aubrey, who was not sentimental, praised him as a man 'of a magnificent and munificent spirit'. It would therefore not be surprising if in 1609, when he was sick at heart as well as physically ill, Donne thought that having recently dedicated some of his religious poems to Magdalen Herbert he would send others to her brother-in-law.

John Carey has (perhaps wisely) dismissed this little debate about whether 'E. of D.' was the earl of Dorset, of Derby or of Danby. In his edition of Donne's poetry (1990, p. xxviii) he suggested that the Holy Sonnets may 'belong to Donne's relationship with the Countess of Bedford' and may be essentially a lament about the poet's social and financial humiliation although this basically secular concern is clothed in religious language in order to take account of 'the Countess's Calvinism'. But no solid argument was added to this theory. Equally questionable is the theory of Arthur

Marotti that these poems 'encoded' Donne's dissatisfaction with unemployment and illness. However, in his earlier book on Donne Carey offered an interpretation which was more probable. Then he found in the Holy Sonnets a 'need for God', a fear of damnation', a 'fear that he belongs to the devil', a 'writhing in the trap' because the Protestant insistence on an emotional faith which he could not feel was for Donne 'a recipe for anguish' (pp. 35–43). That emphasis on the genuinely religious content of these poems – of course not excluding the influence of the experiences of unemployment and illness – does much more justice to what Donne wrote.

Carey's earlier emphasis on the poet's genuine 'anguish' also illuminates the fact that Donne turned to the formal structure of the fourteen-line rhyming sonnet in order to express painfully real religious emotions. The sonnet had been used in English love poetry since Sir Thomas Wyatt and Henry Howard, Earl of Surrey, had imitated and developed Petrarch's *Canzoniere*; both men had died in the 1540s. Shakespeare had of course written sonnets of a wider character, and Henry Lok published *Sundry Christian Passions Contained in Two Hundred Sonnets* while Donne was writing about other passions in the 1590s, but Donne was the first major English poet to use the sonnet for a definitely religious purpose, to be followed by Milton among others. In 'La Corona' the formality had contributed to the impression of some shallowness in the emotions but now the passion was obviously profound and it seems that Donne kept it within the sonnet's structure not merely in order to please a patron but mainly so as to keep in order this torrent of religious emotion. Sonnets had been used like the banks of a river in order to control feelings about women which might be very strong; Petrarch had made such poems when he could not get near Laura. Donne made them now when he could not get near God.

In these 'Holy Sonnets' God is addressed by a man who is extremely anxious because he has not yet been given any sign that he is one of the 'elect' predestined to salvation. According to Calvinism, the God who was merciful to the 'elect' also gave them the assurance that they had been chosen, together with the power to 'persevere' and (it was often added) health, happiness and prosperity as encouragement. Donne felt no such power in him and enjoyed no such blessings in his life of unemployment and sickness. He was genuinely interested in religion, as his previous poetry had shown, but his rejection both of his Catholic heritage and of an Anglican parish had shown he had found no institution in which his spirituality could find a home and flourish. Since he had been taught – by Roman Catholics and Anglicans alike – that God is active, he now begged God to act decisively, to clear up the mess which was Donne, to give him faith and peace, to show him the way ahead. These were deeply sincere emotions and, to give them shape, he worked them out in a series of sixteen sonnets.

In various sonnets, surely we hear from a heart:

> Except thou rise and for thine owne worke fight,
> Oh I shall soone despaire, when I doe see
> That thou lov'st mankind well, yet wilt not chuse mee . . .
>
> Oh my blacke Soule! now thou art summoned
> By sicknesse, death's herald and champion . . .
> Or wash thee in Christ's blood, which hath this might
> That being red, it dyes red soules to white.
>
> This is my playe's last scene, here heavens appoint
> My pilgrimage's last mile; and my race
> Idly, yet quickly runne, hath this last pace,
> My span's last inch, my minute's latest point . . .

Teach me how to repent; for that's as good
As if thou hadst seal'd my pardon, with thy blood . . .

And mercy being easie, and glorious
To God, in his sterne wrath why threatens hee?
But who am I, that dare dispute with thee?

In these sonnets Donne entered a new depth in his relationship with Christ. He could say to Christ's enemies

Buffet and scoffe, scourge and crucifie mee

but he felt that he was one of the enemies: 'I crucifie him daily'. He could see the 'strange love' of the Eternal being incarnate in the crucified when

God cloth'd himselfe in vile man's flesh, that so
He might be weake enough to suffer woe

but he knew that his vision of that love was intermittent:

I runne to death, and death meets me as fast,
And all my pleasures are like yesterday,
I dare not move my dimme eyes any way,
Despaire behind, and death before doth cast
Such terrour, and my febled flesh doth waste
By sinne in it, which it t'wards hell doth weigh;
Onely thou art above, and when towards thee
By thy leave I can looke, I rise againe
But our old subtle foe so tempteth me,
That not one houre my selfe I can sustaine . . .

So he prays that 'Thy Grace may wing me' to the security for which he longs; that his 'iron heart' may be drawn by the magnet of 'Grace'.

In one sonnet he tried to persuade himself that death is not terrible: presumably that is what he tried to believe when contemplating suicide. He claimed that death is only 'rest and sleepe' and that 'our best men' show that they prefer it by dying young. Alternatively, anything can make us die – Fate, chance, kings, desperate men, poison, war, sickness – so why not accept it calmly? But in this same year he wrote other poems which took a more realistic view – St Paul's view of death as 'the last enemy':

> Th' earth's face is but thy Table; there are set
> Plants, cattell, men, dishes for Death to eate.
> In a rude hunger now hee millions drawes
> Into his bloody, or plaguy, or sterv'd jawes.
>
> Man is the World, and death th' Ocean,
> To which God gives the lower parts of man.
> This Sea invirons all, and though as yet
> God hath set markes, and bounds, 'twixt us and it,
> Yet it doth rore, and gnaw . . .

Thus he lamented the deaths of Cecilia Boulstred and Lady Marckham.

In two sonnets he expressed his emotions in a way which has shocked many readers and commentators. Their complaint has been that in addition to any excess of emotion about Christ he spoils the poem by a reference to sex which seems wholly inappropriate if the devout emotion is genuine; to John Carey this is 'hideous piffle' (p. 33). But for Donne himself, religion at its most intense is best described by comparing it with the other experience which has meant most to him: rightly or wrongly he thinks that the sex in the poem does not wreck, it illuminates. So he writes:

> Marke in my heart, O Soule, where thou dost dwell,
> The picture of Christ crucified, and tell
> Whether that countenance can thee affright.
> Teares in his eyes quench the amasing light,
> Blood fills his frownes, which from his pierc'd head fell,
> And can that tongue adjudge thee unto hell,
> Which pray'd forgivenesse . . . ?

And then, at this moment which to any sensitive believing Christian must be the most sacred of all moments, he remembers saying 'to all my profane mistresses' that beauty in a face is a sure sign of pity in a heart. How extraordinary! How inexcusable! Yet something can be said for Donne, even in this situation. He had praised pretty faces and soft hearts in order to persuade girl-friends not to send him away disappointed – and however oddly, that memory helps him to see that the 'beauteous forme' of the dying Christ shows a 'pity' which means that he is not being told to go to hell. The poem begins with the question: 'What if this present were the world's last night?' It gives the answer: you must be serious. And however strange or repulsive this may seem, Donne is being serious when at the foot of the cross he recalls the intensity of sexual experience. If tonight were to be the end of the world, it is likely that this last night would find this man (at this stage of his life) thinking about two subjects with a supremely important connection between them: God and sex. And if we are still shocked, it may help us to forgive Donne's error of taste if we remember that even poets who are usually praised for their impeccable taste can lapse when they use 'conceits' which make their impact precisely by being unexpected. Thus George Herbert can lapse into a suggestion that Christ on the cross teaches the music which the poet loves:

> His stretched sinews taught all strings what key
> Is best to celebrate this most high day.

And he can get worse:

> Christ left His grave-clothes, that we might, when grief
> Draws tears or bloud, not want an handkerchief.

In the most powerful and famous of these 'Holy Sonnets' sex is again introduced into a solemn meditation, for the poem ends with this extraordinary prayer to the Holy Trinity:

> Take mee to you, imprison mee, for I
> Except you enthrall mee, never shall be free,
> Nor ever chast, except you ravish mee.

And, not surprisingly, commentators whose belief is that Donne is not really talking to the real God have not been slow to offer suggestions about the fantasy in which he is indulging. Perhaps he is imagining himself as a woman who fantasizes that she is being raped? Or perhaps he is still aware that he is a man and he is imagining the homosexual pleasure of sodomy? Or perhaps he is a sado-masochist, begging for the delight of being made to suffer pain? To Edmund Gosse 'nothing could be more odious' than this closure to the poem.

However, an interpretation which is not quite so sensational is possible if we remember that in company with most of his contemporaries Donne believes not only in the ultimate reality but also in the utter holiness of God. Long before any critic can rebuke him he sees how dangerous it is going to be to end the poem with the image of his soul – his soul which by convention is spoken of as being feminine – being ravished by God. At the start of the poem he says that his 'heart' must be the target of God's attention and that God is 'three person'd' – Father, Son and Holy Spirit, not a man. He goes on to say that so far his experience of God has been too feeble. The God he has known has been too like a tinker asked to mend some old kitchen utensil: as yet, God has not been known by him to do more than 'knocke, breathe, shine and seek to mend'. He prays that God will now use his almighty force less gently. He must 'brake, blowe, burn and make me new'. His heart and soul need this drastic treatment because he can compare himself to a town which tries to admit its proper lord into its gates, 'but Oh, to no end', since at present it is under the control of a usurper and the ruler who was appointed by the lord has proved 'weake or untrue'. In yet other words, he is married to God's 'enemie' and God must act to secure his divorce. Reason, which is intended to be God's 'viceroy' ruling over his evil passions, is unable to exert the power required.

What he means by this succession of images is that he feels that he is the prisoner of Satan – but he can say to God 'dearely I love you' and he longs to be able to 'rise and stand' when he is 'free'. And by 'free' he does not mean free to enjoy a form of sex which is condemned by the Christian tradition's understanding of the Law of God. He means being free to be 'chast' – free to be cleansed thoroughly from his sexual behaviour in the past and from any lingering thoughts which are unclean, free to be chaste within a Christian marriage (he does not ask to be celibate).

In 1608 and 1609 Donne went through a spiritual crisis, almost a mental breakdown, which in some moods later he tried to forget, and the depth of this crisis would have been unknown to the world had these poems not survived for publication. Without them, we should have known only that he grumbled about depression in the countryside and wrote a muddled and unprintable book half-defending suicide.

After this time of mental suffering Donne seems to have known a period of calm, for the Holy Sonnets include one where the soul is asked to 'digest' in 'wholesome meditation' the fact that God 'hath deign'd to chuse thee by adoption' as one of his sons, destined to the glory of heaven. And another sonnet gives thanks to God for 'thy all-healing grace' and for the command which in the end requires only 'love'.

Donne's experience of sickness was not over, but it seems that when confined to his bed once again in the winter of 1609–10 he composed a 'Litanie' of prayers and sent copies to a few of his closest friends. A letter to Henry Goodyer in which he says that 'since my imprisonment in my bed' he has 'made a meditation in verse, which I will call a Litany' is not dated. Helen Gardner thought it possible that Donne wrote it before all or most of the 'Holy Sonnets', partly because another letter to Goodyer which includes some phrases echoed in the Litany is known to have been written in September 1608. But it seems best to attach more importance to the tone of the Litany, which suggests a recovery of balance after the highly disturbed sonnets of 1608–09. Donne may then have repeated phrases used in an earlier letter.

In these prayers we meet a poet who surprises us not by being sexual but by being sensible. He begins by saying, as in the Holy Sonnets, that he has 'growne ruinous', adding that he is still tempted to suicide:

> My heart is by dejection, clay
> And by selfe-murder, red . . .

And he prays for the known cure:

O be thou nail'd unto my heart,
And crucified againe . . .

But he now feels able to add other prayers to the petition in the sixth of the Holy Sonnets, which was 'Impute me righteous' (because I am a sinner, my only hope is that I may be reckoned to be righteous by being mercifully considered by God as Christlike). Some of the new prayers echo, while silently reforming, his Roman Catholic past. Others are influenced by the Anglican spirit, which instinctively prefers the 'middle way' as a compromise between more dramatic positions at the extremities.

He uses Catholic prayers although he makes a Protestant alteration: here, he does not pray to anyone except God. He thanks God for the Virgin Mary:

For that faire blessed Mother-maid,
Whose flesh redeem'd us; That she-Cherubin,
Which unlock'd Paradise, and made
One claime for innocence . . .

He even thanks God for 'her prayers'. When ordained as an Anglican, he was going to renounce this remnant of Popery, preaching that 'the Virgin Mary had not the same interest in our salvation as Eve had in our destruction; nothing that she did entered into that treasure, that ransom that redeemed us' (1:200).

He thanks God for the angels, for the patriarchs of Israel ('those great Grandfathers of thy Church'), for 'thy Eagle-sighted Prophets', for the apostles, for the martyrs, for the confessors, for the virgins, for the 'doctors' who taught the Church on earth, for the whole of 'that Church in triumph' in heaven. And he adds appropriate prayers about himself. When considering the prophets he prays to be delivered from 'excesse in Poëtiquenesse' and when praising the apostles he asks that his own 'comment' on Scripture will not merely 'make thy word mine'. When admiring the martyrs he remembers that his own escape from the fates of martyred members of his family must not mean the end of heroism for him, for in more complicated situations

> Oh, to some
> Not to be Martyrs, is a martyrdome.

And when admiring past teachers of the Church, he remembers that they may have 'misdone or mis-said' when they were not faithful to 'thy Scriptures': so, 'Lord let us . . . call them stars, but not the Sunne'.

Donne's own psychological needs come out even more clearly when he asks to be given the wisdom to avoid the many pitfalls of daily life – which for him must often mean not rushing to extremes. Thus he prays to be made neither 'anxious' nor 'secure' and to be prevented from thinking either that 'all happinesse' lies in 'great courts' or that no happiness is there. He must seek God with all his might but must not think that 'this earth is only for our prison fram'd'. He must trust in the blood of Christ but also attend to the welfare of his own soul. He must be spiritual but also perform 'our mutuall duties'. He must avoid both 'Vanitie' and excessive 'humilitie'; he must resemble the Christ who calmly accepts both 'Povertie' and 'kings' gifts'. And he must learn to reject his own most pressing temptations: to wish to die 'ere this world doe bid us goe' and to 'seeme religious only to vent wit'. Instead of his present 'Pietie' which depends on moods, he asks that he may 'change to evennesse', hearing the 'musique of thy promises'.

It seems, however, that his prayer for the peace of 'evennesse' was never granted – and could not be, granted that he had the perpetually uneasy temperament which made him what he was.

The poem which grew out of his meditation while on horseback on Good Friday in 1613 showed that he still had a troubled relationship with the Christ whom he now regarded as his Saviour. He was 'riding westward', to the family home of the Herberts in Wales, as he often rode on 'pleasure or businesse'. Yet he was far from relaxed, since on Good Friday 'my Soule's forme bends towards the East', towards Jerusalem with 'Christ on this Crosse'. He felt 'almost glad' that

I do not see
That spectacle of too much weight for mee

for he had no natural wish 'to see God dye'. Yet he did know that 'thou look'st towards mee' and so he prayed:

O Saviour, as thou hang'st upon the tree;
I turne my backe to thee, but to receive
Corrections, till thy mercies bid thee leave.
O thinke me worth thine anger, punish mee,
Burne off my rusts, and my deformity,
Restore thine Image, so much, by thy grace,
That thou may'st know mee, and I'll turne my face.

In 1619 he was asked to embark on another journey, this time across the English Channel. He greatly exaggerated its dangers but it gave him the stimulus for his 'Hymne to Christ'.

In what torne ship soever I embarke,
That ship shall be my embleme of thy Arke;
What sea soever swallow mee, that flood
Shall be to mee an embleme of thy bloode;
Though thou with clouds of anger do disguise
Thy face; yet through that maske I know those eyes,

Which, though they turne away sometimes,
They never will despise.

He was still troubled; he would not be Donne if he had not been. He was still being witty; it was his way of expressing himself. In reality his ship for the brief crossing to France was going to be safe enough to carry the leadership of the most expensive diplomatic mission ever financed in seventeenth-century England, but here is some evidence that his main response to the image of Christ had developed between 1613 and 1619. He had turned and now could say 'I know those eyes'.

He was still troubled in the two poems which were written as companions to his *Devotions* in prose after his grave illness in 1623. One was his 'Hymne to God my God, in my sicknesse'. It bore all the marks of his practice of meditation using the method taught by St Ignatius Loyola, with four stages: the soul must be prepared, the scene must be imagined, an analysis of its meaning must be thought out, prayer must be made for divine assistance in living out that meaning. After a time when 'I tune the Instrument here at the dore', Donne pictures his body, lying 'flat on this bed' under the eyes of the worried physicians. He compares this with a 'mapp' unrolled under the eyes of 'Cosmographers'. He sees on this one map both West and East and to him the West, where the sun sets, means Death. He imagines the 'Pacifique Sea' far in the West and reflects that the 'streights' through which that ocean is entered are symbols of the dire straits in which he finds himself as he suffers. But as he contemplates the prospect of a painful death, his imagination fastens on a new symbol. Reviving the legend which he mentioned in *Metempsychosis*, he sees that at the centre of the world is 'Adam's tree' which became 'Christ's Crosse' and he prays:

As the first Adam's sweat surrounds my face,
May the last Adam's blood my soule embrace.

Finally he preaches 'my Sermon to mine owne' (himself), with the lesson that 'the Lord throws down' in order to 'raise'. From the ocean of Death he may be raised to Resurrection, as 'Easterne riches' may be found by sailing into the Pacific.

His 'Hymne to God the Father' is much simpler: of its 144 words, 132 are of only one syllable and four are 'forgive'. It was set to music at Donne's request and sung as an actual hymn. But its simplicity includes the admission of 'feare'. He still fears that his sins are so great that he cannot be forgiven and therefore, when he dies, he must perish. He is still witty, but the wit is now restrained: there is only the old pun about God's 'sonne' or the 'sunne' shining into his darkness, added to the pun about 'done' and possibly a pun about 'more'.

And even when he is one of the leading spokesmen of the Church of England he is still capable of writing a poem so unconventional that it must be kept almost entirely secret, surviving in a single copy. He prays about the Church:

> Show me, deare Christ, thy Spouse, so bright and clear.

Is it the Catholic Church, 'richly painted' like a prostitute? Is it the Protestant Church, in a torn dress as it 'laments and mournes in Germany and here' because the Thirty Years' War is going against the Protestant cause? The Roman Catholic Church claims to be infallible – 'and errs'. But what about the equally false Protestant claim that the Catholicism of the Middle Ages was a sleep of a thousand years? And then, in the intensity of his concern about the condition of Christ's Church, comes another tasteless reference to sex. Must Anglicans 'travaile' in order to 'seeke' the Bride of Christ like the 'adventuring knights' of the old tales of chivalry – 'and then make Love'? Or is the Church of England where Donne is now at home, God's 'mild Dove', able to satisfy 'myne amorous soule'? Is it wrong that this Church is so imperfect and untidy because it wants to include the whole English people, Catholic or Protestant? Or is this Bride of Christ 'most trew, and pleasing to thee'

> When she is embrac'd and open to most men?

This comparison between the Bride of Christ and a wife who is encouraged by her husband to be sexually promiscuous is of course startling. That, surely, is what Donne meant it to be – but his motive was not to end a poem with a bang by reverting to the 'libertine' advocacy of promiscuity which is on record in the erotic poetry of the 1590s. He now wanted to say that he knew that the idea of the true Church being tolerant and comprehensive would startle most of the most earnest Christians in that age of the Thirty Years' War. Even in the Church of England uniformity was the official ideal. But he had come to think that being 'open to most men' was indeed the will of Christ for his Church.

How had Donne's religion developed to this maturity? He himself said that he owed more to his faithful wife than to anyone else. Sex had battered his young manhood but through his marriage as well as his conscience God had, he believed, battered his middle age.

9 Admyring her

Here the admyring her my mind did whett
To seek thee God
Holy Sonnets *XVII*

The development of the feminist movement, including related studies, has encouraged research, thinking and writing about Anne More and her marriage with John Donne. Previously it had been generally assumed that very little could be said about her with any confidence. She seemed to have lived and died in the shadows into which almost all the women in history have been banished (including Anne Shakespeare). Even now we cannot know as much as we want. In 1996 M. Thomas Hester edited essays which constituted the first book ever written about Anne, with the title *John Donne's 'Desire of More'*. But when Donne said in a sermon of 1627 that 'God hath implanted in every natural man . . . an endlesse and Undeterminable desire of more, than this life can minister to him' (8:75), did he mean to refer to his wife's surname before their marriage? It seems unlikely. However, I want to argue that something substantial can be known about Anne Donne because of what John Donne wrote.

In *John Donne's Articulations of the Feminine* (1998) H. L. Meakin observed that after all attempts 'Donne scholars are no closer to resolving the question of Donne and women' and added: 'This study seeks to celebrate rather than lament this phenomenon, because it is through the fissures created when Donne's representations of the feminine collide with one another that possibilities emerge for rescuing both the feminine and masculine from essentialism and the false universal.' But I am one of those many readers to whom the evidence suggests, more simply, that Donne was essentially heterosexual. It was an age when differences between the genders were somewhat different from what modern readers expect, as students of Shakespeare have often noted: not only did boys play the women's roles in the theatres but gentlemen expressed devotion to each other and made patronizing or misogynist remarks about women expecting these to be treated as normal or funny. But Donne's position is clear in his epigram:

> Thou call'st me effeminat, for I love women's joyes,
> I call not thee manly, though thou follow boyes.

He went through a development which, if not universal, is common in any age: he was fascinated by women although failing to respect or understand them, then he loved and married one. The most obvious facts about Anne are that John Donne loved her when she was barely an adult, loved her so much that he was prepared to sacrifice his career in order to marry her, loved her through years of unemployment, poverty and illness when she was pregnant for most of the time, and loved her when heartbroken by her death.

However, to modern eyes the glory of this love must be damaged by other facts which cannot be denied. As we have seen, some of Donne's early poems express with a rare eloquence a rare intensity of contempt for women and for the institution of marriage. Perhaps it was a reaction against a dominant mother which became a reaction against that mother's strict religion, or perhaps it was simply the reaction to women of an immature young man. Anyway, it was not a good starting point for a poet of married love. As we shall see, some of Donne's sermons repeat traditionally patriarchal ideas about the inherited status of women, and about their unclean bodily functions including childbirth, in attitudes which are nowadays seen as thoroughly diseased. That was not what is now hoped for from a teacher of married love. And above all other scandals is the terrible fact that Anne died of 'fever' after the delivery of a stillborn child when she was not yet 34 years old. Her body was worn out by the sexual appetite of her husband, who seems to have been feeling proud as he counted up her twelve pregnancies which went to their full term, on the monument over her grave. It is estimated that in this period of English history approximately one birth in every hundred was the direct cause of the mother's death and that statistic becomes all the more dreadful when one knows that many women experienced childbirth as often as Anne did. Her own mother had died in childbirth.

Donne was himself disgusted. He blamed men and women alike. He was ashamed of himself, as we have often seen, but a sermon gave the men of Lincoln's Inn a glimpse of Jezebel, one of the wicked queens of the Old Testament: 'she paints, she curls, she sings, she gazes, and is gazed upon' (2:57). In the same chapel, in 1618, he urged the congregation to wash their beds with tears if they were married, repenting because 'in that bed thy children were conceived in sinne' and 'thou hast made that bed which God gave thee for rest, and for the reparation of thy weary body, to be as thy dwelling and delight, and the bed of idleness and stupidity' – and of 'voluptuousnesse and licentiousnesse' (2:223). In company with countless preachers Donne fully acknowledged the power of sex and did not underestimate its ability to imprison people in evil. He once said that 'it is a lesse miracle to raise a man from a sick bed, than to hold a man from a wanton bed, a licentious bed; lesse to overcome and quench his fever, than to quench his lust. Joseph that refused his mistris was a greater miracle than Lazarus raised from the dead' (4:152). And he could continue in this vein even when the people enjoying sex were married parents. On his last Easter Day in St Paul's he made an approving reference to the married Luther's belief that 'God pardons some levities and half-wantonesses in married folkes' (9:199), but he still thought that such behaviour needed to be forgiven.

In 1618, when he was still trying hard to overcome his memories of enjoying sex within marriage, he preached fiercely at the 'churching' or purification of Lady Doncaster after giving birth to a son who had died. He claimed that for the 'greatest persons', who presumably ought to know better, 'there is more dung, more uncleannesse, more sinne, in the conception and birth of their children' than would be the case for 'meaner and poorer parents', who presumably might be excused because ignorant. A newborn infant was described as a 'barrell of dung' (5:171–2). The mother of this dead baby was only nineteen years old and must have been depressed, yet Donne could talk about 'the Curse that lyes upon women for the transgression of the first woman, which is a painfull and dangerous child-birth' (5:198). Eve had sinned and had lured Adam into sin: therefore every conception of a human being was unclean and every birth of a baby was a potentially fatal ordeal for the mother, because all inherited the original sin of humanity's first parents and deserved punishment. That seemed to be the will of God, revealed in Holy Scripture. Nowadays it must seem strange that the grieving parents were not offended, but within a year Donne was to be the chaplain accompanying a long and delicate mission led by Viscount Doncaster, who was always to be a close friend. Probably they accepted the sermon as something to be expected from a clergyman; perhaps they forgave Donne because they understood why in his bereavement he had become so harsh towards what is natural and so insensitive to their own grief.

Married sex might have been enjoyed and conception avoided by the practice of *coitus interruptus* or by the use of the primitive contraceptives then available in towns (plus a bit of luck), but it was believed that both were contrary to the laws of Nature and God. Donne preached about the story in the Old Testament that Onan was ordered to 'go in to his brother's widow' and beget a child: he went in but 'conceived such an unwillingnesse' to enable the woman to conceive that 'he came to that detestable act, for which God slew him' (5:116). The teaching of St Augustine was repeated: 'Marriage with a contract against children, or a practice against children, is not a marriage, but a solemn, an avowed, a dayly Adultery' (6:270).

Presumably Anne did not dare to contradict anything taught with such august authority and accepted by all, or almost all, of her contemporaries. But it is some consolation to know that the preacher who was her husband and ardent lover, and whose insistence on sex eventually killed her, could also stress the more humane side of the Bible and the Church's tradition.

In a sermon of 1617 he said that when 'the love of woman . . . is rightly placed upon one woman, it is dignified by the Apostle with the highest comparison, *Husbands love your wives as Christ loved his Church.* And God himself forbad not that this love should be great enough to change natural affection (for this, *a man shall leave his Father*), yea to change nature itself, *the two shall be one.*' 'The true nature of a good love,' he declared, 'is a constant union'. It is not fixing the eye on riches or honour; it is not even fascination with beauty. That would be like keeping the eye fixed on a piece of paper which is floating down the river into the sea. True love is 'not onely a contentment, an acquiescence, a satisfaction, a delight in this pureness of love; but love is a holy impatience in being without it . . . and it is a holy fervor and vehemency in the pursuit of it, and a preferring it before any other thing that can be compared to it; That's love' (1:198–200). We may hope that Anne was listening when her husband said this, for she was to die five months later – but that seems unlikely.

Donne could be very positive about marriage. He observed that the Bible is full of celebrations of its joys: 'God is Love, and the Holy Ghost is amorous in his metaphors; everie where his Scriptures abound with the notions of Love, of Spouse, and

Husband and Marriadge Songs, and Marriadge Supper, and Marriadge-Bedde' (7:87). And even his acceptance of doctrines which modern Christians tend to find offensive – doctrines about the subordination of Eve to Adam and about their infectious sinfulness – could be softened as he reflected on his experience of marriage. 'By being a husband', he said, 'I become subject to that sex which is naturally subject to Man, though this subjection be no more in this place, than to love that one woman' (5:117). In the same sermon he accepted that story that Eve was the first to eat the forbidden apple. More than once in his poetry he used this story which blamed the Fall on a woman to supply the 'conceit' that a woman then killed mankind – but he could add that women go on killing, for when enjoying sex a man 'dies'. In a bad mood he could say this about the role of sex in the Fall: 'Man was borne to love, he was made in the love of God; but then man falls in love, when he growes in love with the creature, he falls in love' (6:69–70). But that was not the last word to be spoken by Donne on this subject and on another occasion he liked the suggestion that Adam followed Eve's example in order to demonstrate his love for her, 'lest by refusing to eate, when she had done so, he should deject her into a desperate sense of her sinne' (5:114–15).

'God', he said, 'did not place Adam in a Monastery on one side, and Eve in a Nunnery on the other, and so a River between them' (3:242). On the contrary, although 'Adam was asleep when Eve was made' he 'knew Eve upon the very first sight to be bone of his bone and flesh of his flesh' (8:99). Adam was attracted to her because 'the law of God bindes men in generall . . . to Marriage'. This is mainly because children are needed. 'Man is borne into the world that others might be borne from him' (8:100–1). But Adam was also attracted because Eve had been made to be more than a breeding machine – and Adam knew that in her creation he had been smitten in order to be helped. Eve 'was not taken out of the foot, to be troden upon, nor out of the head, to be an overseer of him; but out of his side, where she weakens him enough, and therefore should do all she can, to be a Helper' (2:346).

The duty of all husbands now began for Adam: he must 'take her to his heart, and fill his heart with her, let her dwell there, and dwell there alone' (3:244). In a word, he must love her – and love 'is so noble, so soveraign an affection, as that it is due to very few things, and very few things worthy of it . . . Love delivers over him that loves into the possession of that that he loves; . . . it changes him that loves, into the very nature of that that he loves, and he is nothing else' (1:184–5).

Donne did not ignore the importance of intelligence in wives. On the one hand, a wife's essential virtues are not 'wit, learning, eloquence, musick, memory, cunning, and such': they are 'chastity, sobriety, taciturnity, verity and such' (2:346). On the other hand, this 'love between man and woman' may 'confess a satiety' unless she does sometimes talk with him – and talk intelligently. 'If a woman think to hold a man long, she provides herself some other capacity, some other title, than merely as she is a woman: Her wit, her conversation, must continue this love; and she must be a wife, a helper; else, merely as a woman, this love must necessarily have intermissions' (1:199). So he was aware that no honeymoon lasts for ever. 'As in all other states and conditions of life, there will arise some encumberances; betwixt all maried persons there will arise some unkindnesses, some mis-interpretations; or some quick interpretations may sometimes sprinkle a little sournesse, and spread a little, a thin, a dilute and washy cloud upon them' (8:97). A marriage, he said, may be 'shaked sometimes by domestique occasions, by Matrimoniall encumberances, by perversenesse of servants, by impertinences of Children, by private whisperings, and calumnies of Strangers' (8:108). And he believed that intelligent talk could drive away that kind of cloud.

Being a man of his time, he was sure that in marriage the man must be the master, having been given more strength by the

Creator; as in his poem 'The Canonization', marriage must be between 'the Eagle and the Dove'. In marriage the husband is like the head while the wife is like the hands; he is like the legs and she is like a staff so that 'he moves the better for her assistance' (3:247). But Donne was also sure that 'God hath given no master such imperiousnesse, no husband such superiority, no father such a soverainty, but that there lies a burden on them, to consider with a compassionate sensiblenesse the grievances that oppresse the other part which is coupled to them. For if the servant, the wife, the sonne be oppressed, worne out, annihilated, there is no such thing left as a Master, or a husband, or a father . . . The wife is to submit herselfe; and so is the husband too: They have a burden both' (5:114).

In these sermons we seem to be given glimpses of the Donnes' domestic life. A letter to Henry Goodyer in 1608 includes another suggestion that this masterful man would accept domestic responsibilities. An eagle, he wrote, 'should not spend a whole day upon a tree staring in contemplation of the majestie and glory of the Sun' while in the nest eaglets waited for food. And in his *Essayes in Divinity*, he gave thanks that Anne and the children had sometimes interrupted his thoughts when they were far from glorious. He was grateful that 'thou hast delivered me, O God, . . . from the monstrous and unnaturall Egypt of painfull and wearisome idleness, by the necessities of domestick and familiar cares and duties'.

Donne knew from his own experience that 'the heates and lusts of youth overflow all' but 'Behold a miracle, such a young Man limiting his affections in a wife'! 'As long as a Man's affections are scattered, there is nothing but accursed barrennesse; but when God says, and is heard and obeyed in it, . . . let all thy affections be settled upon one wife, then the earth and the waters become fruitfull, then God gives us a type and figure of the eternity of the joyes of heaven, in the succession and propagation of children . . . And since thou art bound to love her because she is thy wife, it must be as long as she is so . . . Husbands therefore are to love wives as the Mothers of their Children, as the comforters of their lives; but . . . to avoid fornication, that's not the subject of our love.' He explained that last point by saying that loving a wife is not the same as sex with 'a Mistresse'. Husbands must 'expresse your loves' not only sexually but also in 'a gentle behaviour towards them, and in a carefull providence of Conveniences for them' (5:116–20). So marriage is 'sanctified'. The divine love expressed in Christ's love for the Church must be 'a patterne of Men's loves to their wives here' and will be 'a meanes to bring Man and wife and child to the Kingdome of heaven' (5:129). Indeed, Donne claimed that the Christian ideal of marriage and family life could make a home a 'type' – a promise, a first instalment – of heaven itself. One Whit Sunday he told a congregation that 'the holy Ghost shall accompany you home to your own houses, and make your domestique peace there a type of your union with God in heaven; and make your eating and drinking there a type of the abundance and fulnesse of heaven; and make every daye's rising to you there a type of your joyfull Resurrection to heaven; and every night's rest a type of your eternall Sabbath; and your very dreames prayers and meditations and sacrifices to Almighty God' (5:57–8).

His attitude to his home-making wife seems therefore to have fitted into the more general attitude to women which he expressed in the course of his last Easter sermon. He was clear that women have souls: 'No author of gravity, of piety, of conversation in the Scriptures could admit that doubt, whether women were created in the Image of God, that is, in possession of a reasonable and an immortall soul.' But he went further, saying that 'the faculties and abilities of the soul appeare best in affaires of State, and in Ecclesiastical affaires'. In politics, 'our age hath given us such a Queen, as scarce any former King hath equalled . . . And then in matters of Religion, women have evermore had a great hand, though sometimes on the left, as well as on the right hand.' Women have 'been great instruments for the advancing of true Religion' – although also in the advancement of heresies (10:90).

He warned husbands 'not to call the sociableness of women prostitution' (6:239), but he was more ambiguous in his public reactions when women made themselves attractive by more than their charming conversation. He approved of slimming: 'the lesse flesh we carry, the liker we are to angels' (7:106). But was makeup really respectable? As a younger man he had argued (in a 'paradox') that the woman should be encouraged who shows her 'great love to thee' by taking pains 'to seem lovely to thee' – so 'women ought to paint'. As a preacher in a good mood he could say that 'if they that beautifie themselves meane no harme in it, therefore there should be no harm in it'. The Bible mentioned that during a famine in Israel a poor woman had one jar of oil left – no doubt, oil for cooking. Perhaps not very seriously, Donne interpreted and condoned the contents as 'oyle for unction, aromaticall oyle to make her looke better' (5:302–3). But in other moods he was not so approving. Perhaps it should be left to God on the day of resurrection 'to glorifie our bodies with such additions' (6:269)? He quoted the severe Tertullian: 'there's prostitution in drawing the eye to the skin'. And he complained: 'Our women expose their nakedness professedly, and paint it, to cast bird-lime for the passenger's eye. Beloved, good dyet makes the best Complexion . . .' (3:104). And at least once while preaching, he said that he was simply undecided. 'Scarce can you imagine a vainer thing than the looking-glasses of women' – but the preacher saw two circumstances which might excuse a lady's vanity in front of a mirror: a man looking at her as she looked at herself might be more vain, and secondly, Moses had decreed that mirrors were useful as showing women 'the spots of dirt which they had taken by the way' (8:224).

No communication between husband and wife was included when their son John edited extracts from grander correspondence: these were, as the title boasted, *Letters to Severall Persons of Honour*. But it seems almost certain that letters were written. The two were parted for more than a year and a half when they were engaged to marry in 1600–01; parted for about a year while John was abroad in 1605–06 (and their son George was born during this period); and parted again for ten months in 1611–12 (and during his absence Anne had to bury a stillborn child). If Donne got some letters to her during these absences despite the great difficulties in communicating, they were lost. We have no picture of Anne, no writing by her, no signature. But some letters mentioning her do survive.

One was written to her father asking for his consent to their secret marriage. It has been claimed that he never expected the father to be angry (John Carey, p. 57, says this), but this seems impossible. Donne was not such a fool as to ignore the risks he was running in disobedience both to the Church's law and to social conventions (as I summarized the situation on pp. 62–4). It cannot have been easy to persuade Christopher Brooke, who had shared a chamber with Donne in Lincoln's Inn, to be the witness who 'gave away' the bride in her father's place, and his brother Samuel had to be persuaded to be the officiating priest in this furtive ceremony. Neither was without intelligence, respectability or ambition: Christopher was to be a successful lawyer, often a Member of Parliament, and Samuel ended up as Master of Trinity College, Cambridge. These properly ambitious men must have known that they were liable to imprisonment if the enraged father, who had influence in high places, demanded this – as happened. When preaching at a wedding in 1621, Donne was to remind his hearers that 'as marriage is a Civill Contract, it must be done so in publick, as that it may have the testimony of men . . . In a marriage without testimony of men they cannot claim any benefit by the Law' (3:243).

The question about the validity of his own marriage was not answered in his favour until 27 April, almost five months after the event. Such risks would not have been run had it been thought possible that Sir George More would lay on a splendid public wedding, followed by a reception in Anne's home in Loseley in Surrey (where some fifty servants were kept) and by the transfer to the congratulated husband of a dowry which would have solved his financial problems even before his career continued in a smooth progress to profitable heights.

As it was, Donne clearly had enough sense to be fearful about the father's reaction. In his fear he made the situation worse by waiting until 2 February before he owned up to a marriage 'a few weeks before Christmas'; and he made the admission not face-to-face as man-to-man but in a confused letter which the Earl of Northumberland (whom we shall meet again on p. 334) had to be persuaded to convey, in the hope that as a neighbour and friend he could act as mediator. When he wrote Donne knew that Sir George already knew – and was furious. In part of the letter he did not expect contradiction: 'I know this letter shall find you full of passion' and 'I knew that to have given any intimation of yt would have been to impossibilitate the whole matter', resulting in 'our hindrance and torment'.

He had to admit that he had been deceiving Sir George for some time before the marriage. He had found 'meanes' to see Anne 'twice or thrice' while she had been back in London accompanying her father during the Parliament which had begun on 27 October, and on one of those occasions they had promised each other to marry. Donne's defence was that they had 'adventurd equally' knowing 'the obligacions which lay upon us' once they had made this 'promise and contract' – a defence which was unlikely to silence Sir George, since it amounted to saying that the two had been equal in deceiving him but did not admit that Donne, who as the man had made the proposal, was more responsible than the young

Anne. The nervous husband expressed the hope that 'my endevors and industrie, if it please you to prosper them, may soone make me somewhat worthyer of her'. But this apparently manly ambition to earn more implied the admission that he needed Sir George's blessing if his career was to continue at all. All that he could offer was the argument that since the marriage was 'irremediably donne' (did he make a pun, even in this situation?) the logical result was for the father to accept it and subsidize it, if only in the interests of his daughter and of any future grandchildren. This was the strongest of Donne's arguments and after a cooling-off period it was to persuade Sir George to accept the *fait accompli*, but the letter could have put the matter more tactfully.

Nine days later he wrote again to Sir George, more humbly. He now declared that 'all my endevors and the whole course of my lyfe shall be bent to make myselfe worthy of yor favor and her love, whose peace of conscience and quiett I know must be much wounded and violenced if your displeasure sever us'. This was of course a reference to Anne's insistence on defying her irate father although she had to remain in his house, a tearful prisoner. But still Donne could offer no assurance that he could make his way in the world without Sir George's support. He could deny a charge that he still loved a 'corrupt religion' but not the fact that he had been educated by people who did love it. He could claim that stories that he had 'deceivd some gentlewomen' were 'vanished and smoaked away' but he could not deny that he had this reputation which in later years he was to admit was accurate, there being no smoke without a fire. He could say that rumour had 'at least' doubled his debts, but he had to admit that he was in debt.

Writing to Goodyer on 23 February, he had been hopeful that Sir George's 'good nature and her Sorrow will worke something' and that he would be welcomed back to his job when Sir George had softened: 'you know my meanes and therefore my hopes'. But when he made his appeal to his former employer on 1 March, his 'meanes' did not include any careful consideration of Egerton's own feelings about his ex-secretary's clandestine liaison with his innocent young niece.

Donne concentrated on the consequences for himself if he was not reinstated in his job. The 'sweetnes and security of a freedome and independency' which he had enjoyed as a student had ended because he had worked through his father's legacy; he had no savings because as one of Egerton's secretaries he had been 'not dishonest nor gredy'; and now it would be 'a madness' to think that anyone else would give him a suitable job, because 'every great man' to whom he might apply would think that he had been 'flung away' by Egerton for some 'great fault'. He saw 'no way before me' if Egerton did not take him back – and it seems probable that even before his marriage he had realized that unemployment was at least a risk, for like the Brooke brothers he was not an innocent babe in the woods of reality.

His letters both to Sir George and to Sir Thomas read like the cries of a man who had a nightmare before waking up to find real life no better. He begged Sir Thomas to allow him back into his presence. 'Affliction, misery, and destruction are not there; and everywher else where I ame, they are.' But Egerton was not to be persuaded. He had dismissed Donne when urged to do so by Sir George and did not now wish to show weakness by cancelling his decision because Sir George had somewhat relented – but there was another factor in the situation: despite his abilities and charm which had earned him his employer's satisfaction, the ex-secretary had become unwelcome in circles which demanded the maintenance of dignity within the acceptance of society as it was. Donne had caused a scandal even while the anti-Establishment cynicism of his poetry remained hidden from view.

All these documents were used in R. C. Bald's biography in 1970 but later, in 1986, in a collection of articles with the title *The Eagle and the Dove*, an American scholar, Iona Bell, put forward another letter as belonging to this crisis and as being one of three surviving 'love letters' to Anne. It had been found among papers once belonging to Donne's friend Sir Henry Wotton and had been printed in 1924, but it had not then been thought to be what Bell now claimed. It is certainly unlike the polished *Letters to Severall Persons of Honour.* It begins abruptly, without giving the name of the person being addressed, and it is ungrammatical, presumably because written in agitation and haste. It expresses 'wonder and grief' that Lord Latimer had spread a story that the writer had 'dishonored yo' and that this story had been taken by 'yr father' as 'good fuell of anger against mr davis & me to'. The exact meaning of the letter is not clear but it may well have been scribbled by a panic-stricken Donne in love. The greatest puzzle about it is why it was kept in the first place, and then sent to Wotton. If Anne kept it as a kind of love letter, why was it not destroyed? If it was sent to Wotton because he was planning to write a biography of Donne, who sent it? It reads like a mere draft of a letter, but it is not in Donne's handwriting; so why was a scribe told to make this copy and what happened to the original? The same unanswerable questions can be asked about the other two documents claimed by Iona Bell to be 'love letters'.

But more eloquent than any of these letters is the refusal of both John and Anne to agree that their marriage was invalid. When John saw the full cost of being married he could have withdrawn his petition to have the wedding ceremony declared legal – and when Anne experienced her father's full fury during months when she was at his mercy in their home she might have ended the relationship which had caused so much trouble, and might have consoled herself with the prospect of a 'good' marriage in the class of the alliances into which her sisters entered without any controversy or ill effects. The persistence with which both John and Anne wanted their marriage to be recognized by the archbishop's court seems to have made the decisive impression on the ecclesiastical judges although they were under strong pressure from her father to deny the legality (and there would have been precedents if a bribe had been offered). And sooner or later the whole of Anne's family accepted the marriage, supported Anne and made friends with her legally wedded husband.

More coherent letters to other correspondents sometimes give us glimpses of the lovers' married life. One letter records the husband's great anxiety about the wife's 'anguish' during the birth of their son Francis. That night in January 1607 was 'the saddest night's passage that I ever had' and John had thought about ending his own life if Anne died: 'I should hardly have abstained from recompensing for her company in this world, with accompanying her out of it.'

A happier scene surrounded the composition of a letter to Henry Goodyer 'from the fire side of my Parler and in the noise of three gamesome children'. He was sitting 'by the side of her whom, because I have transplanted into a wretched fortune, I must labour to disguise that from her by all such honest devices as giving her my company and discourse'. The reply to Goodyer had to be short because 'I steal from her all the time which I give this Letter'. The letter has been interpreted by John Carey as showing that Donne regarded conversation with the 'virtually uneducated' Anne as 'scarcely more than a benign duty' (p. 60), while in her short study of *John Donne* (1994) Stevie Davis found it 'difficult to believe' that he accepted more than 'a duty of allegiance'. She thought she could detect an 'aghast quality in his experience of the aftermath of marriage . . . Poverty, dependency, boredom, illness, and claustrophobia in the company of a growing family of children bred melancholy and aggravation.' But the surviving evidence does not demonstrate either that Anne's head was empty or that her husband's heart had grown cold. On the contrary, the letter just quoted shows that they treated one another with sensitivity: Donne felt that 'I melt into a melancholy as I write' but he must hide it because 'I sit by one too tender towards these impressions' and he must not cause 'sad apprehensions'.

We know that in some rich families daughters could receive an education from tutors although only boys were sent to the grammar schools and universities, and we also know that Anne had been sent to be polished in the sophisticated household of a lawyer-statesman in London. If she could hold an intelligent conversation with men there when scarcely into her teens, years later she was surely capable of interesting Donne with her mind. As we have noted, he seems to have told Izaak Walton that she had been 'curiously and plentifully educated', 'curiously' then meaning 'unusually'. If – a big 'if' – the letter about Lord Latimer does refer to Donne's relationship with Anne, it expresses dismay that Sir George should find 'any defect' in her when he had been an instrument in 'ye building of so fayre a pallace as yo are and so furnishing it as his care hath done'. In other words, having seen to her education he ought not to have been surprised when she fell for a brilliant scholar such as Donne instead of marrying a man who merely possessed land. And that letter ends with a kiss to the woman's 'fayre, learned hand'.

When lamenting his own unemployment to Sir Robert Ker whose life was happily busy, Donne wrote that 'I stand like a tree which once a year beares, though no fruit, this mast of Children', 'mast' meaning acorns or other droppings fed to pigs. But that bitter remark need not be taken as proof that he was permanently angry with his wife and children for existing and with himself for being connected with them. On the contrary, he was inviting his busy friend to act as godfather to the latest baby and was assuring him that the request would not be repeated every year. When he called himself a 'tree' he may have been making a between-men joke about the tall and fertile member of his body; in a poem about a mistress ('Nature's lay

Ideot') the phrase had been 'I planted life's tree in thee'. And the comparison of his children to acorns may have been an affectionate look at their potential for growth.

It is natural to suspect that Donne was cold-hearted if he wrote all or any of the very tender 'valedictions' preserved among his poems – and then went abroad leaving his wife to cope alone with the last months of pregnancy. Helen Gardner, for example, thought it 'impossible' that the poems could have been addressed to Anne in such circumstances. But whether or not they were, the evidence does not seem to support a very severe condemnation of Donne. Both of the journeys abroad which he undertook after his marriage, in 1605–06 and in 1611–12, were essentially business trips, when he seems to have acted as companion, translator and secretary to rich patrons who presumably paid for his services and expenses and who might be expected to continue to reward him in the future. And on both occasions he left Anne and the children in the care of a sister who had her own household and no financial worries.

In February 1605 a licence was granted to Sir Walter Chute to travel abroad with Donne, two servants and four horses, for three years. It was an opportunity for Donne to escape gracefully from his stay with Sir Francis Wolley at Pyrford in Surrey. It was embarrassing that this cousin kept a mistress by whom he had a daughter while his own wife remained childless. The Donnes already had two children and must have hoped for a place of their own. The most attractive way to recover financial independence was for him to be taken back into the service of the government and a free trip abroad seemed an opportunity to acquire a further qualification. The travellers spent time both in Paris and (almost certainly) in Venice, where Donne's newly knighted friend Wotton was the ambassador. They may also have visited Spain (now at peace with Britain) where Donne could have deepened his knowledge of the language and the literature. In the event he was back in England by the beginning of April 1606 and although no job was forthcoming the house in Mitcham could be afforded.

In July 1611 another licence to travel abroad was issued, also for three years. It allowed Sir Robert Drury to take his family and a coach with twelve horses. Walton says that Anne protested so strongly against the idea that Donne should accompany the Drurys that he decided not to go, only to change his decision with Anne's reluctant consent, when his patron insisted. The offer made must have seemed irresistible, for on the strength of it the Donnes ended their tenancy of the house at Mitcham although a gloomy farewell letter to Goodyer shows that they were heavily in debt. Then Drury was delayed by business affairs and it was November before the Channel was crossed; a pack of hounds and some hawks were taken along with the very worried Donne.

On 7 February he wrote to Anne's brother Sir Robert enclosing a letter to her which has not survived and begging for news of her condition: 'this silence doth somewhat more affect me than I had thought anything of this world could have done'. On 14 April he complained to Goodyer that 'I have received no syllable, either from herself, nor from any other, how my wife hath passed her danger'. He did not then know that on 24 January a stillborn son had been buried with a note in the parish register that the mother was the 'best of women'. However, his employer did not allow him to return to England until September. It seems reasonable to conclude that communications between rural England and France were not easy but that Donne felt it necessary to work for his patron because he so badly needed the money for himself and his family, while Anne took the children to stay with her sister on the Isle of Wight.

One reason why Donne had missed his wife is hinted at in a letter he wrote to Wotton in 1612: 'You (I think) and I are much of one sect in the Philosophy of love; which though it be directed upon the minde, doth inhere in the body, and find prety entertainment there.' (The 'piety' of the printed version needs correction into 'prety'.) Nine months after his return home, he was given another son – and Francis had been born nine months after an earlier return, in 1606. Anne recovered from the birth of Nicholas (who was to die very soon) by taking a holiday away from their new home in London and in a moment of freedom from domestic cares Donne joked to Goodyer that 'I have now two of the best happinesses which could befall me; which are, to be a widower and my wife alive'. It is not inconceivable that Anne was also happy, to have a break from his moods and his sexual needs. But his good humour did not last. In February 1614 he was reporting that Anne had had a miscarriage and 'fallen into an indisposition, which would afflict her much, but that the sicknesse of her children stupefies her'. A month later he was writing that 'my wife hath now confessed her self to be extremely sick; she hath held out thus long to assist me, but is now overturn'd & here we be in two beds, or graves'. His depression made him tell Goodyer bitterly that 'if God should ease us with burialls' among the sick children he did not know how he would be able to pay for their funerals. To us it is of course surprising that Izaak Walton printed that outburst, presumably thinking that it showed only how sadly his hero 'did bemoan himself', but it was an age when people believed that God controlled the deaths of innocent children, took care of them in eternity and relieved the suffering of those who had watched them die. In such an age this would not be an extreme example of Donne's insensitivity. In fact his daughter Mary died. He recovered: as he wrote, 'I have paid death one of my Children for my Ransome'. Again we may be shocked, although we need not jump to the conclusion that the cost of this 'Ransome' seemed cheap to an entirely selfish Donne.

We need to understand why he felt that he had to apologize to Goodyer for including such a 'homely' fact as 'the death of one of my Children' in a letter. Goodyer, a Warwickshire squire to whom he wrote every week partly because of his correspondent's financial generosity, would have been expecting an elegant letter of philosophy presented as literature. He might have been embarrassed when he was sent instead domestic news of illness and tragedy. And even parents were not meant to display too much grief after a child's death, because children died so often. Donne knew Goodyer well enough to write to him now that 'I loved it well' but the 'it' may have been his polite bow to that social convention which was meant to be merciful. How he reacted in private we do not know. Ben Jonson wrote poems about his children but if Donne did they have not survived. Yet we shall shortly see that he knew how to grieve and we do know that his children's deaths gave him causes to do so. Of his four sons who survived birth, Nicholas died in infancy and Francis did not live to be eight. Of his six daughters who survived birth, Lucy did not live to be nineteen and Mary did not live to be four.

He could grow so depressed during his years of unemployment, financial anxiety and solitary (and perhaps pointless) study that he could moan to his men friends that his marriage had ruined him. In 1608, writing to Lord Hay (the future Viscount Doncaster), he lamented 'that intemperate and hastie act of mine' which had been 'the worst part of my historie' but the one best remembered by potential employers. Amid his gloom in 1612 he told Goodyer 'I must confess, I died ten years ago'. But two years later he was reminding Sir Robert More (her brother) that he and Anne 'had not one another at so cheap a rate, as that we should ever be wearye of one another'. In that letter he was worrying about Anne being lonely without him; he was lonely himself although he had his books. And pregnancies continued to suggest how their reunited love was enacted. Back in 1602 he had assured her father that 'my love is directed unchangeably' upon 'her whom I tender more than my fortunes or my lyfe', and fifteen years later the keeping of their marriage vows was reflected in the epitaph which he composed for Anne's monument in their London parish church, St Clement Danes, which was later rebuilt with the loss of the monument although written copies of his words had been made.

He listed some of her distinguished ancestors and the copy of his draft which was kept in their family's seat, Loseley Park, shows that this final act of reconciliation was very acceptable. He publicly recorded his wish to be buried in the same grave (although when he had become Dean of St Paul's he was to think that his body belonged there). He did not explicitly mention Christ as the Saviour, but he may well have implied much when recording that she had died at the traditional age of the Saviour's death. Nor did he explicitly mention the Christian hope of resurrection, but there was probably that significance in his mind when he gave the date of her death, for 15 August was the date of the Catholic Church's celebration of the Assumption of the Blessed Virgin Mary into heaven.

This epitaph praised Anne as

A woman most special, most beloved,
a spouse most dear, most chaste,
a mother most dutifull, most indulgent,
having completed fifteen years in marriage
seven days after giving birth for the twelfth time,
with seven surviving children,
she was carried off by a ravishing fever.
Commanding this stone to speak
because grief made him as speechless as an infant,
a husband most wretched, once dear to the dear,
pledges his own ashes to hers
in a new marriage (if God bless it) together here.
She withdrew
in her 33rd year, in the 1617th year of Jesus,
on August 15.

What did he say in poetry about her?

Izaak Walton told his readers that after her death Donne 'betook himself to a most retired and solitary life', and then preached a heart-broken sermon in the church where she was buried: it was on the text 'I am the man that hath seen affliction'. No such sermon has survived and the one that was printed with this text would not support Walton's description, but since he had no wish to exaggerate the importance of Anne (whom he had never met), it seems reasonable to accept his account. What we know for certain is that Donne wrote some deeply felt poems about her death. One said that marriage to her had been his religious education:

> Since she whom I lov'd hath payed her last debt
> To Nature, and to hers, and my good is dead,
> And her Soule early into heaven ravished,
> Wholly in heavenly things my mind is sett.
> Here the admyring her my mind did whett
> To seeke thee God: so streames do show their head . . .

Commentaries on it have shown that the significance of this poem can be debated and it has even been suggested that he thought that her death had been 'good' for him because he wanted to get rid of her – or more subtly, that he accepted that being dead she could no longer do 'good' to herself or to him. It is much more likely, however, that what he meant was that it was 'good' for her to be in heaven and for him to have to concentrate on loving God. Walton says that he now told his children that he would never marry again – a considerable sacrifice, and not only because he would miss the sex, the love and all that he meant by a wife being a 'help'. His household including six younger children now had to be run by his daughter Constance, in 1617 only fourteen years old, and the domestic problems were increased when he soon became Dean of St Paul's. But it seems that he had made his decision partly out of loyalty to Anne and partly because her death intensified his conviction that his only ultimate good, beyond death, was God. What he meant by that is shown in a prayer at the end of a sermon which he preached four months after losing her: 'O glorious Beauty, infinitely reverend, infinitely fresh and young, we come late to thy love, if we consider the past daies of our lives, but early if thou be pleased to reckon with us from the houre of the shining of thy grace upon us' (1:250).

He was adapting what St Augustine had said about what he had sought and found when sexual activity had been put into the past. He was doing, or trying to do, what other great poets had had to do before him – Dante when he saw beyond Beatrice to 'the Love', Petrarch when he had to turn from Laura to God, and among the Elizabethans what Sidney and Spenser had also found necessary. He was taking, or trying to take, the advice which he had given to his distressed mother when Anne was still alive: God's purpose was 'to keep your Soul in continuall exercise, and longing and assurance of comming immediately to him' and 'to remove out of your heart all such love of this world's happinesse, as might put Him out of possession of it. He will have you entirelie.' And he was achieving, or trying to achieve, what he had urged after Elizabeth Drury's death:

> Up, up my drowsie soule, where thy new eare
> Shall in the Angels' songs no discord heare . . .
> And what essentiall joy canst thou expect
> Here upon earth? . . .
> Onely in Heaven joie's strength is never spent . . .

It is difficult for commentators who think that any idea of joy's strength in heaven is an illusion to appreciate why Donne developed his poem about 'she whom I lov'd' into a meditation about his own relationship with God, but the matter is seen differently if it is understood that Donne actually believed that if he handled this supreme relationship aright he would join Anne in heaven. It was in this belief that he continued the poem as a prayer. She had persuaded him to drink from a river which came from God, with the result that 'I have found thee, and thou my thirst hast fed'. But there had been a further result: his thirst for God had become 'a holy thirsty dropsy' – an unrestrainable thirst. He told himself that it was mad for him to 'begg more Love' from Anne More or from God, when he could already say to God 'thou dost wooe my soule'. God had Anne's soul in his keeping and offered to share with this mourner's soul the whole of his own eternal reality and glory; it was as if God longed to marry both souls. And God was entitled to 'thy tender jealousy' if Donne gave his love instead to 'things divine' such as mere 'Saints and Angels' or if he shut God out of his life in favour of 'the World, Fleshe, yea Devill' – the 'fleshe' including carnal thoughts about Anne.

Another poem about Anne's death is called 'The Dissolution' and ends with her maiden name. It begins 'Shee is dead' and recalls that they were 'made of one another' so that 'my body then doth hers involve'. Since her body is dead he finds that memories of marriage only increase

> My fire of Passion, sighs of ayre,
> Water of teares, and earthly sad despaire . . .
> And I might live long wretched so . . .

Yet he is also 'amaz'd that I can speake' of a life beyond the death of her body, a life where he can join her:

> And so my soule more earnestly releas'd,
> Will outstrip hers; As bullets flowen before
> A latter bullet may o'rtake, the pouder being more.

And the significance of that last word may be an example of a general rule which Donne propounded in the pulpit: 'in all Metricall compositions . . . the force of the whole piece, frame of the Poem is a beating out of gold, but the last clause is the impression of the stamp, and that is it that makes it currant' (6:41).

However, it was not easy for him to forget the passion, the sighs and tears, the despair and ecstasy, of his love for Anne More. In 1613 he had written the best of his marriage songs, celebrating the wedding on St Valentine's Day of the king's only daughter (Elizabeth) with one of the Protestants' strongest hopes (Frederick, Elector Palatine). Its tone was very different from his juvenile effort contributed to the students' revels in Lincoln's Inn, but it was no less physical as it pictured a union of man and wife where she was no longer the moon reflecting the masculine sun and sex was no longer the payment of a 'debt' which the married pay reluctantly.

> He comes and passes through Spheare after Spheare,
> First her sheetes, then her Armes, then any where.
>
> Here lies a shee Sunne, and a he Moone here,
>   She gives the best light to his Spheare,
>   Or each is both, and all, and so
> They to one another nothing owe,
>   And yet they doe, but are
> So just and rich in that coyne which they pay,
> That neither would, nor needs forbeare nor stay;
> Neither desires to be spar'd, nor to spare,
>   They quickly pay their debt, and then
> Take no acquittances, but pay again:
> They pay, they give, they lend, and so let fall
> No such occasion to be liberall . . .

It was not easy for the Donne who had written that poem to sacrifice marriage and to bury his memories of its earthly joys. In 1619 he wrote a 'Hymne to Christ' in which he once again told himself that he must move on – to the love which God offered and to death. He was so depressed that he expected his death to occur in the near future, completing his sacrifice.

> I sacrifice this Iland unto thee,
> And all whom I lov'd there, and who lov'd mee . . .
> As the tree's sap doth seeke the roote below
> In winter, in my winter now I goe
>   Where none but thee, th' Eternall root
>   Of true love I may know.

And so he prayed for help to forget, after two years:

> Thou lov'st not, till from loving more, thou free
> My soule . . .

But does Christ really want him to forget Anne More?

> O, if thou car'st not whom I love
>   Alas, thou lov'st not mee.

At this time he wrote in a letter: 'I leave a scattered flock of wretched children, and I carry an infirm and valetudinary body, and I goe into the mouth of such adversaries, as I cannot blame for hating me, the Jesuites, and yet I goe . . .' He felt that he had to go, because the king had ordered it and also because he depended on the king's support for his own future if he lived. It was not the letter of a man who found it easy to sacrifice his 'I-land' (puns had become a habit) or his family or his memories. But it was also not the letter of the man described by John Carey, who argues that Anne's death brought to a head the 'obsession' still caused by 'the early crisis of his apostasy from Rome', so that 'he found it impossible to believe that he was loved enough, even by God' (p. 45). On the contrary, Donne attacked himself for loving humans too much, when the 'Eternall root of true Love' is God.

In the end he did manage to pray that all the loves of his past, good or bad, might be married not to him but to Christ:

> Seale then this bill of my Divorce to All,
> On whom those fainter beames of love did fall;
> Marry those loves, which in youth scattered be
> On Fame, Wit, Hopes (false mistresses) to thee.

And so far from packing for a holiday he looked forward to death:

> Churches are best for Prayer, that have least light:
> To see God onely, I goe out of sight:
>   And to scape stormy dayes, I chuse
>   An Everlasting night.

Naturally that negative mood faded as the intensity of his bereavement grew less. In a sermon on Easter Day 1622 he spoke positively about what he called 'the first Resurrection': 'Let that be, The shutting of thine eyes from looking upon things in things, upon beauty in that face that misleads thee, or upon honour in that place that possesses thee; And let the opening of thine eyes be, to look upon God in every object, to represent to thyself the beauty of his holiness, and the honour of his service in every action' (4:76). The spring sunshine was perhaps warming his mind as he said that, and as he added: 'Man is but a vapour; but a glorious and blessed vapour, when he is attracted and caught up by this Sun, the Son of Man, the Son of God'

(4:82–3). Two years later he consoled a widow by assuring her that God's purpose is to reunite husband and wife: 'that piece which he takes to himselfe is presently cast in a mould, and in an instant made fit for his use . . . That piece which he leaves behinde in the world by the death of a part thereof growes fitter and fitter for him by the good use of his corrections, and the intire conformity to his will. Nothing so disproportions us, nor makes us so uncapable of being reunited to those whom we loved here, as murmuring . . . We are not bound to think that souls departed have devested all affections towards them whom they left here; but we are bound to think that for all their loves they would not be here again.'

But, especially when he was out of the pulpit and alone, the cold and the dark could return.

His 'Nocturnall upon S. Lucie's Day' is weeping in the dark. It refers to the night offices of the Roman Catholic Church during what was popularly regarded as the longest night of the year, 'the yeare's midnight', before the commemoration of St Lucy on 13 December. An intimate self-disclosure of which few copies seem to have been made, it clearly mourns someone who is dead and has been loved:

> Study me then, you who shall lovers bee
> At the next world, that is, at the next Spring:
> For I am every dead thing,
> In whom love wrought new Alchimie.

The experience of loving Anne has produced for him not the *elixir vitae* which would be a 'cordial' or magic medicine curing all diseases, as was the dream of the experimenting alchemist in that age, but something which is the essence of Nothing,

A quintessence even from nothingnesse,
From dull privations, and leane emptinesse
He ruin'd mee, and I am re-begot
Of absence, darknesse, death; things which are not.

He mourns his loss of a woman who has shared many sorrows with him:

        Oft a flood
    Have we two wept, and so
Drowned the whole world, us two, oft did we grow
To be two Chaosses, when we did show
Care to ought else; and often absences
Withdrew our soules, and made us carcasses.

'By her death (which word wrongs her)' he has become 'None'. There seems to be no one except Anne about whom such words could have been written – and written after her death. However, some scholars have taken literally Donne's announcement that he was abandoning poetry in 1614 and have done their best to find a date before that. Because of its reference to 'Lucy' in its title Herbert Grierson suggested in 1912 that the 'Nocturnall' was written in 1612, when Lucy, Countess of Bedford, was severely ill – but she was Donne's aristocratic patron, not his partner in sorrows and in sex, and Grierson had the wisdom to say that this was a 'hazardous suggestion' about a poem which remained 'enigmatical'. With less wisdom Arthur Marotti suggested that the woman being mourned was not the Countess of Bedford but a 'transcendent female' of the poet's imagination, so that Donne probably composed the 'Nocturnall' about the same time as the 'Anniversaries' – to which the reply must be that the artificiality of the lament for Elizabeth Drury in the 'Anniversaries' is totally different from the heartbreak in the 'Nocturnall'. Other scholars, recognizing that it must be about his wife, have connected the poem with one or other of the times when he was afraid that Anne was going to die. But in the poem he has been reduced to despair by 'her death', unambiguously.

So was the poem written soon after her death?

It may have been but if so, there is a problem about why St Lucy's Day in particular should have released such a flood of grief and despair. Another problem – which does not seem to have been taken into account – is that on the day after St Lucy's Day in 1617 Donne delivered a sermon before Queen Anne and her courtiers (1:236–51) which sounds like a declaration of faith by a man who is trying to replace worldly loves which were tainted by sin – is trying, and not entirely failing. It claims that the soul 'that hath been transported upon any particular worldly pleasure, when it is intirely turn'd upon God and the contemplation of his all-sufficiency and abundance, doth find in God a fit subject, and just occasion, to exercise the same affection piously and religiously, which had before so sinfully transported and possest it . . . So will a voluptuous man who is turned to God find plenty and deliciousness enough in him to feed his soul . . . Solomon, whose disposition was amorous and excessive in the love of women, when he turn'd to God, he departed not utterly from his old phrase and language, but . . . conveyes all his loving approaches to God, and all God's gracious answers to his amorous soul, into songs . . .' And Donne goes on to quote St Augustine's disgust with his memories of 'sensual love' in comparison with love for God: women had led to 'nothing but to be scourg'd with burning iron rods, rods of jealousie, of suspicion and of quarrels'.

Such references to King Solomon and St Augustine may well have been coded hints to Queen Anne that she could find in a passionate religion a substitute for the disappointment in her sexual relationship with King James, but it does not seem likely that Donne could have preached that sermon if two nights previously he had been so profoundly grief-stricken that his poem could say that by his own wife's death he had been reduced to the 'quintessence' of 'nothingnesse' without a glimpse of God. And in November 1617 a sermon had already reflected some confidence that he was not defeated in the struggle to think positively about Anne's death. He had then claimed that 'this death, this dissolution, this change, is a new creation; this Divorce is a new Marriage; this very Parting of the soul is an Infusion of a Soul and a Transmigration thereof out of my bosome into the bosome of Abraham' (1:231–2). No doubt his moods varied, and no doubt his sermons did not tell the whole story about his private feelings, but this evidence suggests that as winter began in 1617 he had made a recovery from the early intensity of his natural grief after her death. He was now preaching to himself that sex must be over, that Anne must be in heaven, and that he could look forward to joining her there. And through any remaining tears he was trying to see the eternal God.

It seems certain that the 'Nocturnall', which was an outburst of uncontrolled and totally desolating grief not mentioning God, was written about Anne – and it seems probable that it was written ten years after her death. My suggestion is that when Donne thought about Anne as St Lucy's Day began in 1627 his continuing sense of what he had lost when she had died was intensified by mourning after other deaths and by depression over other events which had brought sadness to himself, his family and his country – and then the river of grief burst its banks. If we are looking for a St Lucy's Day whose long, black eve would have revived memories of the damage which he had received in 1617, 13 December 1627 is it.

In January his daughter Lucy had died: she had barely reached the age of eighteen. In May her godmother Lucy, Countess of Bedford, had been buried after a long decline in health and glamour: Donne was no longer close to her but death made the distance greater. Magdalen, Lady Danvers, had joined her in death, and on

1 July he had preached about her the most personal of all his surviving sermons. Walton remembered his tears in the pulpit.

In other ways also, it had been a miserable year. One incident must have suggested to Donne that although he could still preach with power he was becoming yesterday's man. He had been asked to preach in defence of the marriage of the new king with Henrietta Maria, who was unpopular as being both French and Catholic. Cautiously, he had admitted that 'very religious kings may have had wives that may have retained some tincture, some impressions, of error, which they may have sucked in their infancy, from another Church' (7:409). It was a guarded admission of a possible defect in the new queen, but not guarded enough for King Charles, who sent for a copy of the sermon through his favourite bishop, William Laud. Donne sensed danger and begged his friends at court to use their influence. The king, 'who hath let his eye fall upon some of my Poems', ought to see that the 'study and deligence' bestowed on them was less than the care which Donne had taken over this and every sermon, in this case care to support the king – but would Charles see? Donne grew so anxious that he had to apologize in a letter to Robert Ker, a friend at court: he had knocked on Ker's front door, had grown too nervous, and had run away before the door could be opened. Eventually Laud examined the sermon and found nothing in it which was clearly intended to be disloyal; Donne apologized for 'certain slips' (as Laud recorded in his diary); and the king forgave him. But Donne was warned: he could not rely on the steady support which King James had given him.

In 1627 it was difficult to remember that recently James had dreamed of securing peace by a royal marriage, first with Spain and (when that failed) then with France: Britain was now at war with the combined forces of Spain and France. Donne was patriotic in the pulpit but his private correspondence showed intense concern at the collapse of the peacemaking policy, to add to the disaster of the Protestant defeats in Germany. And his soldier son George had been lucky to return to England after the disaster of the expedition led by the Duke of Buckingham to the Isle de Ré in the autumn of 1626, from which half the English force did not return. George did not stay in England for long: he was soon sent to command a small garrison in the Caribbean and was taken to Spain as a prisoner: his father never saw him again. Buckingham was to be assassinated by a naval officer with a grievance in 1628.

It was probably in the Lent of 1627 that Donne said in the pulpit that 'if there were any other way to be saved and to get to Heaven, than by being born to this life, I would not wish to have come into this world' (7:359). At Easter 1627 he preached about the resurrection of the dead but did not conceal his own grief after his unmarried daughter's death. 'If I had fixt a Son in Court, or married a daughter into a plentifull Fortune, I were satisfied for that son and that daughter. Shall I not be so, when the King of Heaven hath taken that son to himselfe, and married himselfe to that daughter, for ever? . . . This is the faith that sustaines me, when I lose by the death of others or when I suffer by living in misery my selfe, That the dead, and we, are now all in one Church, and at the resurrection shall be all in one Quire' (7:384).

In May he preached about the 'tendernesse' of God, saying that 'many of us are Fathers' and should 'learne' from that. On Whit Sunday he preached about the 'comfort' (strengthening) given by the Holy Spirit. But he ended that sermon: 'Onely consider that Comfort presumes Sadnesse . . . In great buildings the Turrets are high in the Aire; but the Foundations are deep in the earth. The Comforts of the Holy Ghost work so, as that only that soule is exalted, which was dejected' (7:451).

In November he preached at the wedding of the grand-daughter of Sir Thomas Egerton, whose patronage had meant so much, to the eldest son of Lord Herbert of Cherbury, who as Sir Edward Herbert had been a close friend of his. Briefly noting that the purposes of marriage were well known and that the happy couple had good examples in their parents, he concentrated on the fact that after death there would be no marriage in heaven. The most that he thought possible was recognition without the restoration of the old union. 'In the Resurrection there shall be no Marriage, because it conduces to no end; but if it conduces to God's glory and to my happinesse (as it may piously be believed that it does) to know them there whom I knew here, I shall know them' (8:100).

Soon he was preaching in St Paul's on the text 'Say unto God, how terrible art thou in thy works!' He took the opportunity to mention that 'it is not the king that commands but the power of God in the king' (8:115), but also to stress that, like the king, God is to be feared. 'Not only a feare of God must, but a terror of God may, fall upon the Best', as when 'a horror of great darkness fell upon Abraham . . . I cannot look upon God in what line I will, nor take hold of God, by what handle I will; Hee is a terrible God, I take him so; and then I cannot discontinue, I cannot break off this terriblenesse, and say, Hee hath been terrible to that man, and that is the end of his terror; it reaches not to me. Why not to me? In me there is no merit, nor shadow of merit' (8:123–4).

Donne did not forget to add that 'this Terriblenesse' is 'Majestic not Tyrannical' but his sermon reached its climax in a vision of God's power: 'It must be power . . . his power extended, exalted . . . his power magnified, his power multiplied upon us.' And on Christmas Day 1627 Donne did not proclaim God's love, or preach with any other seasonal message. Instead he was eloquent about the difficulties of God's spokesmen and the evils of the world to which they must speak, offering only the hope that God 'will not be angry with us for ever' (8:156). A month later he was preaching about St Paul's warning to the elders of the Church in Ephesus that they would 'see my face no more'. He sounded as if he was about to disappear also: 'When you come to heare us here, heare us with such affection as if you heard us upon our death-beds' (8:171).

The depression expressed in such sermons is compatible with the suggestion that he wrote the 'Nocturnall' in December 1627. But the depression lifted. Preaching on the national Fast Day in April 1628 he told the king and the courtiers not to be permanently depressed. 'They must have teares first', he said, 'first thou must come to this weeping, or else God cannot come to this wiping' (8:201). A little later he preached to the court about the martyrdom of St Stephen. He might have been grim after this ominous start: 'He that will dye with Christ upon Good-Friday, must hear his own bell toll all Lent . . . We begin to hear Christ's bell toll now, and is not our bell in the chime? We must be in his grave before we come to his resurrection, and we must be in his death-bed before we come to his grave: we must do as he did, fast and pray . . .' But his sermon was not depressed. It offered 'two general considerations: first, that every man is bound to do something before he dye; and then to that man who hath done these things which the duties of his calling bind him to, death is but a sleep' (8:174–5). That sermon ended with some glorious words about heaven (quoted on p. 350).

The Easter sermon for 1628 promised the 'light of glory' in comparison with which 'the light of honour is but a glow-worm; and majesty itself but a twilight'. God 'crownes all other joyes and glories' but 'this very crown is crowned', for '*we shall be made partakers of the Divine nature*; Immortal as the Father, righteous as the Son, and full of all comfort as the Holy Ghost' (8:232, 236).

Other poems have been thought to refer to Anne More, particularly since they include the word 'more' or reach a climax with it. One is the 'Hymne to God the Father' where twice the confession of sins ends with 'I have more' and in most of the manuscripts the poem ends with 'I have no more'. This can suggest that Donne thought that his spiritual troubles would be over when he had finally escaped from his relationship with Anne More. But it seems highly unlikely that he did think this: his other poems testify against it, although as we have seen they are eloquent about the need to love God even more than her. We know that this poem was set to music as a hymn, and Izaak Walton said that it was often sung in St Paul's Cathedral in Donne's presence – which makes it unlikely that its climax was intended to be a shocking attack on his dead wife. It is probable that the poem ended with 'I feare no more' in the printed versions from 1633 onwards in order to avoid this misunderstanding.

The 'Valediction of my name, in the window' is by far the most light-hearted of the four surviving 'Valedictions'. It does not sound like a farewell to a wife but conceivably may come from the days of courtship. It may imagine Anne More seeing her own face in a window where he has carved his name with a diamond:

> 'Tis more, that it shews thee to thee
> And cleare reflects thee to thine eye.

And it may tease her by saying that one day while they are separated she may look out of that window and see another lover advancing through the garden. If so, his name 'scratch'd' in the glass will still be there to rebuke any temptation:

> So since this name was cut
> When love and griefe their exaltation had,
> No doore 'gainst this name's influence shut,
> As much more loving, as more sad,
> 'Twill make thee; and thou shoulst, till I returne,
> Since I die daily, daily mourne.

But there is at least one snag in any attempt to link this poem with Donne's courtship of Anne. It is very unlikely that he would have dared to carve his name in a window, either in York House where she lived while in London or in her palatial home in the country. If the poem was inspired by Anne, it was an imaginative exercise.

This difficulty raises again a bigger question: is it sensible to connect any poem with Donne's courtship or marriage?

In her introduction to her edition of the 'Songs and Sonets' Helen Gardner argued that Donne's love poems 'are too far from the reality of what we know of for us to speak of them as written to Ann More or even about her'. She divided the 'Songs and Sonets' which ever since 1633 had been printed as a jumble into two 'sets', before and after 1602, but she stressed that 'it is not the mark of the second set . . . that they all handle the theme of love as union': instead, 'their distinction lies in their more subtle and complex conception of form and style'. Her emphasis on reading rather than loving was so firm, so securely academic, that she believed that Donne was attracted by 'authors whose speculations had already fascinated him by a theory of love radically different from the naturalistic view' – and she 'would add' (no more) that he was also influenced 'by his own experience' when he 'lost the world for love'. She thought that he resumed 'considerable literary activity' in 1607, more than five years after his marriage, and she suggested that when he celebrated the faithful union of lovers the poet 'turned to his own uses his reading in the Neoplatonists'. This was in keeping with her basic attitude to the poems, which was that 'each expresses its mood with that lack of hesitation, or equivocation, that purity of tone, that gives sincerity to a work of art and makes it appear veracious, or imaginatively coherent'. But surely we can agree that every poem is a 'work of art' without supposing that 'reading in the Neoplatonists' is sufficient to account by itself for passionate poetry about love. Echoes suggest that Donne was influenced by Serafino's poetry and Ficino's philosophy, but common sense suggests that he was more decisively influenced by his relationship with Anne. He was more bookish than most men have been, but he allowed himself to be controlled by only one book – the Bible. In a letter which seems to have been written around 1600 he said that 'to know how to live by the booke is a pedantry, and to do it is a bondage'. In later life he could not claim, as he did in this letter, that 'I am no great voyager in other men's works: no swallower or devourer of volumes nor pursuant of authors' – but even when he became a learned scholar he did not rely on 'other men's works' to tell him 'how to live'.

Gardner gave no good reasons for her belief that 'the empty period in Donne's literary career is from 1599 to 1607'. There are, on the contrary, strong grounds for thinking it probable that having worked on *Metempsychosis* until August 1601 Donne wrote poetry inspired by two situations which he had never experienced before and which changed the course of his life: courting a young woman whom he desperately wanted to marry despite the obvious difficulties, and being married in defiance of society's code of conduct and at the cost of his career. It is interesting that Arthur Marotti, whose *John Donne, Coterie Poet* (1986) was the most extensive exploration yet made of probable or possible intentions to write for a restricted 'coterie' of fellow students or male friends, accepted that Donne wrote also for Anne's enjoyment, although he reckoned that an earlier scholar, J. B. Leishman, went too far in believing that twenty poems should be listed in this category. Marotti argued that knowing what were the conventional attitudes in Donne's 'coterie' of ambitious and often promiscuous men, and knowing also that Donne continued to long for a career, helps us to see the serious courage of the poet's love for his wife, whom he married 'for love'. 'Romantic without being soft-headed', 'intellectually and emotionally complex', these poems connected with Anne are in Marotti's verdict 'Donne at his best'.

Donne met Anne More while she was staying in London as the guest of Lady Egerton: her mother had died and she was being shown this kindness partly because Lady Egerton had a son by a previous marriage, Francis Wolley, who after her husband's death was brought up by the Mores in their great home in Surrey. The lovers seem to have developed quite a deep relationship before Lady Egerton died in January 1600, after which Anne was taken back into her own family's home. She did not return to London before October 1601. It does not seem stupid to believe that poetry was used by Donne to keep their love alive during this physical separation lasting almost two years. Presumably it was impossible for them to meet and Donne had to rely on smuggled letters if these could be arranged. He could scarcely have hoped to please her by sharing with her the completely unromantic *Metempsychosis* but if he could write it would be natural for him to use his rare ability as a poet. When they could not communicate at all, it would be equally natural for him to pour his anxiety into a poem. And when he had succeeded in marrying her, the failure of his career must have helped to concentrate his thoughts on her. It therefore seems allowable to consider some possibilities that he wrote to or about her.

In 'Love's Exchange' the speaker has fallen in love – without naming Anne, but in an experience which actually overwhelmed John Donne in his relationship with Anne. Love, he says, makes a man weak and blind; it is childish; when others knew about it, it results in embarrassment, in a 'tender shame'; it tortures, kills and cuts up a man – and he is glad, for he has seen

> This face, which whereso'er it comes
> Can call vowe'd men from cloisters, dead from tombes,
> And melt both Poles at once, and store
> Deserts with cities . . .

In 'The Broken Heart' love is a developing disease and the speaker asks

> Who will beleeve me, if I sweare
> That I have had the plague a yeare?

Indeed the beloved has been a surgeon, cutting out his heart:

> If 'twere not so, what did become
>   Of my heart, when I first saw thee?
> I brought a heart into the roome,
>   But from that roome, I carried none with mee . . .

She cannot have kept his heart, otherwise she would have shown 'more pitty unto me', but he has discovered some remnants of it in himself, so

> My ragges of heart can like, wish, and adore
> But after one such love, can love no more

– and she had better mend his heart by proving that she loves him.

'Lovers' Infinitesse' may be another example of teasing Anne More during their courtship. The speaker says that he has run out of sighs, tears and promises after their engagement:

> And all my treasure, which should purchase thee,
> Sighs, teares, and oathes, and letters I have spent,
> Yet no more can be due to mee,
> Than at the bargaine made was meant . . .

But his love had continued to grow:

Hee that hath all can have no more,
And since my love doth every day admit
New growth, thou shouldst have new rewards in store . . .

In 'The Anniversarie' the speaker refers to the passing of a year since the two 'first saw' each other, but he may well mean 'really saw', as lovers. And he refers to 'kings' including his beloved, but this does not mean that the poem cannot have been written in the reign of Elizabeth I.

The Sun it selfe, which makes times, as they passe,
Is elder by a yeare, now, than it was
When thou and I first one another saw . . .

The lovers are not (yet) entitled to the single tomb of the married:

Two graves must hide thine and my coarse,
If one might, death were no divorce . . .

But they are not bored with each other:

All other things, to their destruction draw,
 Only our love hath no decay;
This no to morrow hath, nor yesterday . . .

They feel that they are 'Prince enough in one another', that

Here on earth, we are Kings, and none but wee
Can be such Kings, nor of such subjects bee;
Who is so safe as wee? where none can doe
Treason to us, except one of us two.

They have no need to fear such treason, so

Let us love nobly, and live, and add againe
Yeares and yeares unto yeares, till we attaine
To write threescore, this is the second of our raigne.

'Aire and Angels' is a sophisticated poem about which critics have disagreed. Helen Gardner disarmingly confessed that 'it has had many unsuccessful readers, of whom I am one'. It is not a poem which a sensible poet would address to a girl of Anne's age. But it makes fairly simple sense if we spot a familiar topic, lust, beneath the sophistication. (Therefore no sensible poet would have addressed it to the Countess of Bedford, despite a modern commentator's suggestion.) It seems possible that it originated in Donne's turbulent emotions as he asked himself whether his relationship with Anne would ever become physical – and as he tried to keep his balance by his old trick: write a witty poem.

It begins by saying that this woman looked like an angel, like a 'lovely glorious nothing' or a 'shapeless flame', when he first saw her. But love must 'take a body' and be fixed on 'thy lip, eye, and brow',

For not in nothing, nor in things
Extreme, and scatt'ring bright, can love inhere . . .

However, even when a relationship of love becomes physical the woman can still be angelic because angels have 'face and wings of aire'. These pieces of equipment are not so pure as the angels' souls but they are necessary if there is to be any contact with embodied humanity. In much the same way, 'women's love' must be physical if it is to be 'my love's spheare' – which seems to mean: if it can be like the sun circling round the earth in the old Ptolemaic and medieval picture of the sky. This argument seems to refer to the teaching (of St Thomas Aquinas, for example) that angels have strange bodies of air, and in a sermon at a wedding Donne was to explain more solemnly that angels 'are Creatures, that have not so much of a Body as flesh is, as froth is, as a vapour is, as a sigh is, and yet with a touch they shall moulder a rocke into lesse Atomes, than the sand that it stands upon' (8:126). But then the speaker lowers the level of argument by claiming that his own love is so superior that it is always like 'Angells' puritie' – when it is evidently nothing of the kind. He has begun by saying that the woman cannot remain purely angelic if he is to love her fully; now he ends by saying that a man can be earthy and yet remain pure. He is being Donne, very witty and very masculine, alluding to the man-made tradition that it is the woman who most wants the sex.

A redeeming feature in Donne's character is the honesty which surfaces. 'Love's Growth' was perhaps a further meditation about Anne and the 'love which cures all sorrow with more'. The man now confesses that he is longing to embrace the woman:

> I scarce beleeve my love to be so pure
>   As I had thought it was . . .
> Love's not so pure, and abstract, as they use
> To say, which have no Mistresse but their Muse,
> But as all else, being elemented too,
> Love sometimes would contemplate, sometimes do.

The same theme runs through 'The Extasie', a poem which C. S. Lewis once found 'singularly unpleasant' because it argues that the flesh is inferior to the spirit, yet can be used well – precisely the Christian attitude to the spiritual side to human nature, as Joan Bennett reminded Lewis in her reply. (This was before Lewis was 'surprised by joy' and married.) 'The Extasie' begins with a picture of the lovers gazing at each other 'all day', their 'eye-beames' united as if by 'one double string' and their hands 'firmely cimented' by the sweat of excitement. And we may be excited by this teasing overture: the bank on which they lie is 'pregnant' because 'like a pillow on a bed' and perspiration accompanies the 'propagation' of images in their eyes. But they only contemplate; they do not 'do'. 'Wee said nothing, all the day', and 'it was not sexe'. (Donne is listed in the Oxford English Dictionary as being the first writer to use the late medieval word 'sex' as referring to 'the sum of those differences in the structure and function of the reproductive organs on the ground of which beings are distinguished as male and female'.) But the speaker is hoping for action which 'interanimates two soules' and can control 'defects of loneliness' in a 'dialogue of one'. If that action is open to the procreation of children when 'our blood labours to beget Spirits', it will be 'that subtile knot, which makes us man' – but if there is no such action, 'a great Prince in prison lies'. Previously the poets' comparison to a prince in prison had referred to the imprisonment of the soul in the body until released into eternity by death, but now release is to come by the action which can create a new generation on earth. The speaker's down-to-bed message is clear enough:

> Love's mysteries in soules do grow,
> But yet the body is his booke . . .

If that is the message, it seems that Helen Gardner was wrong to think that the proposal made in the poem is 'the perfectly modest one that the lovers' souls, having enjoyed the rare privilege of union outside the body, should now resume possession of their separate bodies and reanimate these virtual corpses'. She thought that this teaching that physical contact is best avoided supplies 'the key to Donne's greatest love poetry' and was put into the poet's mind not by what the body teaches but by a study of Leone Ebreo's book *Dialoghi d'Amore.* We may ask whether Donne, a very physical poet, would not have laughed when he had overcome his astonishment at reading such a bookish suggestion. A more realistic comment was made by

A. J. Smith, who saw in 'The Extasie' 'people who are in the act of making a momentous self-discovery intelligible to themselves' – the discovery that the deepest reality about sexual love is that the joy of union is consummated, not automatically produced, by physical sex. The lovers' commitment to each other is spiritual and sexual intercourse is a sign, almost a sacrament of it, in accordance with what Donne said in his Easter sermon of 1623: 'All that the soule does, it does in, and with, and by the body' (4:358).

A poem which in 1650 was given a strange title, 'A Lecture upon the Shadow', is a rather simpler expression of a courting lover's impatience and John Shawcross believed that a connection with Anne was 'unavoidable'. The speaker has been on a walk with his girl 'these three houres' and when 'the Sunne is just above our head' he lectures her about the implications of the fact that they no longer have separate shadows. In the past

> Disguises did, and shadowes, flow,
> From us and our cares; but, now 'tis not so.

But danger lies ahead! Earlier in their walk together their shadows separate in order to 'blinde others' since their love has had to be kept secret. But he warns that if they walk on in this secrecy, still avoiding the publicity of marriage, new shadows will form and will blind their own eyes, for the lovers will begin to keep secrets from each other. They may think that they are merely continuing their walk into the afternoon,

> But oh, love's day is short, if love decay.

> Love is a growing, or full constant light;
> And his first minute, after noone, is night.

However, if the married walk through life they cannot always be together physically. Just as it seems likely that Donne used his power as a poet when courting Anne, so it seems probable that he did so as emotions arose when they parted for a long period. Some commentators have stressed that this cannot be proved, which is of course the case. But an appeal may be made to common sense. There are three poems called 'Valedictions' which are different from every other poem which Donne wrote: they are consistently personal and tender; they offer comfort to the sadness of someone else, and are not about his own emotions; and they are about partings before long absences. Only a few such absences occurred in his life. Three were when he went to Italy and Spain as a tourist and when he went on expeditions against the Spaniards, and we know that the emotions in these poems were not his emotions then. His other long absences came after his marriage and common sense asks: from whom could he have parted with such tenderness, if not from his wife? And if the answer should be that all the poems arose from an unusually vivid imagination, common sense asks another question: how could he so well imagine feeling like that, if in all his life he had never actually felt the pain of good-bye? And if he actually felt it only once, directly inspiring only one poem, that would be an interesting connection with his wife.

The 'Valediction to his Booke' may refer to a book which once existed and which collected their love-letters written when they were parted in 1600–01:

> Study our manuscripts, those Myriades
>   Of letters, which have past twixt thee and mee,
>   Thence write our Annals, and in them will be
> To all whom love's subliming fire invades,
>   Rule and example found . . .

And certainly this poem suggests that Donne would have had no objection in principle to an attempt to see whether any of his writing is about his own courtship and marriage; he would not have dismissed the possibility with the scorn which we find in some of the twentieth-century commentators. The poem suggests that love letters can instruct 'Divines' (theologians) about love as a reality which is not entirely spiritual:

> Love this grace to us affords,
> To make, to keep, to use, to be these his Records . . .
> Here Love's Divines (since all Divinity
> Is love or wonder) may find all they seeke . . .
> For though minde be the heaven, where love doth sit
> Beauty a convenient type may be to figure it.

Yet part of the 'wonder' of this love which is physical, not heavenly, is that it need not die when the lovers are separated physically, for

> How great love is, presence best tryall makes,
> But absence tryes how long this love will bee . . .

The 'Valediction Forbidding Mourning' may also have been a good-bye to Anne; Walton thought that it was, in 1611. Helen Gardner thought this impossible: a wife would not be expected to keep her grief at her husband's departure private or to be involved in 'the romantic conception of passionate love as the *summum bonum*'. These objections, however, do not necessarily apply either to all marriages or to the relationship between the highly emotional John and the usually pregnant Anne. At least, the poem is about the parting of two people, real or imagined, who have been physically very close, who have achieved a spiritual union also, and who must now be content that for a while their relationship will be spiritual. Other lovers, it says, may indulge in 'teare-floods' and 'sigh-tempests' when they part – and there is a hint that the woman is now doing precisely that.

> But we by a love, so much refin'd,
>   That our selves know not what it is,
> Inter-assured of the mind,
>   Care lesse, eyes, lips, hands to misse.
>
> Our two soules, therefore, which are one,
>   Though I must goe, endure not yet
> A breach, but an expansion,
>   Like gold to ayery thinnesse beate.

This suggestion that the union of souls need not be destroyed by a geographical separation seems fairly simple and common, but there has been much critical discussion about the rest of the poem, which compares the parted lovers to two legs of a compass. Donne was not the first poet to use this 'conceit' in order to talk about a separation which is also a continuing union, but it has often been objected that in a poem which is beautifully tender the cold artificiality of the compass is out of place. This objection deserves some thought.

As used by Donne, this image does not minimize the difficulty caused by the separation. Just as gold beaten until it is as thin as air (as 'gold leaf' used in decoration) is not the same as the gold ring which symbolizes the full union of marriage, so the legs of a compass are definitely parted when only one leg is making a circle. Indeed, the comparison with the compass is introduced by the admission that the lovers' souls, about which it has just been said that they 'are one', in fact 'are two'. But the point now made is that the 'fixt foot' (the woman who stays behind) remains 'fixt' in the sense of being constant, but 'doth move' in the sense of turning in sympathy as the other moves (so the woman can follow her man's movements in her mind). Even when 'the other far doth rome' the 'fixt foot' moves towards the other and 'leanes and hearkens after it', until the circle (with detours) is completed when the other 'comes home'. Then the 'fixt foot' is delighted and 'growes erect'. Somewhat as beaten gold leaf remains gold and is not entirely different from the metal which can be melted into a coin or a bracelet, the two legs of the compass are not completely out of touch and can be completely united again. In brief, the speaker very gently begs the woman (Anne?) to stop crying and to think about how she must be loyal and hopeful when they are parted, until her 'firmnes' enables him to 'end where I begunne' – with her.

The mood is the same in a song which seems to have been written to accompany an existing tune (and which Walton also associated with their parting in 1611):

> Sweetest love, I do not goe,
> For wearinesse of thee,
> Nor in hope the world can show
> A fitter Love for mee . . .

Here, too, the beloved is begged not to weep:

> When thou sigh'st, thou sigh'st not winde,
> But sigh'st my soule away,
> When thou weep'st, unkindly kinde,
> My life's blood doth decay . . .
>
> But thinke that wee
> Are but turn'd aside to sleepe;
> They who one another keepe
> Alive, ne'r parted bee.

In the 'Valediction of Weeping' the word 'more' may well be a clue to the identity of the lover to whom this farewell is addressed. In response to her tears which are 'emblemes of more' he has to 'powre forth' his own tears. But still having his wit, he is afraid that if they both go on crying like this the water may 'overflow this world' in a Flood of biblical size even before he embarks on his risky voyage:

O more than Moone,
Draw not up seas to drowne me in thy sphere,
Weepe me not dead in thine armes, but forbeare
To teach the sea, what it may do too soone . . .

And he begs the lady not to create a great 'winde' by her sighs, pointing out that 'thou and I sigh one another's breath': the one who 'sighes most' is 'cruellest' without meaning to be.

Since 'A Feaver' combines teasing with an intimate tenderness, it may well have been addressed to Anne, who was often ill. (It was clearly not addressed to the Countess of Bedford.) The beginning would be offensive if the speaker were not tolerated and loved by the recipient:

Oh doe not die, for I shall hate
All women so, when thou art gone,
That thee I shall not celebrate,
When I remember, thou wast one.

But by its end the poem has become an outburst of uncomplicated, sexual love:

These burning fits but meteors bee,
Whose matter in thee is soon spent.
Thy beauty, and all parts, which are thee,
Are unchangeable firmament . . .

For I had rather owner bee
  Of thee one houre, than all else ever.

Three poems which are much happier almost certainly record the ecstasy of the early days and nights of their married love, when they first fully owned each other. One of these, 'The Canonization', seems to date from the reign of a king not a queen, for it mentions 'his stamped face' on coins. It is addressed to friends who regard the speaker's absorption in love as an error, and begins dramatically

For Godsake hold your tongue, and let me love . . .

and asks 'who's injur'd by my love?' The world's business has not been interrupted as the lovers 'dye and rise' (familiar slang for sexual intercourse) 'at our own coste'. And the poet assures friends that this love is inspiring poetry which will be their memorial:

We'll build in sonnets pretty roomes;
As well a well wrought urne becomes
The greatest ashes, as half-acre tombes . . .

So there is irony in the fact that the reference to a 'well wrought urne' as a monument which 'becomes' (suits) 'the greatest ashes' was used as the title of the book which in 1947 was a manifesto of the 'new criticism'. *The Well-Wrought Urn* by Cleanth Brooks argued that the attempts of earlier critics to find autobiography behind poetry were futile. Yet Donne himself said that like an urn holding the ashes of an aristocrat so 'sonnets' can be rooms holding the spirits of lovers who once 'did the whole world's soule contract' into their love which would be a 'patterne' to future lovers.

'The Sunne Rising' also seems to date from after their marriage, since it seems later than the accession to the throne in 1603 of King James. His enthusiasm for hunting is, it appears, mentioned:

> Goe tell the Court-huntsmen, that the King will ride.

The sun is rebuked for calling on the lovers to get out of a bed which contains 'both the Indias of spice and Myne' (both the spices of the East and the gold of the West) plus all the kings of the earth, 'all here in one bed'. The speaker exults:

> She is all States, and all Princes, I.
> Nothing else is.
> Princes do but play us, compar'd to this,
> All honor's mimique; All wealth alchimie . . .

And the end of the poem transcends the traditional *aubade*, where the dawn is merely resented as an intrusion on love. Now the lovers' bed is the centre of the universe and 'if her eyes have not blinded thine' the sun is instructed to circle round the room and to warm 'us' with its beams:

> Shine here to us, and thou art every where;
> This bed thy center is, these walls, thy sphere.

But if the sun should be unable to do its duty that will not matter, for it has already been reminded that deep love is a foretaste of eternity:

> Love, all alike, no season knows, nor clyme,
> Nor houres, dayes, moneths, which are the rags of time.

'The Good-morrow' is a poem with the same mood of joy as sunshine pours into the bedroom after a night of love. This love is different from the fumblings of adolescents as they explore bodies and emotions.

I wonder by my troth, what thou, and I
Did, till we lov'd? were we not weaned till then?
But sucked on countrey pleasures, childishly? . . .
'Twas so; But this, all pleasures fancies bee
If ever any beauty I did see,
Which I desir'd, and got, t'was but a dreame of thee.

And now good morrow to our waking soules,
Which watch not one another out of feare;
For love, all love of other sights controules,
And makes one little roome, an everywhere.

The love-intoxicated speaker dismisses the 'new worlds' being opened up by 'sea-discoverers' and the new stars now shown on maps of the night sky. What matters as 'true plain hearts' come to rest is 'let us possesse one world, each hath one, and is one', for eternity is here:

If our two loves be one, or, thou and I
Love so alike, that none can slacken, none can die.

Thus a number of Donne's love poems may be connected with Anne: nothing in them makes this impossible and we do not know of any other woman who could arouse in the poet feelings so deep, so tender and so wise. It seems sensible to think it highly probable that Donne wrote poetry about his love for his wife, for it would be extraordinary if he did not. But it would be wrong to claim certainty about the background to any particular poem. In 1982 a scholar, Patricia Pinka, could publish *The Dialogue of One* as a detailed study of the 'seven types of lover' on view in the 'Songs and Sonets' without ever mentioning Donne's wife. 'More' need not always be a pun on her surname before marriage; valedictions have been written by many poets as literary exercises; many poets have imagined situations not belonging to their own lives; many men have had lovers in short or long relationships who were not their wives. Only one conclusion is, it seems, undeniable: marriage with Anne contributed decisively to the deepening and purification of Jack Donne. He said so himself: admiration for her when she was his physical partner made him seek God and after her death intense grief deepened both his emotions and his prayers. Also, his sermons celebrated married love as 'union' in addition to their less attractive echoes of the traditional subordination of the wife to the husband. The contrast with his attitudes as a young poet makes this transformation by marriage little less than a new birth psychologically. And since these were facts, we should not be surprised to find it probable that he could still find himself in an agony of bereavement ten years after Anne's death.

Why, then, did he in the end decide to be buried in the cathedral where he had preached instead of in her grave as he had intended in 1617? And why did he take no steps to make sure that the poetry of their love was kept in the text which he had written, and in an intelligible order? It was, I suggest, because he had been captured by a vocation which he believed to come from God, and thus he felt that he was under the pressure of a love even greater than their married love.

10 The Trumpet

Thou art the Proclamation; and I ame
The Trumpet, at whose voice the people came.
'The Second Anniversarie'

Donne's sermons may have been neglected as evidence about what he really was but they have often been praised as one of the glories of English literature, as eloquence not unworthy of a major poet. They combine grandeur and intimacy, tenderness and drama, reminding us that this was the age of the Authorized (or King James) Version of the Bible and also the age of Shakespeare. Attention was drawn to his many-splendoured eloquence by Coleridge in the nineteenth century but more effectively by the publication of *Donne's Sermons: Selected Passages*, first in 1919 and later in many reprints. However, the editor, Logan Pearsall Smith, felt that a rather nervous introduction was necessary since the sermons had 'received no very adequate attention'. He recognized that it was not only their 'great number and length which daunts the reader; there is much in the writing itself which is difficult and distasteful to the modern mind'. The editor signalled to the reader, however, that he was himself 'secular minded' and that his purpose was not 'theological, didactic or even historical': it was to make known a great writer of enjoyable prose.

He had to rely on the texts printed during the seventeenth century: on the six sermons published during Donne's lifetime, on the seven which the Cambridge University Press brought out in 1631–34, and on the three folio volumes which were edited by Donne's son. One problem was carelessness in editor or printer.

When Donne began writing out a collection of his sermons in 1625, he told a correspondent that he hoped that publication would bring benefit to his son John, then aged 21. But the son's ordination was delayed and during his last illness Donne entrusted his sermons and other papers to the more reliable care of Henry King, his closest friend among his colleagues in the cathedral, without mentioning them in his will. However, King became too busy to complete the work still needed and in the end the unsatisfactory son did have the honour of arranging the publication.

In a fit of rage one day in 1634 John Donne junior struck a boy who subsequently died and although he was acquitted of manslaughter he thought it wise to leave Oxford for further study in Italy. On his return to England in 1637 he got hold of his father's papers by some action which left Henry King aggrieved; he did some work on them while drawing incomes from a number of rural parishes; and in 1640 a handsome volume was published containing 80 sermons. During the civil war and the Cromwellian regime he lived in London and edited (more or less) more of his father's works: a volume of 50 sermons in 1646, the book on suicide in the same year, a new edition of the poems in 1650, followed by the letters and a collection of short pieces. He made a mess of the letters, not arranging them in any sort of order and often not saying correctly to whom they were addressed. He rushed out 500 copies of some more sermons in 1660, taking advantage of the restoration of the Church of England along with Charles II (who accepted the dedication), and on the title page claimed that the contents were 26 sermons instead of the actual 23. He died in 1663, the last of John Donne's sons to survive; his brother George had had various adventures as a soldier but had died in 1639 while on a voyage to Virginia.

John Donne junior has usually been treated as a son who remained prodigal. Anthony Wood wrote about him as 'an atheistical buffoon, a banterer, and a person of over free thoughts'. A parishioner (called by him 'a pitifull ignorant Baker') rebuked him publicly as 'an idle man' who 'never preached' – as we know from a letter in which he defended himself as having been busy with his father's sermons. However, his will, made in 1662, was impressive: one earl was named as his executor, another witnessed his signature. He returned the cabinet which had contained his father's papers to King and his intention was that King (now Bishop of Chichester) should be sent all the summaries of books. He also intended that Walton should receive all the other papers. But in a letter written in November 1664, which Walton printed with King's agreement, King expressed dignified regret that the papers had disappeared: 'how these were got out of my hands . . . is not now seasonable to complain' and the unexplained fact was that they had now been finally 'lost both to me and to your self'. They had also been lost to posterity.

Logan Pearsall Smith confessed that the volumes edited by John Donne junior 'stood for years on my bookshelves' before 'it occurred to me that it might be interesting to read them' – and eighteen years passed before the publication of the extracts which he edited. In 1839 a young clergyman, Henry Alford, had published an edition of many of the sermons with some censorship, and also modernized spelling, in the hope of interesting Victorian readers, but his work had attracted few readers and no praise from scholars; his publisher had told him to abandon his hopes of editing more Donnean material (although he went on to become Dean of Canterbury). A text taking account of the printed versions and of many of the manuscripts, with a useful commentary, became available only in 1953–62, when the University of California Press undertook the publication of 160 sermons. In the triumphant introduction to the final volume there was a cool glance at anthologies: 'In the selection of purple passages the morbid and the rhetorical will always have too large a place. It is only by reading four or five sermons that we can realize Donne's sense of form, the carefully thought out scheme by which he arranged his material, his common sense, his shrewdness, his psychological insight, and his real religious fervour.' This major feat was achieved by an English scholar, Evelyn Simpson, with the collaboration of George Potter until his early death.

Their labours eased the path of a number of other good scholars who since then have published studies of the sermons considered either as theology or as literature. But the problem has remained that if many potential readers are to find it easily digestible the material has to be chopped up. On what principle should this be done? It seems best to concentrate on the message of the preacher, for this is what Donne wanted to deliver. But this does not exclude the enjoyment of his unique eloquence, for that is what he offered his congregations with all the work and skill required.

Unlike his poems, his sermons seldom begin with a phrase which arrests attention. Instead the introduction often includes a *divisio*, a division of the text taken from the Bible into small sections each of which will be expounded. Questions about translation from the Hebrew or the Greek may be mentioned but there is no immediate translation of the biblical words into everyday speech about everyday events. It seems to be taken for granted that the congregation will be as fascinated by the Bible as the preacher is, and eager to hear how he is going to handle this precious material.

After this introduction it is assumed that Christians of the seventeenth century will be impressed, edified and even delighted by a sermon which piles quotations from the Bible on top of one another, supporting them with many references to the Fathers of the Church who had interpreted Scripture but had been dead for more than a thousand years. It seems probable that this scholarly apparatus was enlarged when he wrote out sermons for the printer, but equally probable that he took not a few quotations with him into the pulpit. And modern Christians can scarcely believe that their predecessors enjoyed it all. Even in the Victorian age, when preachers were still heard patiently in England, one of Donne's successors as Dean of St Paul's, Henry Milman, wondered how a large congregation could have been attracted to 'these interminable disquisitions, to us teeming with laboured obscurity, false and misplaced wit, fatiguing antitheses'.

What Dean Milman said in the pulpit has been entirely forgotten. Whether he was right in his verdict on Donne should be decided after some study of what Donne actually said.

He had to find his own voice as a preacher and we are not surprised to be told by Izaak Walton that it took a little time: what is astonishing is how little was needed. Accompanied by a friend, this middle-aged apprentice would visit churches which would allow him to experiment in the pulpit. Not all the experiments worked, it seems. A sermon survives from a visit to the parish church in Greenwich and Donne must have been proud of it, for years later he wrote it out with a view to publication. He did what he could for an audience which cannot have been highly cultured, and made references to commerce; and one hopes that the references to Latin and Hebrew were added later. But it is unlikely that he bridged the intellectual space between that pulpit and that congregation. Indeed, it is so unlikely that it has been suggested that he was preaching to the court of Queen Anne, whose palace at Greenwich was being reconstructed at that time – but nothing in the sermon itself suggests this. Essentially he was still talking to himself and warning himself against covetousness, which he often attacked as the sin of men no longer young.

The contrast between that early effort and the mature style, which was emotionally as well as intellectually strong, can be seen at its extreme in one of the best known of his sermons, preached to the Virginia Company before a feast in November 1622 (4:264–82).

The young English colony was extremely insecure as Donne spoke. The boundless hopes of 1606 – voiced, for example, in Michael Drayton's 'To the Virginian Voyage' – had been dashed and the sponsoring company was now deeply divided between those who still believed that Virginia might be the Paradise of a new life in a new world and those who impatiently waited for a return on the investment. Many of the settlers had recently been massacred by the 'Indians' and those who survived found it difficult to earn a living before tobacco was exported after being grown by slave labour. In England, the venture had attracted supporters who were suspected by the government and two and a half years after this sermon the Virginia Company was to be dissolved. But that afternoon, almost four hundred people gathered in the church to hear this preacher as he raised morale.

He did not do this by urging a war of vengeance against the 'Indians': instead, 'preach to them Practically' by 'your Justice and (as far as may consist with your security) your Civilitie'. Nor did he advocate emigration by people who found England unsatisfactory. Nor did he recommend Virginia as a good investment. 'Those whom liberty drawes to goe', he declared, 'or present profit draws to adventure, are not yet in the right way.' Nor did he think that the main motive ought to be politics, whether conservative or radical: 'if you seeke to establish a temporall Kingdome there, you are not rectified'. His glowing vision was of a religious mission to the new world, taking the Gospel of the kingdom of God across the Atlantic as the children of Israel had once taken themselves across the Red Sea. For once, Donne did not treat the West as the area of sunset. On the contrary, if the Virginia Company dedicates itself to the conversion of the 'Indians' that will be a part of the building of a new part of Christendom in the new world. 'You shall have made this Iland which is as but the Suburb of the old world a Bridge, a Gallery, to the new; to join all to that world which shall never grow old, to the Kingdome of heaven.'

The obvious danger of the emotionalism of this style was that the rhetoric could lapse into irrationality. Sometimes he lapsed in order to raise the tone above everyday reality (but did Donne the preacher remember that he had once applied for the down-to-earth job of being secretary to the Virginia Company?) and sometimes in order to make the flesh creep. A notorious example is when he used a plague to warn his congregation that they must reckon with death – as if that was not already causing them enough grief. 'Have you not left a dead son at home, . . . whom you should have beaten with a rod, to deliver his soul from hell, and have not?' He imagined 'men whose lust carried them into the jaws of infection in lewd houses, and seeking one sore perished with another; men whose rapine and covetousnesse broke into houses, and seeking the wardrobes of others stole their own death'. And he imagined the dust which was all that remained of the bodies of the dead blowing around the church: 'Every puff of wind within these walls may blow the father into the son's eyes, or the wife into her husband's, or his into hers, or both into their children's, or their children's into both' (6:362, 389). This was said to people who had just buried those whom they loved.

But these performances were not what he said on the average Sunday and so far as we know he remained on good terms with the anxious supporters of the Virginia Company, who arranged for the sermon to be printed, and with the congregation of St Dunstan's, who remained astonishingly loyal. The explanation seems to be that when he preached people liked the preacher even while they did not like – or perhaps did not choose to hear? – what he said. (One secret about the art of preaching is that a congregation is often more interested in the messenger than in the message.) It seems that what mattered most on those occasions was that Donne showed that he was moved to eloquence by what was moving his hearers to fears or tears; he really cared about Virginia, he was really upset by the deaths in the plague, what he actually said might be silly or deeply offensive but his 'nearnesse' pierced.

Izaak Walton often heard him preach, and remembered him: 'A Preacher in earnest; weeping sometimes for his Auditory, sometimes with them, always preaching to himself, like an Angel from a cloud, but in none; carrying some, a S. Paul was, to Heaven in holy raptures, and inticing others by a sacred Art and Courtship to amend their lives; here picturing a vice so as to make it ugly to those that practised it; and vertue so as to make it beloved even by those that lov'd it not; and all this with a most particular grace and an unexpressible addition of comeliness.' That memory does something to compensate for a truth in Donne's letter when he sent a copy of a sermon requested by the Countess of Montgomery: 'I know what dead carkasses things written are, in respect of things spoken.'

His sermons have the disadvantage and the advantage of being based on the belief that from cover to cover the Bible had been dictated to 'secretaries of the Holy Ghost'. The disadvantage is obvious to most modern people, and it is intellectual: his understanding of how the literature called *ta biblia* ('the books') was compiled could not be modern. For example, he believed that Moses had been the secretary to whom God dictated the first part of Holy Scripture. Consequently, Moses knew more than any scientist of whom Donne was aware and 'to depart from the literall sense . . . in the book of Genesis is dangerous, because if we do so there, we have no history of the Creation of the world in any other place to stick to' (6:62). He does not seem to have doubted that Genesis was reliable: he reminded the court of Charles I that in 'our age' people had sailed round the world but he still believed that God had taken only six days to create 'that earth and that heaven' (9:47).

In Donne's view a king of Israel could also be a king of literature, for David wrote all the psalms and Solomon all the 'wisdom' literature traditionally connected with him. That made David a 'better Poet' than Virgil (4:140). Solomon was 'wiser than Adam, than Moses, than the Prophets, than the Apostles' – and Donne added to that list which he drew from medieval sources. Since the Virgin Mary was not a marvel 'of natural and civil knowledge' she, too, was less wise than Solomon (3:48).

The advantage in this essentially medieval attitude to the Bible was that it inspired great care in the preacher's study, meditation and exposition, with close attention to both Testaments. Of the 160 of Donne's sermons which have survived, almost exactly half began with a text taken from the Old Testament and almost as many were based on a psalm as on a gospel. The preacher felt that he was standing in line with the Fathers of the Church as he preached from the divinely dictated Bible, and he was sure of his authority to do so. He quoted St Augustine of Hippo some seven hundred times in his surviving sermons, and one quotation was this: 'that which the Scripture says, God sayes, for the Scripture is his word; and that which the Church says, the Scriptures say, for she is their word, they speak in her; they authorize her and she explicates them' (6:282). But this following of the Fathers was not slavish, for as the Fathers had admitted, and as this preacher was not afraid to demonstrate, they could make mistakes: 'Let us follow the Fathers as Guides, not as Lords over our understandings' (9:161). As Donne put it, 'to that Heaven which belongs to the Catholique Church I shall never come except I go by the way of the Catholique Church . . . To beleeve according to ancient beliefs, to pray according to ancient formes, to preach according to former meditations' (7:61). But he was also a Protestant for whom the Catholic Church could never be superior to what the Bible said and should never be dogmatic where the Bible was silent. And he was a scholar who appealed to reason and to facts as seen by educated people in his time, holding that 'faith without a root, without reason, is no faith, but an opinion' (5:102). St Paul's Cathedral had been dedicated in honour of one of the giants of the Bible, built during the Middle Ages when the power of the Catholic Church rose above the little city, and taken over by the Protestant National Church in the early modern age – and when Donne preached in it, his sermons suited that formidable background.

One consequence was that he did not present the Jesus of the gospels as being human and attractive, the homeless friend of the poor and of women, of those excluded from respectable society and of those who were hungry for spiritual food not on offer from official religion. Inevitably he accepted what was thought by scholars in his own time: that Matthew's was the earliest of the gospels, written for Jews, and that Mark's was a 'just and intire history of our blessed Saviour' written for 'the Western Church' and based on 'Peter's Dictates'. John 'handleth his Divinity and his Sermons' while Luke merely 'cut off excesse and superfluity' (5:239–40). Earlier he had more sensibly thought that John's gospel was the last to be written (3:348). But his dismissal of Luke as an abbreviator shows how much he missed.

On Christmas Day in 1625 he told the congregation: 'He had a heavenly birth by which he was the eternall Son of God, and without that he had not been a person to redeem thee; He had a humane birth by which he was the Son of Mary, and without which he would not have been sensible in himself of thine infirmities and necessities; but this day (if thou wilt) he hath a spiritual birth in thy soul, without which both his divine and his humane births are utterly unprofitable to thee, and thou art no better than if there had never been Son of God in heaven, nor Son of Mary on earth' (6:335). This passage makes it appear that Donne believed that even in the congregation of St Paul's Cathedral, a quarter of the way through the seventeenth Christian century, there were people who needed a 'spiritual birth' and it may be thought that he would have been a more effective evangelist had he drawn more attention to the Jesus of Luke's gospel.

But Luke's account of Paul's conversion in the Acts of the Apostles did mean a great deal to this Dean of St Paul's who had himself been converted – although less dramatically – and he seized opportunities to preach about it. And the accounts of the crucifixion in all four gospels meant everything to him. 'I know nothing, if I know not Christ crucified' (5:276). He rejected the Calvinist's idea of God's 'irresistible' grace, because he remembered for how long he had resisted it himself, but now he accepted with his whole heart the teaching of Calvin and many others, Catholic and Protestant, about the cross as the supreme suffering and sacrifice. The devout emotion which he had tried to stir up and to increase in the poems written before ordination now flooded out. He told people: 'The Son of Man . . . hath himself formerly felt all our infirmities, and hath had as sad a soule at the approach of death, as bitter a Cup in the forme of Death, as heavy a feare of God's forsaking him in the agony of death, as we can have . . . The sins of all men, and all women, and all children, the sins of all Nations, all the East and West, all the North and South, the sins of all times and ages . . . were at once upon Christ' (6:275).

To him this was more that a 'theory of the atonement'. It mattered supremely that 'Christ doth suffer in our sufferings' (6:221); that after Christ's substitution of himself for us on the cross, 'Christ is the sinner and not I' (6:239); that 'no man hath any work of righteousness of his own, as can save him; for howsoever it be made his, by that Application or Imputation, yet the righteousness that saves him, is the very righteousness of Christ' (7:158–9). 'If I could dye a thousand times for Christ this were nothing, if Christ had not died for me before' (2:302). 'Preaching must be a continuall application of all that Christ Jesus said and did, and suffered, to thee' (7:232).

And how great were the gains when the Bible was read closely and lovingly by a major poet! One reason why he loved the psalms was that he knew what work went into a poem which 'requires diligence in the making and then when it is made can have nothing, no syllable taken from it, nor added to it' (2:50). He believed that in the Bible the poet's work was done by the Holy Spirit. 'The Holy Ghost in penning the Scriptures', he said, 'delights himself, not only with a propriety, but with a delicacy, and harmony, and melody of language and height of Metaphors, and other figures, which may work greater impressions upon the Readers, and not with barbarous, or triviall, or market, or homely language . . .' (6:55). Again: 'The Holy Ghost is an eloquent Author, a vehement and an abundant Author, but yet not luxuriant; he is far from a penurious, but as far from a superfluous style too' (5:287).

He did his best to repay the Bible in its own coin by using images which were either substantial metaphors provoking thought or else little pictures which could be flashed to keep a congregation awake. In the first category came more than one elaborate meditation on what the sea meant to Christians. London was then a very busy port, and England was then the base for the exploration of the oceans, so that many of his contemporaries were fascinated by maps and globes, but the impression made on Donne by his voyages in the 1590s still seems to fill his own imagination with salt air. 'A Sea is subject to stormes and tempests . . . And then, it is never the shallower for the calmnesse . . . It is as bottomlesse to any line which we can sound into it, and endlesse to any discovery which we can make of it' (2:306). Christians could be exhorted to embark bravely on voyages to heaven, choosing a sound ship with the safety given by the ballast in the hold but the speed given by the sails up aloft. They would face many dangers including the possibility that an innocent-looking fisherman might turn out to be a pirate (3:54), but the preacher could promise a rich profit on the cargo after a happy landing. He could use nautical terms accurately: 'we can ride out a storm at anchor; we can beat out a storm at sea, with boarding to and again; . . . though we be put to take in our sayls, and to take down our masts, yet we can hull it out' (3:184–5). And he could compare the mysterious vastness of eternity with the ocean: 'Give God sea-roome, give him his latitude' (8:318).

In his *Devotions* and in his 'Hymne to God my God' Donne also meditated elaborately on the spiritual lessons to be learned from sickness, and the scene when doctors probed the secrets of his body reminded him of a need which he had urged when preaching: 'Let every one of us dissect and cut up himself' (1:273). His sermons included many shorter references to medical knowledge and physical sufferings – topics of special interest to his fellow Londoners, as well as to him, since their city was overcrowded, insanitary and at the mercy of epidemics. A doctor's stepson and the patient of many other doctors, Donne was not nervous when pointing to parts of the human body. 'We know . . . the capacity of . . . the stomach of man, how much it can hold; . . . and we know the receipt of all receptacles of blood . . . ; and so we doe of all the other conduits and cisterns of the body . . . When I looke into the larders, and cellars, and vaults, into the vessels of our body for drink, for blood, for urine, they are pottles and gallons; when I look into the furnaces of our spirits, the ventricles of the heart and the braine, they are not thimbles' (3:236). He could even preach about the penis, that 'sewar of all sinne', reflecting that Abraham was wise to have himself circumcised when 99 years old (6:190–3). But all this frank acceptance of human physicality was connected with his acceptance of the Bible, which of course says a great deal about flesh.

He was unambiguous about the supremacy of the Bible. 'All knowledge is ignorance except it conduce to the knowledge of the Scriptures, and all the Scriptures lead us to Christ' (4:124). So the Scriptures must be supreme over the Church and over all human life. 'The Scriptures are God's Voyce; the Church is his Eccho' (6:223). And the Scriptures can teach things not known to 'Reason': 'though Reason cannot apprehend that a Virgin should have a Son, or that God should be made Man and dye', yet 'when our Reason hath carried us so far as to accept these Scriptures for the Word of God, then these particular Articles, a Virgin's Son and a mortall God, will follow evidently enough' (9:355). 'The Scripture is our Judge, and God proceeds with us according to those promises and Judgments, which he hath laid down in the Scripture.' There is even a sense in which 'the Scripture is a Judge by which God himself will be tryed' (8:281–2) – meaning that God does not hold himself free to act in contradiction of the holy love which he has revealed in Scripture. But the main point about the Bible is that the Christian must use it for life. There is little to be gained when a Christian is proudly able 'to ruffle the Bible and upon any word to turn to the Chapter and to the verse'. Truly to 'search the Scriptures', Donne said, 'is to finde all the histories to be examples to me, all the prophecies to induce the Saviour for me, all the Gospel to apply Christ Jesu to me' (3:367). A Christian ought to use the Bible 'as thou wouldest search at a wardrobe, not to make an Inventory of it, but to finde in it something fit for thy wearing' (3:367).

What matters most about the psalms is their power to speak about the deep things of God as people recite them and meditate on them, in generation after generation. More than once he claimed that if the rest of the Bible were to be lost the psalms would still enable the Christian faith to be known and spread. That was an obvious exaggeration but he was strict to maintain the custom of St Paul's Cathedral 'that the whole booke of Psalmes should every day, day by day, bee rehearsed by us who make the Body of this Church in the eares of Almighty God' (6:293). He recited the five psalms allocated to him daily and showed in his preaching that he had absorbed them with a special care, but the whole psalter fed his soul and was on hand as food for the congregation. One of his sermons was based on a text from one of the psalms (63:7) which were his daily ration: 'Because thou hast been my helpe, therefore in the shadow of thy wings will I rejoyce.' 'As the spirit and soule of the whole booke of Psalmes is contracted into this psalme, so is the spirit and soule of this whole psalme contracted into this verse' (7:52).

This love of the psalms may well have been the main reason why he began to study Hebrew seriously amid all the problems of his life in 1613. In contrast, the extent of his knowledge of Greek is questionable and it seems that he never thought it necessary to fill this gap left by his education. As we have already noted, Latin had been no problem to him since boyhood: his instinct was to quote the Bible first in Latin – or at least, this is suggested by the sermons which he prepared for future publication.

Donne was perfectly clear that the high authority of the sermon derived mainly from this authority of the Bible, not from the preacher's own holiness. 'I doubt not of mine own salvation; and in whom can I have so much occasion of doubt, as in my self? When I come to heaven shall I be able to say to any there, Lord! how got you hither? Was any man less likely to come thither than I?' (8:371). 'Whatsoever any Preacher can say of sinne, all the way, all that belongs to me, for no man hath ever done any sin which I should not have done if God had left me to my selfe' (5:41). His frequent identification of himself as a sinner was what made acceptable his equally frequent denunciations of 'all the wantonnesses of your youth, all the Ambitions of the middle years, all the covetous desires of your age' (5:182). And it was now his ambition, or at least his prayer, that how he lived might not contradict how he preached.

'Every minister of God', he told his parishioners in London, must have 'the courage of a Lion, the labourisness of an Oxe, the perspicuity and cleare sight of an Eagle, and the humanity, the discourse, the reason, the affability, the applicableness of a Man.' And he meditated in detail on the challenges offered by the traditional symbols of the four gospel-writers in the New

Testament. Lion-like courage must be 'proof against Persecution (which is a great) and against Preferment (which is a greater temptation); that neither Feares nor Hopes shake his constancy'. The ox-like minister will 'preach for the saving of soules, and not for the sharpening of wits'. Like an eagle who can look directly at the sun the minister must 'dare to looke upon other men's sins' although 'he is guilty of the same himself' – but must not look 'through other men's spectacles'. And being human, the minister requires 'a gentle, a supple, an appliable disposition, a reasoning, a perswasive disposition' (8:41–2).

A preacher who had to struggle to live up to those ideals also had to speak to sinners who would refuse to hear his message because they were in church in order to impress. 'The worldly man will hear thee', he told himself, 'yet though it be but to beget an opinion of holiness in others' – so that the preacher's task was to 'put thorns and brambles into his conscience'. 'The fashionall man . . . will hear' but only because he will go to church if he knows that 'great men' already go there, perhaps out of curiosity (2:174). It was not the job of the preacher to put 'pillows under great men's elbows' (2:105). On the contrary, prophet-like preachers have been commanded by God to 'see and discern the highest sins of the highest persons, in the highest places; they are not onely to look down towards the streets, and lanes, and alleys, and cellars, and reprehend the abuses and excesses of persons of lower quality there; all their service lies not below staires' with the servants. Preachers are ordered to 'look into the chamber, and reprehend the wantonesses and licentiousnesse of both sexes there'; they are to go 'unto the house top' and attack the 'ambitious machinations and practises' needed to climb up there; and they are to climb themselves, into a 'watchtower' where they must denounce sins 'done so much more immediately towards God, as they are done upon colour and pretence of Religion' (2:164–5).

If any sinner dared to reply by claiming to be guilty of no more than small sins, Donne could point out that 'as men that rob houses thrust in a child at the window, and he opens greater doores for them, so lesser sins make way for greater' (9:302). 'As a spider builds always where he knows there is most access and haunt of flies, so the Devil that hath cast these light cobwebs into thy heart, knows that that heart is made of vanities and levities' – so that 'lascivious glances' become adultery, 'covetous wishes' can lead to theft, and angry words can end up in murder (1:195).

Whether sins are full-grown or ominously pregnant, Donne claimed that the sinner ought to be glad that inside every church was a stone, namely Christ the Judge and Saviour – not a bed of flowers, not a pillow of feathers, not a river 'to disport, and refresh, and strengthen himself in his sinne', but a stone to stop him falling into hell (2:190). And in the Church 'the Ordinance of preaching batters the soule, and by that breach the Spirit enters; His Ministers are an Earth-quake and shake an earthly soule; They are the sonnes of thunder and scatter a cloudy conscience; They are the fall of waters and carry with them whole Congregations' (7:396). That vision of the preacher's momentous task explains why he thought it legitimate for a preacher to batter, shake, alarm and move sinners by shock tactics, and it may help us to forgive the rhetoric. And his preaching was not all melodramatic. He could preach as practical pastor. Having experienced them, he could speak about night thoughts when the Devil tempted and God seemed distant or hostile, but he recommended a defence – a 'shaking hands with God' at bedtime, 'and when thou shakest hands with God, let those hands be clean' (9:217). And he could preach with love. 'Who but myselfe can conceive the sweetnesse of that salutation, when the Spirit of God sayes to me in a morning, Go forth today and preach, and preach consolation, preach peace, preach mercy?' (7:133).

It can come as a shock to modern readers when they see that the preacher's commission to denounce the sins of the 'highest persons' was believed to stop short of the king. Like many other preachers who praised the princes governing as well as reigning in that age, Donne taught that 'Obedience to lawfull Autoritie is always an Essentiall part of Religion' (6:258). In particular is obedience due to a king. 'All forms of Government have one and the same Soul, that is Soveraignty . . . and this Soveraignty is in them all from one and the same Root, from the Lord of Lords, from God himself, for all Power is of God: But yet this form of a Monarchy, of a Kingdome, is a more lively and a more masculin Organ and Instrument of this Soul of Soveraigntie than the other forms are' since 'God himselfe, in his Unity, is the Modell, He is the Type of Monarchy' (4:240–1). Accordingly he endorsed the common description of kings as 'Lieutenants and Images of God', 'of whom God hath said, *Ye are Gods*' (4:334, quoting as many others did Psalm 82:6). This preacher who had once poured scorn on royal courts could now even bring himself to say that 'a Religious King is the Image of God, and a Religious Court is a Copy of the Communion of Saints' (8:336). And this royal chaplain made his loyalty clear in practical terms, for example in a sermon to lawyers. He maintained that the king 'is accountable to God only, and neither to any great Officer at home, not to the whole body of the people there, nor to any neighbour Prince or State abroad' (4:137).

In another sermon he put the Crown at the apex of a class structure which was like a pyramid. He claimed that despite his rough appearance and his diet of locusts and wild honey John the Baptist was 'of a good family and extraction', indeed was of the 'nobility', with 'his father a Priest, and his mother also descended from Aaron'. It had to be admitted that John's mother was not a virgin like the mother of his cousin Jesus, but 'to be born of a Virgin is but a degree more than to be borne of a barren woman'. The Baptist received a good education and enjoyed a good reputation: he was full of 'knowledge' and was 'reputed an honest man' (4:146–7). His dress and diet were not of the high quality to be expected of a member of a high class, but Donne's point was that this only showed how remarkable the Baptist was: 'for a Sonne of such Parents, an onely Sonne, a Sonne so miraculously afforded to them, to passe on with that apparell and that diet is certainly remarkable, and an evidence of an extraordinary austerity, and an argument of extraordinary sanctity' (4:154).

He knew perfectly well that the Baptist denounced his own king as a sinner and tyrant, but he had no intention of preaching about the unconventional sex life of King James or the consequent alcoholism of his queen. Nor did he directly attack the favourites of the happily married King Charles. He excused himself with the argument that Christian monarchs were responsible to God – as both James and Charles admitted – and would be judged by him, and that meanwhile God had not instructed either popes or preachers to take his reserved place (2:303). But this royal chaplain now exposed himself to the question he had asked in his 'Second Anniversarie':

> Shalt thou not finde a spongy slack Divine
> Drink and sucke in th' Instructions of Great men,
> And for the word of God, vent them agen?

The contempt which Donne the layman had felt for flattering preachers is bound to be shared when modern people accustomed to democracy listen to Donne the preacher. However, it needs to be remembered that when Donne preached that kings were 'such Images of God as have eares and can hear; and have hands and can strike' (9:59), no one in his congregation would have been disgusted. He belonged to an England where it was commonly agreed that monarchy was the only realistic alternative to anarchy and in that period Puritan preachers were among those who agreed. James was personally unpopular after 1619 – he seemed to be unpatriotic as he tried to be the ally of Spain and unwise as he relied on ministers who were corrupt or incompetent or both – but complaints were not rebellion. Within a dozen years of Donne's death the atmosphere had changed and King Charles was on his way to the executioner's scaffold erected outside the Banqueting House in the palace of Whitehall, but only a few years later order was to be restored very firmly by Oliver Cromwell, who was a king in all but name. After another short period, Charles II (a worse king than either his father or his grandfather) was to be restored the throne of his ancestors amid popular rejoicing. His brother James had to become a Roman Catholic without discretion in order to lose that throne. And two of the three monarchs in whose reigns Donne lived were people who knew how to survive exceptional dangers by the exercise of exceptional skills. Elizabeth, once addressed by Donne as 'Greatest and fairest Empresse', ruled men by dazzling them and the less glamorous James, once called by him 'the learnedst king that any age hath produced' (10:161), ruled them by being indispensable. Both survived a number of plots to assassinate them and it was truly said about them both that a nation survived because its monarch did.

Donne's first sermon which invited publicity and criticism by being preached in the open air at Paul's Cross came in 1617, remarkably soon after his ordination (1:183–221). It was 'exceedingly well liked generally' according to the critical and gossipy John Chamberlain who was there. This was because 'he did Quene Elizabeth great right' and said even more to honour King James, whose accession to the throne was being celebrated – and did all this in the context of a plea for peaceable Christian living which could not be regarded as at all controversial.

If such a sermon is now thought to be an example of the blind preaching to the blind, we should remember that Donne once said that 'Princes are God's Trumpet, and the Church is God's Organ, but Christ Jesus is his voyce' (6:217). So far from being a complete Cavalier, he had much in common with the Puritans who were to give such trouble to the Stuart dynasty. He shared their enthusiasm for preaching based on the Bible. He shared their insistence on at least the struggle for holiness ('sanctification') after the personal acceptance of Christ as the Saviour who shared his righteousness so that sinners might be treated as righteous ('justification'). 'God', he says, 'requires the heart, the whole man, all the faculties of that man, for onely that is intire, and indivisible, is immovable' (9:196). He shared their Protestant patriotism. He could still denounce the cruelty of the full Calvinist system in theology, but he now used Calvin as a biblical scholar and called him 'a very great man' (5:65). He could laugh at the Puritan who 'imagines a Church that shall be defective in nothing' and sometimes imagines himself 'to be that Church' (9:168–9), and he could warn Puritans who thought that crossing the Atlantic was necessary in order to be pure: 'we shall not need any re-Reformation, or super-Reformation, as swimming Brains must needs cross the Seas for' (4:107) – but he knew that most Puritans in his time had no wish to leave England or the Church of England.

He belonged to the sizeable group in the Church under James I which was in important ways Puritan without being fully Calvinist. That was why the senior lawyers of Lincoln's Inn were willing to have him as their preacher; many of them were Puritans, Donne's predecessor and successor in the office were both definite Puritans, and a chaplain who assisted Donne but attacked Puritans too personally was sacked. It is also significant that Donne maintained close friendships with Lincoln's Inn lawyers who had opposed the king during the 1614 Parliament, of which he himself had been a member. When invited to preach before Queen Anne and her courtiers in 1617, without mentioning the well-known fact that Her Majesty was a Roman Catholic he produced eloquence in praise of the Protestant Church of England of which any Puritan would have been proud. And when he delivered the first sermon which Charles I heard as king (6:241–61), he spoke in a style to which no Puritan could object, for he spoke of a kingdom where king and subjects, Church and State, were united in maintaining laws which should not offend any reasonable Christian's conscience. Maybe it was a dream – but it was an ideal which, if it had consistently inspired the king's policies, could have saved the country from civil war.

We should not dismiss Donne as a mere courtier and snob. One great test came in September 1622. King James had recently issued 'Directions to Preachers' forbidding any clergyman who was not a bishop or a dean from discussing in the pulpit the main theological controversy of the day – and no preacher was to 'meddle with matters of state and the differences between Prince and people'. Emotions were running high because the people were agitated about the disasters which seemed to be overwhelming the Protestants in central Europe while the king seemed more interested in an alliance with Catholic Spain to be cemented by a marriage between his son and heir and the king of Spain's daughter. Rumours spread that King James was going to become a Roman Catholic like his wife and that 'Papists' were going to be tolerated (secretly James I agreed that such toleration could follow such a marriage, and it was to happen under James II, causing a revolution). Puritan and some other preachers were loud in affirming their Protestantism and their patriotism, calling for war, not alliance, with 'Papists'. Some private correspondence of Donne's has survived which shows that he fully shared the general anxiety, and he wrote the very anxious poem 'Show me deare Christ' although this was not made public before 1899.

He was instructed to explain and defend the king's 'Directions' in a sermon at Paul's Cross, outside the cathedral of which he had recently been made dean. A large, excited and distinguished congregation assembled to hear him perform; most had to listen standing, for over two hours. What they heard pleased the king, who told the Earl of Carlisle to assure the preacher that the sermon was 'a piece of such perfection, as could admit neither addition nor diminution'. By royal command it was printed, as the first of Donne's sermons to receive that degree of fame, and the pamphlet was dedicated by permission to the king's first minister, the Duke of Buckingham. Yet a layman in the congregation, John Chamberlain, told a friend that the preacher had given 'no great satisfaction, or as some say spake as yf himself were not so well satisfied'.

In fact Donne had performed with high skill. On the one hand, he had no wish to criticize his royal master's plan to banish theological controversy from pulpits in the parishes. A pastorally minded preacher in a parish had more than enough to do if he preached 'the Gospell, onely the Gospell, and all the Gospell' (5:261). He snubbed the ignorant impertinence of lay or clerical commentators on current affairs: 'Pretend not thou who art but a private man, to be an Overseer of the Publick' (4:137). And the royal supremacy over the Church of England, now being invoked in order to control pulpits, did not trouble Donne at this stage: he thought it right that the king should have 'the same autoritie in causes Ecclesiastical that the godly Kings of Judah, and the Christian Emperors in the primitive Church, had' (4:199). And this authority should be extensive: 'The rituall and ceremoniall, the outward worship of God, the places, the times, the manner of meetings, are in the disposition of Christian Princes, and by the favours of those Churches which are in their government' (10:221).

On the other hand, like the Puritans whom the king was trying to muzzle Donne did not think that 'Catechizing' would be enough for the average congregation. The 'Directions to Preachers' ordered that this exercise should take place every Sunday afternoon although they allowed a sermon in the morning, and in the next reign the emphasis of bishops such as William Laud was to be on catechizing rather than preaching. One reason for this preference was that this substitute for a sermon, being intended mainly for the instruction of children, was based on the catechism of questions and answers printed in the Book of Common Prayer. The clergymen were expected to add only reinforcements of the Prayer Book's answers – and what was taught was in part this: 'My duty towards my neighbour is . . . To honour and obey the King, and all that are put in authority under him: To submit myself to all my governors, teachers, spiritual pastors and masters: To order myself lowly and reverently to all my betters: . . . To keep my hands from picking and stealing . . . To do my duty in that state of life, in which it shall please God to call me.' Donne would not have disagreed with any of that but he wanted, and offered, a preacher's appeal to the mind and the heart of an adult, pointing to the Bible rather than to any lesser authority.

He therefore based this tricky sermon in 1622 on an obscure text in the Old Testament: 'the stars in their courses fought against Sisera'. He interpreted this text as meaning that preachers, being 'Starrs', would always fight against error. He offered no detailed defence of the new directions, merely arguing that the king had reaffirmed the Church of England's traditional position, which surely all of its clergy would also wish to endorse. While avoiding all criticism of the monarch he was unenthusiastic in public and in a private letter to a friend he said that his hope was that his hearers had 'received comfortable assurance of His Majestie's constancy in Religion', which meant the rejection of 'the superstition of Rome'. In the event the 'Directions to Preachers' were ineffective since, led by Archbishop Abbot, the bishops were not willing to enforce censorship on their clergy and James lost interest in seeking it. Also the plan for a Spanish alliance came to nothing. Within two years Puritan preachers were in the pulpit which Donne had occupied, expounding the controversial Calvinist theology which had been forbidden. Nor did Puritan preachers avoid political controversy.

On 5 November that year Donne preached on another occasion when political tensions came to a head. He could not preach at Paul's Cross because of the rain, but to those who took refuge inside the cathedral he expounded a celebration of the deliverance of the king from 'the Powder Treason'. He combined this with discreet admissions that the king was being criticized on a number of grounds: he signalled his loyalty to his royal master but also a feeling that the critics needed to be reassured. 'Many times a Prince departs from the exact rule of his duty' he admitted, before adding that this need not be 'out of his own indisposition to truth, and clearnesse', but could a tactic designed to 'countermine underminers' as when rival tunnels were dug in the siege of a city. With the same cunning a Prince could be 'crafty and perchance false' with neighbours – a clear hint that Donne thought that James was being both secretive and devious in his negotiation with Catholic Spain, but had a strategy in mind. 'When Princes pretermit in some things the present benefit of their Subjects, and confer favours on others . . . you may think the King an ill King' – a hint that Donne understood the resentment of the English against favourites chosen by James partly because they came from Scotland. Another criticism mentioned was against a king who 'exercises his Prerogative without just cause' – the charge laid against James by the opposition in Parliament. And Donne even dared to mention a complaint against 'that King that gives himselfe to intemperate hunting' – a frequent complaint against James, who was said to neglect the business of the kingdom because he was out hunting. Accusations against kings might have some substance in them, so that they should be referred to the judgement of God; meanwhile those who have 'that great honour and that great charge' of having access to a king have a duty to warn him of dangers, for instead of killing kings 'we must endevour to preserve their persons' (4:249–50). King James sent for a copy of the sermon and, no doubt by his decision, it was not given the wider publicity of print. Donne had risked losing his support permanently.

Another test of his integrity came in April 1625 when he preached to the courtiers assembled 'at Denmark House, some few days before the body of King James was removed from thence, to his burial'. Of course it had to be a sermon in mourning and the preacher's grief was, no doubt, genuine, for he owed much to this patron. He ended: 'let none of us goe so farre from him or from one another, in any of our wayes, but that all we that have served him may meet once a day, the first time we see the Sunne, in the eares of Almighty God, with humble and hearty prayer that he will be pleased to hasten that day in which it shall be an addition even to the joy of that place, as perfect as it is and as infinite as it is, to see that face again, and to see those eyes open there, which we have seen closed here' (6:291). And of course the king was praised, eloquently. But this sermon was not only a courtier's tribute to the 'anoynted of the Lord', the 'breath of our nostrils' (4:250). It was also eloquent in a silence, for while praising James as a man who had been powerful and wise, and in these ways Godlike, Donne did not praise him as a man who had been good. And he did emphasize that James was now a man who was 'dead': the word came five times in the sentence which was the climax of the tribute. His alarming eloquence about corpses did not falter even now, with one – and such a one – near him and the royal household gathered round. And in the printed sermon only two pages are occupied by references to James, while nine and a half deploy the same eloquence in celebration of the one deathless king, Christ as proclaimed by Bible and Church. One wonders how many other royal chaplains would have kept this sense of proportion in that situation, in the seventeenth century or in any other age, with the conviction that 'so are all men, one kind of dust' (6:228).

Finally we may notice that during the constitutional crisis of 1629, when the House of Commons was accusing King Charles of breaking the law and destroying the liberty of England, Donne was summoned to preach before the king – and spoke about the necessary combination of law and liberty. It was the same vision as in 1620, when he had preached to the court of the wiser King James about the unity of 'Prince and people' in 'Peace, Plenty, and Health' (3:90). But in March 1629 Charles dismissed Parliament and began his personal rule, also aiming at 'Peace, Plenty, and Health' but believing that he knew what was best for his subjects without needing the advice of the House of Commons. At the time protests were on a small scale (five ships, the famous 'first fleet', sailed in April taking Puritans to Massachusetts). However, the day would come when the king needed the taxes which only the Commons could authorize. Summoned to vote for taxation, in the end the Commons voted for a civil war.

In 1625 Donne wrote out many of his sermons while taking refuge from the plague in the house of Sir John Danvers, who had married Magdalen Herbert. In 1649 Danvers was to be one of the 'regicides' who signed the condemnation of Charles I to death.

We have seen that in politics Donne was a royalist who refused to be tied down to the unquestioning royalism which was to be called Cavalier. When preaching his approach was essentially the same: he was a conservative who refused to be tied down to the kind of orthodoxy which was to be called fundamentalism. He felt the power of the old images – of the Holy Trinity as three co-operating persons, of eternal life as the resurrection of the flesh, of eternal death as the torments of hell, of sinfulness as the poison which began to flow when Eve ate the apple, and so forth. But he also knew that these traditional images needed interpretation to some of those who heard him in that early modern age.

'Almost every meanes between God and man suffers some adulterings and disguises: But Prayer is best' (5:232). That was for him the key to many problems in theology and its communication. Human religion has to be imperfect – but there can be prayer, and intelligent prayer, to the God who is real, as a key to open a huge door which will resist merely human battering.

It should not be assumed that because he accepted and repeated the standard imagery when expounding the doctrine of the Trinity Donne was naïve when thinking about God. There could be other imagery. 'God', he said, 'is not onely a multiplied Elephant, millions of Elephants multiplied into one, but a multiplied World, a multiplied All, All that can be conceived by us, infinite many times over' (10:35). And no imagery could fully express the reality: 'We can expresse God himselfe in no clearer termes, nor in termes expressing more dignity, than in saying we cannot expresse him' (8:105). Donne was no philosopher, yet by meditating on the self-revelation of God to Moses in the story of the burning bush ('I am'), he reached a philosophical conclusion: 'Jehovah is a name that denotes Essence, Beeing: Beeing is the name of God, and of God onely; for . . . the name of the Creator is *I am* but of every creature rather I am not, I am nothing' (8:145).

'The Trinity is the most mysterious part of our religion, and the hardest to be comprehended . . . But these mysteries are not to be chawed by reason, but swallowed by faith' (5:46–7). Why should they be swallowed? Donne's basic answer was that because of a combination of God's own self-revelation with human experience a Christian can 'apprehend not onely that I am in the care of a great and a powerful God, but that there is a Father that made me, a Sonne that redeemed me, a holy Ghost that applies this good purpose of the Father and Sonne upon me, to me' (9:52).

He taught that the mystery of the Trinity is illuminated by the experience of existing instead of being the alternative,

'Nothing'; and of being saved by Christ instead of the alternative, hell; and of reading the inspired Scriptures and finding that an inspired response arises in the mind and the heart. Often he stressed the power of the Father, the wisdom of the Son and the goodness of the Holy Spirit (as in 5:88) although in his final sermon while keeping 'power' he spoke chiefly of 'mercy' and 'comfort' (10:231). This belief in the threefold God found in Christian experience fitted in well with his frequently expressed conviction that the human desire for community and love is rooted in the being of God, in whose image human nature has been created. And even in the individual he found the work of the threefold Creator: 'finde impressions of the Trinity in the three faculties of thine own soule, thy Reason, thy Will and thy Memory' (as in 3:359). Elsewhere he put memory before will. But he took all this, as he took so much else, from St Augustine and certainly he did not believe in three gods. On the contrary, like St Augustine he usually referred to 'God' in the singular. 'These notions that we have of God, as a Father, as a Son, as a Holy Ghost . . . are so many handles by which we may take hold of God, and so many breasts by which we may suck such a knowledge of God, as that by it we may grow up into him' (3:263).

He often used the picture of God as the Circle, beginning and ending in simple perfection. So he began his praise of 'the translation of the Psalmes by Sir Philip Sydney, and the Countess of Pembroke his Sister', with this invocation:

> Eternall God, (for whom who ever dare
> Seeke new expressions, doe the Circle square,
> And thrust into strait corners of poore wit
> Thee, who art cornerlesse and infinite)
> I would but blesse thy Name, not name thee now . . .

It seems that one reason why he welcomed that translation was that it preserved the sense of wonder in the psalms while a version often used in churches at that time, the metrical version of 1562, was doggerel (but the Sidney translation, not printed until 1823, was never used). And although his imagination delighted in the spectacle of the resurrection of the body by God's supermiracle, here too he was not completely naïve in his thinking about a part of the Church's tradition.

In the eighteenth meditation of his *Devotions*, he thinks that 'every body is sure' that someone who has just died had a soul, and of course he agrees. But 'if I will aske mere Philosophers, what the soule is, I shall finde amongst them some that will tell me it is nothing but the harmony . . . of the elements in the body, which produces all those faculties, which we ascribe to the soule . . . If I will ask . . . Philosophicall Divines how the soule, being a separate substance, enters into Man, I shall finde some that will tell me, that it is by . . . procreation from parents . . . ; and I shall finde some that will tell mee that it is by immediate infusion from God . . . If I will aske not a few men but almost whole bodies, whole Churches, what becomes of the soules of the righteous at the departing thereof from the body, I shall bee told by some, They attend . . . a purification in a place of torment; By some, that they attend . . . in a place of rest, . . . of expectation; By some that they passe to an immediate possession of the presence of God.' And so the experts differ. 'But yet I have . . . mine owne Charity; I aske that; and that tels me, He is gone to everlasting rest, and joy, and glory.' And charity combined with faith bids him pray for more than that, since the 'Saints in heaven lacke yet . . . the consummation of their happinesse' – and so he prays for the soul's 'joyful reunion to that body which it hath left'.

As we saw in connection with his love poetry, he preached that 'all that the soule does it does in, and with, and by the body' (4:358). Accordingly he believed that since this was the case before death the resurrection of the dead could not be fully glorious if it did not include the body. But he did face some questions which are likely to arise if it is believed that bodies will literally 'live again'. 'Where be all the splinters of that Bone which a shot hath shivered and shattered in the Ayre? Where be all the Atoms of that flesh which a corrasive hath eat away, or a Consumption hath breath'd, and exhal'd away from our arms and other Limbs? In what wrinkle, in what furrow, in what bowel of the earth, ly all the graines of the ashes of a body burnt a thousand years since? In what corner, in what ventricle of the sea, lies all the jelly of a Body drowned in the generall flood?' He did not shrink from asking how there could be a reunion 'between that arm that was lost in Europe, and that legge that was lost in Afrique or Asia, scores of yeers between'. Nor did he shirk questions about bodies deformed by disease, when 'a Dropsie hath extended me to an enormous corpulency, and unweildenesse' or when 'a Consumption hath attenuated one to a feeble macilency and leannesse'. Nor did he escape from such problems by believing (as many Christians including St Paul have done) that the 'body' of the resurrection will be a new, spiritual body, so that what is really believed in is the resurrection of the personality. He insisted: 'I shall have my old eies, and eares, and tongue, and knees, and receive such glory in my body my selfe as that, in that body, so glorifyed by God, I also shall glorify him' (8:98).

Those last words give the clue about Donne's motive in imagining so exuberantly that final world of stupendous miracles. He believed that all three persons of the Trinity had been involved in the creation of human bodies and would not rest content until what had been created was brought to perfection. 'In those infinite millions of millions of generations, in which the holy, blessed and glorious Trinity enjoyed themselves one another, and no more, they thought not their glory so perfect, but that it might receive an addition from creatures; and therefore they made a world, a materiall world, a corporeall world, they would have bodies' (4:47). Donne often quoted Genesis 1:26: '*Let us make man*, that consultation of the whole Trinity in making man, is exercised even upon this lower part of man, the dignifying of his body.' So he was not surprised that 'very many of the Fathers' had taught that 'the soule of man comes not to the presence of God, but remaines in some out-places until the Resurrection of the body' (6:266). He thought that the human body was the 'Master-piece' of the physical creation (4:294) and expected the work to be completed triumphantly on the day of resurrection. 'All dies, and all dries, and moulders into dust, and that dust is blowen into the River and that puddled water tumbled into the sea, and that ebbs and flows in infinite revolutions, and still, still God knowes . . . in what part of the world every graine of every man's dust lies; and . . . he whispers, he hisses, he beckons for the bodies of his Saints, and in the twinckling of an eye, that body that was scattered over all the elements, is sate down at the right hand of God, in a glorious resurrection' (8:98).

Here Donne the preacher put into spoken rhetoric what Donne the poet had imagined almost twenty years before:

> At the round earth's imagin'd corners, blow
> Your trumpets, Angells, and arise, arise
> From death, you numberlesse infinities
> Of soules, and to your scattered bodies goe,
> All whom the flood did, and fire shall o'erthrow,
> All whom warre, dearth, age, agues, tyrannies,
> Despaire, law, chance, hath slaine . . .

Thus Donne enjoyed imagining the physical resurrection of the body, but he admitted that it would be incredible were it not part of the Apostles' Creed, which he believed had been composed by

Christ's apostles (4:62). 'There are so many evidences of the immortality of the soule, even to a naturall man's reason, that it required not an Article of the Creed, to fix this notion of the Immortality of the soule. But the Resurrection of the Body is discernible by no other Right, but that of Faith, nor could it be fixed by any lesse assurance than by an Article of the Creed' (7:98). And he could be cautious about detailed predictions of heaven, even while he accepted the Church's creed. 'Of these new heavens, and this new earth', he once said, 'we must say at last, that we can say nothing.' This was because eternity is 'where every thing is every minute in the highest exaltation, as good as it can be, yet super-exalted, infinitely multiplied, by every minute's addition; every minute infinitely better than it was before' (8:82).

Like many others in the history of Christian beliefs about life after death, Donne used various comparisons with life before death and was not able to fit them together into a smoothly logical system. At the time of the tenth of his 'Holy Sonnets' he concentrated on the comparison with sleep as he addressed Death:

> From rest and sleepe, which but thy pictures bee,
> Much pleasure, then from thee, much more must flow . . .
> One short sleepe past, wee wake eternally,
> And death shall be no more, death, thou shalt die.

He did not then discuss what we should enjoy when 'wee wake eternally' – but then, he did not mention God in that poem. In a sermon some fifteen years later he used another image, which did not involve any contrast between sleeping and waking. He said that 'true joy in this world shall flow into the joy of Heaven as a River flows into the Sea; That joy shall not be put out by death and a new joy kindled for me in Heaven'. He expected that 'my soule, as soon as it is out of my body, is in Heaven and does not stay for the possession of Heaven . . . but without the thousandth part of a minute's stop as soon as it issues is in a glorious light, which is Heaven'. He summed up: 'that soule that goes to Heaven meets Heaven here' (7:70–1). But he saw, it seems, that it was not altogether logical to say that immediately after death the soul 'meets Heaven' if we must also say that the resurrection of the body is needed for the fullness of joy. In another sermon he sounded as if he had seen this problem, saying defensively and illogically that 'though those Joyes of heaven, which we shall possesse immediately after our death, be infinite, yet even to these infinite Joyes, the Resurrection gives an addition, and enlarges even that which was infinite' (5:212).

Of course it was a mosaic or muddle of images, but at different times – probably without any clear development in systematic thought – Donne let his imagination work on different parts in the rich tradition which he accepted: rest in sleep, the soul's immortality, physical resurrection. His essential belief was, it seems, that everything depends on God – that 'whom God loves, he loves to the end: and not onely to their own end, to their death, but to his end, and his end is that he might love them still . . . The Sun is not weary with sixe thousand yeares' shining; God cannot be weary of doing good' (6:173–4).

Donne the preacher was always eloquent about the inevitability of death. In an early sermon he was already ridiculously gloomy: 'It is but our mistaking, when we call any thing Health . . . Before we can craule, we runne to meet death' (2:80). He was fascinated by deathbeds, including his own. But for him the deathbed's drama need not end in darkness. 'The sun is setting to thee, and that for ever; thy houses and furnitures, thy gardens and orchards, thy titles and offices, are departing from thee; a cloud of faintnesse is come over thine eyes, and a cloud of sorrow over all theirs.' And yet! – 'when his hand that loves thee best hangs tremblingly over thee to close thine eyes . . . behold then a new light, thy Saviour's hand shall open thine eyes, and in his light thou shalt see light' (2:267). In death a human being dies like an animal, yet for humanity death is the fulfilment of the lifelong feeling that something better must lie ahead: 'Creatures of an inferiour nature are possest with the present, Man is a future creature. In a holy and usefull sense wee may say that God is a future God; to man especially he is so; Man's consideration of God is specially for the future' (8:75).

That belief that the good God is trustworthy in life and death is a simple belief, but it can be clothed in rhetoric as splendid as any passage that Donne ever achieved. 'God hath made no decree to distinguish the seasons of his mercies: In paradise the fruits were ripe the first minute, and in heaven it is always Autumne, his mercies are ever in their maturity . . . If some King of the earth have so large an extent of Dominion in North and South as that he hath day and night together in his Dominions' – preaching in London on Christmas Day 1624, Donne did not like to refer directly to the king of Spain – 'much more hath God mercy and judgement together: He brought light out of darknesse, not out of a lesser light; he can bring thy Summer out of Winter, though thou have no Spring; though in the Wayes of fortune, or understanding, or conscience, thou hast been benighted till now, wintred and frozen, clouded and eclypsed, damped and benummed, smothered and stupefied till now, now God comes to thee, not as the dawning of the day, not as in the bud of spring, but as the Sun at noon to illustrate all shadowes, as the sheaves in harvest to fill all penuries; all occasions invite his mercies and all times are his seasons' (6:172).

As we have seen, Donne has sometimes been condemned as a hellfire preacher who terrified his ignorant congregation, and a part of the truth is that he did indeed use the traditional images of everlasting torment. No preacher of that age could think of depopulating hell and no poet with Donne's imagination could fail to be fascinated by hell's horrors – 'the intensenesse of that fire, the ayre of that brimstone, the anguish of that worm, the discord of that howling, and gnashing of teeth' (4:86). It is also true that he could be frightening about the possibility of a quick removal from sin on earth to hell in eternity. 'God is the Lord of Hosts', he warned, 'and he can proceed by Martial Law: he can hang thee on the next tree; he can choak thee with a crum, with a drop, at a voluptuous feast; he can sink down the Stage and the player . . . in to the mouth of hell; he can surprise thee even in the act of sinning' (1:176–7). Donne could conjure up a picture of the sinner who 'thought death his end; It ends his seventy yeares, but it begins his seventy millions of generations of torments, even in his body, and he never thought of that' (6:277).

However, when his preaching is taken as a whole what stands out in this connection is his insistence that the traditional images of hell signify most importantly exile from the joy of life in God's heaven, and the traditional doctrine about hell is meant chiefly as a warning given in order to alert and change sinners. Moreover, his only surviving sermon to be entirely about hell was preached (probably in 1622) not to people who could easily be terrified out of their wits because their wits were few, but 'to the Earle of Carlile, and his Company at Sion'. While ranking only as Viscount Doncaster, the Earl of Carlisle had been the head of the lavish diplomatic mission to which Donne had been chaplain, and while merely Lord Hay he had acquired the reputation of being among the courtiers of James I both one of the most sophisticated (he had spent time in France and had a polished courtesy) and one of the most extravagant (he had invented the 'ante-supper', a large display of cold food which guests admired, only to find that it was removed in favour of an even larger meal of hot food). Sion House was one of the houses owned by the Earl of Northumberland, the 'Wizard Earl' so called because he had passed the time by conducting scientific experiments while imprisoned for sixteen years in the Tower of London. Back in 1602 he had carried to Sir George More

Donne's fateful letter announcing his marriage. And we can be sure that the 'Company' included guests who could hold their own in conversation with these two earls.

To that distinguished gathering which had probably assembled in church in a mood of relaxed happiness, Donne said: 'When we have given to those words by which hell is expressed in the Scriptures the heaviest significations, . . . when all is done, the hell of hels, the torment of torments is the everlasting absence of God, and the everlasting impossibility of returning to his presence . . . To fall out of the hands of the living God is a horror beyond our expression, beyond our imagination . . . That that God should loose and frustrate all his owne purposes and practises upon me, and leave me, and cast me away as though I had cost him nothing, that this God at last should let this soule go away as a smoake, as a vapour, as a bubble, and that then this soule cannot be a smoake, nor a vapour, nor a bubble, but must lie in darknesse as long as the Lord of light is light it selfe, and never a sparke of that light reach to my soule; What Tophet is not Paradise, what Brimstone is not Amber, what gnashing is not a comfort, what gnawing of the worme is not a tickling, what torment is not a marriage bed to this damnation, to be secluded eternally, eternally, eternally, from the sight of God?' (5:265–7).

Speaking to a more mixed congregation in St Paul's Cathedral on Easter Day 1622, Donne quoted St John Chrysostom to the effect that 'Hell is not a monument of God's cruelty, but of his mercy. If we were not told of hell, we should all fall into hell; and so there is mercy in hell . . . We are bound to praise God as much for driving Adam out of Paradise, as for placing him there, And to give him thanks as well for hell as for Heaven. For whether he cauterise or foment, whether he draw blood, or apply Cordialls, he is the same Physitian, and seekes but one end (our spirituall health) by his divers ways' (4:82). Rightly or wrongly, Donne was one of the preachers who have believed that when the aim is the conversion of sinners a vivid picture of hell complete with all the traditional horrors can be more effective than a less alarming exhortation to see warnings around them now – to 'see your dishonesty in your accounts, looke upon your ward-robes and know your excesses, looke upon your children's faces and know your fornications' (4:150). But it does not follow that he thought that all the images of hell must be taken literally. In his 'Hymne to God the Father' he expressed his own fear of what might become of him after his death: this mature fear was that 'I shall perish', not go to hell.

Repeatedly Donne treated himself and all who listened to him as sinners. He had been converted and he preached in order to convert others. 'I came to a feeling in my selfe, what my sinfull condition was', he recalled. 'This is our quickning in our regeneration and second birth; and till this come a sinner lies as the Chaos in the beginning of the Creation' (9:299). Without question he accepted and expounded the account of the origins of this human condition given by Bible and Church as understood by all Christians in his time. 'We were all wrapped up in the first Adam, all Mankind', he preached in 1618, 'so that we inherit death from him, whether we will or no; before any consent of ours be actually given to any Sin we are the children of wrath and death.' 'Miserable men!' he exclaimed in that sermon delivered as a chaplain to the royal court. 'A Toad is a bag of Poyson, and a Spider is a blister of Poyson, and yet a Toad and a Spider cannot poyson themselves; Man hath a dram of poyson, originall-Sin, in an invisible corner, we know not where, and he cannot choose but poyson himself and all his actions with it' (1:293).

Such words may be dismissed as rhetoric not likely to trouble a courtier or anyone else. But when preaching in St Paul's Cathedral Donne was capable of being more specific about sins in his congregation than any modern preacher would dare to be in such a pulpit. 'Consider that when thou preparest any uncleane action, in any sinfull nakednesse, God is not onely present with thee in the roome then, but then tels thee, that at the day of Judgement thou must stand in his presence and in the presence of the whole World, not onely naked, but in that foule, and sinfull, and uncleane action, which thou commitedst then.' And the sins denounced were not only those of the flesh. 'You rob and spoile, and eat his people as bread, and then come hither, and so make God your Receiver and his house a den of Thieves . . . Let thy Master be thy god, or thy Mistresse thy god, or thy chests be thy god . . . The Lord is terrible above all gods' (7:318).

Thus Donne could bring down to the level of his audiences, and of himself, what to him was the fact that the sin of Adam and Eve lived on. He did believe that they had sinned, as a fact of history, and that since every man was 'in Adam' 'the will of every man concurred to that sin' (2:106), but in another sermon which was more mature and pastoral he showed awareness of the objection that God would be unjust to punish later generations merely because their first ancestors had sinned. 'Adam sinned, and I suffer; I forfeited before I had any Possession or could claim any Interest; I had a Punishment before I had a being. And God was displeased with me before I was I; I was built up scarce 50 years ago in my Mother's womb, and I was cast down almost 6,000 years ago in Adam's loynes; I was borne in the last Age of the world, and dyed in the first. How and how justly do we cry out against a Man that hath sold a Towne, or sold an Army. And Adam sold the World' (7:78). But he thought he was able to answer anyone who would 'cry out' against God, for he insisted that 'Originall sin' was not merely an event in the remote past. Adam and Eve had sinned – but so had every human being, both by being mysteriously present 'in Adam' and by being sinful in his or her own life. That, Donne thought, entitled him to deny that God's punishments are unjust.

In his time the question which dominated religious controversy was how to deal with this ingrained sinfulness. He felt obliged to attack both the Roman Catholic and the Calvinist positions as he understood them. He rejected as 'superstition' a form of Catholicism which now seems to be a parody or corruption of what Catholics really believe. He attacked the belief that admission to heaven could be earned by practices including fresh sacrifices of Christ by priests in the Mass, acts of penitence as prescribed by them and good deeds done as instructed by them with no great emphasis on inspiration by God. And he attacked the teaching that the clergy could draw on a 'treasury of merit' – merit earned by Christ's sufferings which were greater than was strictly necessary and by the good deeds of the saints – in order to secure the early release of sinners from the pains of purgatory after death. Donne also rejected what now seems to be a malicious parody of Protestantism: the belief that admission to heaven was restricted to the few who had been predestined by God for its delights, who had been unable to resist the 'grace' bestowed by God on the elect, but whose sole contribution was the faith that they were indeed among the few who, without any merit of their own, had been saved out of the 'damned mass' of humanity because Christ's unrepeatable sacrifice to the Father had been for their exclusive benefit. He denounced both positions and history has applauded his attacks, for crudities which may (or may not) have been taught and believed by Catholics or Calvinists in the sixteenth or seventeenth century have become incredible to most of their heirs. And, more tragically, history has also vindicated Donne's conviction that there is strong evil in the human heart.

So what is the heart of this preacher's message to people who live and think almost four hundred years after his death? Some writers who have been enthusiastic about his sermons appear to have believed that the message as he expressed it should be repeated in more or less the same form, although they have granted that good sermons may take less than an hour. But it seems more realistic to admit that in countries where it is conceivable that the language of England in his time may still be understood a greater difficulty exists: the age of science, and of science-based technology producing a comparatively affluent materialism, with a technology-based educational system, has meant that for many people the problem is not how to be reconciled to God; it is how to know that God is real.

In his middle period John Donne wrestled with God in the sense of being deeply unsure whether God loved him enough to 'save' him among the 'elect'. But in his preaching years he had far more assurance. 'The Holy Ghost bears witness', he now said, 'that is, he pleads, he produces that eternall Decree for my Election. And upon such Evidence shall I give sentence against my selfe?' (5:67). And he stated some of the evidence on which he now relied, together with the many Christians who surrounded him: 'I am of the number of thine elect, because I love the beauty of thy house, because I captivate mine understanding to thine Ordinances, because I subdue my will to obey thine, because I find thy Son Christ Jesus made mine in the preaching of thy Word, and my selfe made his in the administration of his Sacraments' (8:311). Of course that was not a complete statement of the evidence which had made him convinced, for he could have spoken about his own transformed life, given direction, usefulness and joy despite the dark nights. It was not that he had ever felt himself completely outside the Christian tradition. After a Roman Catholic boyhood had come the years when he had been a young man heated by lust. But he had kept going on the spiritual journey, he had become full of depression and self-accusation, as a pilgrim he had made progress, and eventually he had found his way into the most influential pulpits in the country.

He did not then say that he had come to believe in God, for he had never disbelieved. Even in *Metempsychosis* he had spoken of 'Great Destiny' and 'Infinity' and in other poems he had simply referred to 'God'. He lived in an age when 'atheist' was a term of abuse and a charge which, if pressed, could get anyone into serious trouble, for civilization was thought to depend on acceptance of moral laws decreed by the divine Law-giver. Usually, however, to call someone an 'atheist' seems to have meant no more than that someone was regarded as unorthodox in religion or morality: it did not necessarily mean that someone was so mad as not to believe in any kind of God. Donne thought that even a 'pratique Atheist' who had lived without a thought of God would be able to claim 'at the last day' that 'he was no speculative Atheist, he never thought in his heart that there was no God' (3:87). So he could use the term 'atheist' very imprecisely, about a non-Christian believer in God or about a Christian who was a heretic or a 'melancholique' (3:312).

In an age when modern science was in its infancy, it seemed obvious to almost everyone, even to the few Deists who were sceptical about the miracles in the Bible, that the order, the beauty and the usefulness of the world belonged to one vast miracle, the miracle of divine creation. Donne could claim that 'there is nothing that God hath established in the constant source of nature, and which therefore is done every day, but would seeme a Miracle and exercise our admiration, if it were done but once' (2:175). 'To make a King of a Beggar is not so much as to make a worm out of nothing' (4:86). 'The world is the Theatre that represents God, and every where every man may, nay must, see him' (8:224).

He quoted St Augustine: 'Nothing is Essentially good, but God' and yet 'this Essential goodness of God is so diffuse, so spreading, as there is nothing in the world, that doth not participate of that goodnesse' (6:231). Surely everyone must see the truth of both halves of that proposition: God is good, the world is good? Is not this the lesson taught clearly on every page of 'the whole booke of Creatures' (3:264)? The humble 'Marrigold opens to the Sunne, though it have no tongue to say so; the Atheist does see God though he have not grace to confesse it' (4:170). 'To beleeve in God, one great, one universall, one infinite power, does but distinguish us from beasts; For there are no men that do not acknowledge such a Power' (8:59). 'Ridling, perplexed, labyrinthicall soule! Thou couldst not say that thou beleevest not in God, if there were no God' (8:332).

When he reminded himself that there were, or might be, some such people as genuine atheists, he still found it easy to prove the reality and the rule of the Creator to 'the reason of Man'. It seemed obvious that 'this World, a frame of so much harmony, so much concinnitie and convenience, and such a correspondence and subordination in the parts thereof, must necessarily have had a workeman, for nothing can make it selfe'. It seemed equally obvious to him that 'no such workeman would deliver over a frame and worke of so much Majestie to be governed by Fortune, casually, but would still retain the Administration thereof in his owne hands' (3:358).

He went on to say that this divine workman and boss would expect 'a worship and service to him, for doing so', and would reveal 'what kind of worship and service shall be acceptable to him' – and reveal this in writing. He admitted that it could not be proved ('as that one and two are three') that the Scriptures of the Christians are 'of God' but he claimed that anyone comparing this Bible with other scriptures would reach that verdict. And he claimed that while the 'faint and dimme knowledge of God' provided by nature might be compared with 'one small coale' amid 'cold ashes'. 'If thou wilt take the paines to kneele downe, and blow that coale with thy devout Prayers, and light thee a little candle' of Bible study, that would persuade anyone to 'creep humbly into low and poor places' and 'finde thy Saviour in a Manger'. He was preaching his first Christmas sermon in St Paul's.

Because he had never entered into the mind of an atheist, he produced arguments which would not convince anyone in that position, in his own age or ours. Obviously in our own time many would say that much in the universe seems to be disorderly, or has an order which we cannot understand; that its origin is not to be compared glibly with the making of an object by a human craftsman; that its evolutionary history does not easily suggest its Maker's close control of every event; and that no one can be so unprejudiced as to be able to judge all the scriptures of the world impartially before pronouncing the verdict that the Bible is the Word of God. But Donne could bully the atheist, who to him seemed merely a fool.

Regretable sermons by Donne the hell-fire preacher have already been quoted. Here is another rant: 'Bee as confident as thou can in company; for company is the Atheist's Sanctuary' – but at the day of Judgement, 'when I may see thee upon thy knees, upon thy face, begging of the hills that they would falle down and cover thee from the fierce wrath of God', Donne will ask the victim, 'Is there a God now?' When the atheist is dying and must already 'feele Hell', Donne will already have asked that question by the deathbed. Even 'six houres' after the sermon, at 'midnight . . . wake then; and then in the darke and alone, Heare God aske thee then, remember that I asked thee now, Is there a God? and if thou darest, say No' (8:332–3). However, there were probably not many atheists in the cathedral to respond to this sermon after Evensong one dark and cold afternoon in January 1629; so perhaps no great harm was done.

To many modern people it seems unreasonable to believe that God is both good and powerful, since so much suffering lies within human experience. The question was not raised so sharply or so publicly in the early modern period but Donne was aware of it, partly because his own life had not been a bed of roses. He said about suffering that 'he praises not God, he prays not to God, he worships him not, whatsover he does, if he have not considered it, debated it, concluded it . . .' (1:278). He was no sentimentalist either, but he reached the point in his spiritual journey where he saw God for the most part not as the remote Creator, or as the terrifying Judge on the throne, but as the supreme Lover, coming to him in his own experience including the experience of suffering. He thought that he had to believe that all 'affliction' is either sent or permitted by God, but he also believed that 'that which we call the anger of God, the wrath of God, the fury of God, is the goodnesse of God' (6:238). He held that 'God inflicts no calamity, no cloud, no eclipse, without light, to see ease in it, if the patient will look upon that which God hath done to him in other cases, or to that which God hath done to others at other times' (6:214). In another sermon the point was put more vividly: 'As he that flings a ball to the ground or to a wall intends in that action, that that ball should return back, so even now, when God does throw me down, it is the way he hath chosen to returne me to himselfe' (3:193).

Donne's view of the world included an emphasis on many features which seemed to make atheism unreasonable. But the centre of the true world-view had become for him the crucifixion and resurrection of Christ, for to him that proclamation of the divine love amid great 'affliction' was what demonstrated that God not only exists but also loves and rules. He granted that the resurrection of Christ was, like the resurrection of Christians, 'a mystery, out of the compasse of reason', but he added that 'we beleeve it immediately, intirely, chearfully, undisputably, because we see it expressly delivered by the Holy Ghost' (7:100–1). In this light, the light of God's supreme miracle, Donne held that 'God cannot by any Miracle so worke upon himselfe as to make himselfe not himselfe, unmercifull or unjust' (2:309). 'Let the Devill make me so far desperate as to conceive a time when there was no mercy, and he hath made me so far as an Atheist as to conceive a time when there was no God' (6:170). He liked the speculation that the 'word' by which God made the creation was a song (4:180) and in his ears the song was renewed by Christ's victory. This conviction that the ultimate triumph of the merciful God is assured was what made Donne eloquent about the joy of Christian faith and life, for by temperament he was not an optimist.

'Religion is no sullen thing', he declared, 'it is not a melancholy, there is no such sociable thing as the love of Christ Jesus and Christ is at home with thee, he is at home within thee, and that is the neerest way to find him' (2:246). 'The Church', he said, 'is not a grave: it is a fold, it is an Arke, it is a net, it is a city, it is a kingdome . . . It is a garden worthy of your walking in it' (6:152). And in some moods Donne could look through the church door and see the whole world as a delightful garden, an Easter garden. 'See God in every thing, and then thou needst not take off thine eye from Beauty, from Riches, from Honour, from any thing' (8:69). 'God', he could promise, 'shall give thee the sweetnesse of this world, honour and ease, and plenty' – all the honey which is 'the dew of the flowres'. But he also knew that honey is 'the vomit of the Bee' – and bees can sting (3:233). He could not claim that the whole world is a garden.

He told a congregation in St Paul's: 'Be reconciled to God, and you can have . . . the Innocency of Paradise. Go home, and if you finde an over-burden of children, negligence in servants, crosses in your tradings, narrownesse, penury in your estate, yet this penurious and this encumbered house shall be your Paradise. Go forth into the country, and if you find unseasonablenesse in the weather, rots in your sheep, murrains in your cattell, worms in your corn, backwardnesse in your rents, oppression in your Landlord, yet this field of thorns and brambles shall be your Paradise.

Lock thy selfe up in thy selfe, in thine own bosome, and though thou finde every roome covered with the soot of former sins . . . yet this prison, this rack, this hell in thine own conscience shall be thy Paradise' (10:139).

He once preached in St Dunstan's on the text 'Rejoyce evermore' and he had plenty to say which perhaps we do not expect to hear from him. 'Man passes not from the miseries of this life to the joyes of heaven but by joy in this life too; for he that feeles no joy here shall finde none hereafter . . . Rejoyce in your prosperitie, and Rejoyce in your adversitie too . . . Beasts who are carnall men, who determine all their desires in the sensuall parts, come no farther than to a delight: but men who are truly men, and carry them to the intellectual part, they, and onely they, come to Joy . . . The best evidence that a Man is at peace, and in favour with God, is that he can rejoyce.' And human joy in work well done despite the difficulties is a share in God's joy. 'It is . . . the Essence of God to doe good; and when he does that, he is said to rejoyce . . . To have something to doe, to doe it, and then to Rejoyce in having done it, to embrace a calling, to performe the Duties of that calling, to joy and rest in the peacefull testimony of having done so; this is Christianly done, Christ did it; Angelically done, Angels doe it; Godly done, God does it' (10:214–16).

But he was left with the problem of evil, in particular of suffering, and he knew that it was not enough to say cheerily that what we see as misfortune is really 'the goodnesse of God', so that even then we should 'rejoyce'. His sermon about joy was a companion to another, preached to the royal court in Lent 1623, 'in another place . . . when we handled these two words, *Jesus wept*'. That sermon, too, has survived (4:324–44) and it is more in the style we have come to expect of the adult Donne. 'Jesus was troubled and he groaned; and vehemently, and often, his affections were stirred' – in particular, by grief after death. The text about Christ at the tomb of Lazarus brought back Donne's own mourning: 'Here in this world we who stay lack those who are gone out of it: we know that they shall never come to us; and when we shall go to them, whether we shall know them or no, we dispute.' But he also meditated on Christ's weeping over Jerusalem and the world. He pictured the Saviour sharing compassionately in humanity's sorrow ('every man is but a spunge, and but a spunge filled with teares') but also weeping divinely over humanity's sins.

These sermons about joy and sorrow must have been separated from each other by at least a year but their co-existence is one reminder that this preacher always carried in his own heart the 'spunge' to hold tears. He could call affliction 'our daily bread'. He could say that 'man is more miserable than any other creatures, and good men more miserable than other men', so that 'all our life is a continuall burden, yet we must not groane; A continual squeasing, yet we must not pant; and as in tendernesse of our childhood we suffer and yet are wipt if we cry, so are we complained of if we complaine' (7:54–5).

He took no interest in the attempts of philosophers to persuade people that they ought not to complain. He dismissed the 'stupidity' of allegedly wise men who advise those who suffer 'that no pain should make them say that they were in pain' (2:53). He knew suffering himself, from the inside, and said so. He was well acquainted with grief. But he also thought that he now knew why and how to endure.

In the course of an early sermon he claimed that 'no man hath suffered more than himselfe needed' (2:300) and of course that can sound repulsively complacent. But he was speaking about a solution to the problem of evil which is not intellectual but is something given, strangely and uncomfortably, within a Christian's experience of union with the suffering of Christ, even of union with the suffering of God. 'Every man hath afflictions, but every man hath not crosses. Onely those afflictions are crosses, *whereby the world is crucified to us, and we to the world* . . . As Elisha in raysing the Shunamite's dead child put his mouth upon the child's mouth, his eyes and his hands upon the hands and eyes of the child; so when my crosses have carried me upp to my Saviour's Crosse, I put my hands into his hands and hang upon his nailes, I put mine eyes upon his, and wash off all my former unchast looks and receive . . . a new life into my dead teares, from his teares. I put my mouth upon his mouth, and it is I that say *My God, my God, why hast thou forsaken me?* and it is I that recover againe and say *Into thy hands, O Lord, I commend my spirit*' (2:300). And 'God affords thee this manifestation of his Crosse, in the participation of those crosses and calamities that he suffered here' (8:319). The God who asks us to suffer has his own cross.

And the Donne who taught that suffering must always be a part of a Christian's life had himself suffered. 'Affliction', he said, 'is my Physick; that purges, that cleanses me' (6:237). 'I had rather God frowned upon mee, than not look upon mee; and I had rather God persued mee, than left me to myself' (7:85). Once again he quoted Augustine: 'I feele the hand of a father upon me when thou strokest mee, and when thou strikest me I feele the hand of a father too' (8:320). 'Affliction', he told himself, 'is a treasure and scarce any man hath enough of it. No man hath enough of it that is not matured and ripened by it, and made fit for God by that affliction.' That was a lesson re-learned from his illness in 1623, as he recorded in his *Devotions.* He at least understood a saint's view of affliction: 'It is not that I rejoyce, though I be afflicted, but I rejoyce because I am afflicted' (3:341).

Here he was not being insanely morbid and we should remember that the preacher was also a man who knew the pleasures of the flesh, both the pleasures of hot youth and the cooler pleasures of middle age with enough money: he did not seek suffering. He preached that 'since I am bound to take up my crosse, there must be a crosse that is mine to take up; that is a crosse prepared for me by God, and laid in my way . . . and I must not go out of my way to seeke a cross, for so it is not mine, nor laid for my taking up' (2:301). But he knew that suffering must come and taught that during it God must still be trusted and praised. 'God', he said in a sermon where he seems to have been speaking out of darkness, 'will have low voyces, as well as high; God will be glorified *De profundis* as well as *In excelsis*; God will have his tribute of praise out of our adversity, as well as out of prosperity . . . Even in the depth of any spiritual night, in the shadow of death, in the midnight of afflictions and tribulations, God brings light out of darknesse and gives his Saints occasion of glorifying him, not only in the dark (though it be dark) but from the dark (because it is dark) . . . This is a way unconceivable by any, unexpressible to any, but those that have felt that manner of God's proceeding in themselves, That be the night what night it will . . . they see God better in the dark' (8:53).

So Donne came to believe both that death is the deepest darkness and that God's love shines through it. It is both the supreme affliction and the supreme cause to 'rejoyce'.

He never took death lightly. When he heard someone say 'I care not though I were dead, it were but a candle blown out, and there were an end of it all', he saw Satan at work, and he prayed that 'where the Devil imprints that imagination God will imprint . . . a loathness to die, and fearful apprehension of his transmigration' (8:188). So far as we know he never finally believed that when he died he would be 'but a candle blown out' but his 'Holy Sonnets' show that he had a 'fearful apprehension' about his death and his 'Hymne to God the Father', written some fourteen years later when he was an established preacher, confessed frankly that he still had this 'sinne of feare': even if he escaped the torments of hell he might 'perish' utterly. In his 'Nocturnall' he poured out his grief for his wife, saying that he felt dead: 'I am None', knowing only 'absence, darknesse, death; things which are not'. But amid these fears and griefs, only human in their nature but rare in his ability to communicate passion, the faith prevailed that because to die is to meet God the main emotion should not be fear. 'I shall not live till I see God', he said; 'and when I have seen him I shall never dye' (3:751). When he preached about Magdalen Herbert he said that 'in the new Testament death is a promise . . . We get not Heaven but by death, now' (8:91). Life's journey towards death might, or might not, be pleasant but 'wherever we are, is the suburb of the great City' (3:288).

He had come to think of himself and his hearers as 'way-faring men; This life is but the high-way, and thou canst not build thy hopes here; Nay, to be buried in the high-way is no good marke; and therefore bury not thy selfe, thy labours, thy affections, upon this world' (3:287). Even the greatest men on earth, memorialized in elaborate tombs with flattering inscriptions ('half-acre tombes' was his phrase in 'The Canonization'), had bodies which were not much different from logs in a fireplace. 'The ashes of an Oak in the Chimney are no Epitaph of that Oak, to tell me how high or how large that was; It tells me not what flocks it sheltered while it stood or what men it hurt when it fell. The dust of great persons in the grave is speechless, it says nothing, it distinguishes nothing . . .' (4:53).

On Easter Day 1619 Donne preached to the House of Lords before they received the Holy Communion together. Death was in all their minds, not only because of the season in the Church's year but also because the queen had died a few weeks previously and the king was dangerously ill. Donne told their Lordships that they were 'Prisoners all', all condemned to die; 'and then all our life is but a going out to the place of Execution, to death. Now was there ever any man seen to sleep in the Cart between New-gate and Tyborne? Between the Prison and the place of Execution, does any man sleep?' (2:197).

But it was also his message that light could be seen even in the supreme darkness of death. He had other moods but after those dark nights he returned to his faith. Then he could compare death with the coronation of Charles I: 'The Resurrection being the Coronation of man, his Death and lying down in the grave is his enthroning, his sitting downe in that chayre where he is to receive the Crowne' (6:277). And he could compare the sight of earth from that chair with what an adult sees when watching children's games: when the saints 'look down and see Kings fighting for Crownes', earth's struggles look like 'boyes at stool-ball' (5:75). He promised Charles I and his courtiers that one day they would enter the court of the King of Heaven. It would be like the palace where he was speaking but far more importantly it would be unlike, for now this man of flesh – this poet and preacher who over so many years had taken such trouble to find appropriate words – could produce no image rooted in the earth. In heaven the righteous (not merely the predestined few or the doctrinally orthodox) 'shall awake . . . And into that gate they shall enter, and in that house they shall dwell, where there shall be no Cloud nor Sun, no darknesse nor dazzling but one equall light, no noyse nor silence but one equall musick, no fears nor hopes but one equall possession, no foes nor friends but one equall communion and Identity, no ends nor beginnings but one equall eternity' (8:191).

Further reading

I have used *John Donne: The Complete English Poems*, edited by C. A. Patrides and updated by Robin Hamilton with 1,034 items in its bibliography (J. M. Dent, 1994) and *The Complete Poetry of John Donne*, edited by John T. Shawcross (Doubleday, 1967; New York University Press and University of London Press, 1968). The publication of *The Variorum Edition of the Poetry of John Donne* in ten volumes comparing printed editions with manuscripts began in 1995 (Indiana University Press). Editions with modernized spelling include *John Donne: The Complete English Poems*, edited by A. J. Smith and updated by John Tobin (Penguin Books, 1996) and *John Donne* in the 'Oxford Authors' series, edited by John Carey (Oxford University Press, 1990). Important earlier editions from Oxford University Press were Herbert Grierson's *The Poems of John Donne* (2 volumes, 1912 and 1933), Helen Gardner's *John Donne: The Elegies and the Songs and Sonnets* (1965) and *John Donne: The Divine Poems* (2nd edn, 1978), and Walter Milgate, *John Donne: The Satires, Epigrams and Verse Letters* (1967).

The Sermons of John Donne were edited by George Potter and Evelyn Simpson in ten volumes (University of California Press, 1953–62). Editions of his prose include Helen Peters, *Paradoxes and Problems* (Oxford University Press, 1980), Ernest Sullivan, *Biathanatos* (University of Delaware Press, 1985), Anthony Rapsa, *Pseudo-Martyr* (1993) and *Devotions upon Emergent Occasions*

(1975, both McGill-Queen's University Press), Timothy Healy, *Ignatius His Conclave* (Oxford University Press, 1969), Evelyn Simpson, *Essayes in Divinity* (Oxford University Press, 1952), and *Selected Prose,* edited by H. Gardner and T. Healy (Oxford University Press, 1967) and by Neil Rhodes (Penguin Books, 1987). M. Thomas Hester edited *Letters to Several Persons of Honour* (Scholars' Facsimiles and Reprints, 1976) and has a more comprehensive edition of John Donne's surviving letters in preparation. Evelyn Simpson, *A Study of the Prose Works of John Donne* (3rd edn, Oxford University Press, 1962), is still useful. So is the *Bibliography of Dr John Donne* compiled by Sir Geoffrey Keynes (4th edn, Oxford University Press, 1973).

The standard biography is R. C. Bald, *John Donne: A Life* (2nd edn, Oxford University Press, 1986),. Thomas Docherty, *John Donne, Undone* (Methuen, 1986) is more open to criticism. George Parfit, *John Donne: A Literary Life* (Macmillan, 1989), is shorter, as is the study of *John Donne* by Stevie Davies (Northcote House, 1994). John Carey, *John Donne: Life, Mind and Art* (2nd edn, Faber and Faber, 1990), is discussed in my Chapter 6, as is P. M. Oliver, *Donne's Religious Writing* (Longman, 1997). Derek Palmer, *John Donne and His World* (Thames and Hudson, 1975), includes many illustrations. Presentations of his life with an emphasis on the religion include Frederick Rowe, *I Launch at Paradise* (Epworth Press, 1964), Edward Le Comte, *Grace to a Witty Sinner* (Victor Gollancz, 1965), and Richard Hughes, *The Progress of the Soul* (Bodley Head, London, and William Morrow, New York, 1968). And we should not forget Augustus Jessopp, *John Donne, Sometime Dean of St Paul's* (Methuen, 1897), and Edmund Gosse, *The Life and Letters of John Donne* (2 vols, Heinemann, 1899).

North American scholars have excelled in Donnean studies. A good introduction is Frank Warnke's *John Donne* (G. K. Hall, 1976). Books include N. J. C. Andreason, *John Donne, Conservative Revolutionary* (Princeton University Press, 1967),

James Baumlin, *John Donne and the Rhetorics of Renaissance Discourse* (University of Missouri Press, 1991), Meg Lota Brown, *Donne and the Politics of Conscience in Early Modern England* (Brill, Leiden 1995), Ronald Carthell, *Ideology and Desire in Renaissance Poetry: The Subject of Donne* (Wayne State University Press, 1997), Dwight Cathcart, *Doubting Conscience: Donne and the Poetry of Moral Argument* (University of Michigan Press, 1975), Gale Carrithers, *Donne at Sermons* (State University of New York Press, 1972), John Chamberlain, *Increase and Multiply: Arts-of-Discourse Procedure in the Preaching of John Donne* (University of North Carolina Press, 1976), Charles Coffin, *Donne and the New Philosophy* (Columbia University Press, 1937), Horton Davies, *Like Angels from a Cloud: The English Metaphysical Preachers 1588–1645* (Huntington Library, 1986), Heather Dubrow, *A Happier Eden: The Politics of Marriage and the Stuart Epithalamion* and *Echoes of Desire* on English Petrarchism (Cornell University Press, 1990 and 1995), Dennis Flynn, *John Donne and the Ancient Catholic Nobility* (Indiana University Press, 1995), Donald Guss, *John Donne, Petrarchist* (Wayne State University Press, 1995), William Halewood, *The Poetry of Grace* (Yale University Press, 1970), M. Thomas Hester, *Kinde Pity and Brave Scorne: John Donne's Satyres* (Duke University Press, 1982), Deborah Larson, *John Donne and Twentieth-Century Criticism* (Farleigh Dickinson University Press, 1989), Barbara Lewalski, *Donne's Anniversaries and the Poetry of Praise* (Princeton University Press, 1973) and *Protestant Poetics and the Seventeenth-Century Religious Lyric* (Princeton University Press, 1979), Arthur Marotti, *John Donne, Coterie Poet* (University of Wisconsin Press, 1986), Louis Martz, *The Poetry of Meditation* (2nd edn, Yale University Press, 1962) and *The Wit of Love* (University of Notre Dame Press, 1969), Earl Miner, *The Metaphysical Mode from Donne to Cowley* (Princeton University Press, 1969), Janet Mueller, *Donne's Prebend Sermons* (Harvard University Press, 1971), William Mueller, *John Donne:*

Preacher (Princeton University Press, 1962), Marjorie Hope Nicholson's study of the impact of science in *The Breaking of the Circle* (Columbia University Press, 1960), David Novarr, *The Making of Walton's Lives* (Cornell University Press, 1958), and *The Disinterested Muse: Donne's Texts and Contexts* (Cornell University Press, 1980), T. Anthony Perry, *Erotic Spirituality* (University of Alabama Press, 1981), Patricia Pinka, *The Dialogue of One: The Songs and Sonnets of John Donne* (University of Alabama Press, 1982), Winfried Schleiner, *The Imagery of John Donne's Sermons* (Brown University Press, 1970), Robert Shaw, *The Call of God: The Theme of Vocation in the Poetry of Donne and Herbert* (Cowley Publications, 1981), Terry Sherwood, *Fulfilling the Circle: A Study of John Donne's Thought* (University of Toronto Press, 1984), Deborah Shuger, *Habits of Thought in the English Renaissance* (University of California Press, 1990), Alan Sinfield, *Literature in Protestant England 1560–1660* (Princeton University Press, 1983), Camille Slights, *The Casuistical Tradition in Shakespeare, Donne, Herbert and Milton* (Princeton University Press, 1981), Judah Stampfer, *John Donne and the Metaphysical Gesture* (Funk and Wagnall, 1970), P. G. Stanwood and H. R. Asals, *John Donne and the Theology of Language* (University of Missouri Press, 1986), Arnold Stein, *John Donne's Lyrics* (University of Minnesota Press, 1993), Edward Tayler, *John Donne's Idea of a Woman: Structure and Meaning in The Anniversaries* (Columbia University Press, 1991), Rosamund Tuve, *Elizabethan and Metaphysical Imagery* (University of Chicago Press, 1947), Leonard Unger, *Donne's Poetry and Modern Criticism* (Henry Regnery, 1950), and Joan Webber, *Contrary Music: The Prose Style of John Donne* (University of Wisconsin Press, 1963).

The English Department of the North Carolina State University began to publish the *John Donne Journal* in 1982. Collections of articles include *Just So Much Honor*, edited by Peter Fiore (Pennsylvania State University Press, 1972), *Soliciting*

Interpretation, edited by Elizabeth Harvey and Katharine Maus (Chicago University Press, 1990), *Critical Essays on John Donne*, edited by Arthur Marotti (G. K. Hall, 1994), and *John Donne's Religious Imagination*, edited by Raymond-Jean Frontain and Frances Malpezzi (University of Central Arkansas Press, 1995). Claude Summers and Ted-Larry Pebworth edited *The Eagle and the Dove*, *Bright Shootes of Everlastingnesse* and *The Muses' Commonweal* for the University of Missouri Press in 1986, 1987 and 1988, respectively. M. Thomas Hester edited essays on possible references to Anne Donne as *John Donne's 'Desire of More'* (University of Delaware Press, 1996). Other studies are noted by John Roberts, *John Donne: An Annotated Bibliography of Modern Criticism, 1912–67* and *1968–78* (2 vols, University of Missouri Press, 1982): his scope is international. He edited *Essential Articles for the Study of John Donne's Poetry* (Archon Books, 1975) and *New Perspectives in the Seventeenth-Century Religious Lyrics* (University of Missouri Press, 1994). Paul Stellin studied *John Donne and Calvinist Views of Grace* (Free University Press, Amsterdam, 1983) and Donne in the Netherlands in *So Doth, So Is Religion* (University of Missouri Press, 1998).

But British scholarship has not been completely dwarfed. A. J. Smith edited *John Donne: The Critical Heritage* going up to c. 1900 (Routledge, 1975) and Andrew Mousley more recent criticism of *John Donne* (Macmillan, 1999). Julian Lovelock edited criticism of *Donne: Songs and Sonets,* going to c. 1950 and including the dialogue between C. S. Lewis and Joan Bennett (Macmillan, 1973). Earlier studies included Joan Bennett, *Five Metaphysical Poets* (3rd edn, Cambridge University Press, 1964), Frank Kermode, *Shakespeare, Spenser, Donne* (Routledge, 1971), J. B. Leishman, *The Monarch of Wit* (5th edn, Hutchinson, 1962), A. C. Partridge, *John Donne: Language and Style* (Deutsch, 1978), Murray Roston, *The Soul of Wit* (Oxford University Press, 1974), Wilbur Sanders, *John Donne's Poetry* (Cambridge University Press,

1971), A. J. Smith, *The Metaphysics of Love* (Cambridge University Press, 1985), and William Zunder, *The Poetry of John Donne* (Harvester Press, 1982). Feminist studies have included Maureen Sabine, *Feminine Engendered Faith* (Macmillan, 1992), and H. L. Meakin, *John Donne's Articulations of the Feminine* (Oxford University Press, 1998).

David Norbrook studied *Poetry and Politics in the English Renaissance* (Routledge, 1984) and Lawrence Manley *Literature and Politics in Early Modern London* (Cambridge University Press, 1995). The literary background was also illuminated by *The Cambridge Companion to English Poetry, Donne to Marvell*, edited by Thomas Corns (Cambridge University Press, 1993), and new essays on *Renaissance Poetry* were edited by Cristina Malcolmson (Longman, 1998). Jonathan Post surveyed *English Lyric Poetry: The Seventeenth Century* (Routledge, 1999). The ecclesiastical background was researched in recent studies such as Patrick Collinson, *The Religion of Protestants in England 1559–1625* (Oxford University Press, 1982), Julian Davies, *The Caroline Captivity of the Church* (Oxford University Press, 1992), K. T. Kendall, *Calvin and English Calvinism to 1649* (Oxford University Press, 1979), Anthony Milton, *Catholic and Reformed* (Cambridge University Press, 1995), Nicholas Tyacke, *Anti-Calvinists: The Rise of English Arminianism c.1590–1640* (2nd edn, Oxford University Press, 1990), and Peter White, *Predestination, Policy and Polemic* (Cambridge University Press, 1992). Kenneth Fincham edited essays on *The Early Stuart Church* (Macmillan, 1993) and examined the bishops in *Prelate as Pastor* (Oxford University Press, 1990). For Donne's Roman Catholic background studies include Adrian Morey, *The Catholic Subjects of Elizabeth I* (Allen and Unwin, 1978), Peter Holmes, *Resistance and Compromise: The Political Thought of the Elizabethan Catholics* (Cambridge University Press, 1982), and John Bossy, *The English Catholic Community 1570–1850* (Darton, Longman and Todd, 1975). Good biographies include *Ben Jonson* by David Riggs (Harvard University Press, 1989) and *George Herbert* by Amy Charles (Cornell University Press, 1977). Nicholas Lossky gave a good account of *Lancelot Andrewes the Preacher* (Oxford University Press, 1991).

Other studies include Bettie Doebler, *The Quickening Seed: Death in the Sermons of John Donne* (University of Salzburg Press, 1974), Itrat Husain, *The Dogmatic and Mystical Theology of John Donne* (SPCK, 1938), Millar MacLure, *The Paul's Cross Sermons 1534–1632* (University of Toronto Press, 1958), and W. Fraser Mitchell, *English Pulpit Oratory from Andrewes to Tillotson* (SPCK, 1932). Donne was included in Michael Schmidt's *Lives of the Poets* (Phoenix, 1998) and in L. William Countryman's study of the Anglican spiritual tradition as it has been expressed in *The Poetic Imagination* (Darton, Longman and Todd, 1999).

John Guy edited essays on *The Reign of Elizabeth I: Court and Culture in the Last Decade* (Cambridge University Press, 1995). Linda Peck did the same for *The Mental World of the Jacobean Court* (Cambridge University Press, 1991) and made her own study of *Court Patronage and Corruption in Early Stuart England* (Unwin Hyman, 1990). Roger Lockyear summed up recent studies of *James VI and I* (Longman, 1998), and Maurice Lee called him *Great Britain's Solomon* (University of Illinois Press, 1990). James's use of preachers was studied by Lori Anne Ferrell, *Government by Polemics* (Stanford University Press, 1998), and his visionary ecumenism by W. B. Patterson, *James VI and I and the Reunion of Christendom* (Cambridge University Press, 1997). Jonathan Goldberg explored *James I and the Politics of Literature* (2nd edn, Stanford University Press, 1989) and, with a different emphasis, Curtis Perry studied *The Making of Jacobean Culture* (Cambridge University Press, 1997). Recent social studies have included Michael MacDonald and T. R. Murphy, *Sleepless Souls: Suicide in Early Modern England* (1990), David Cressy, *Birth, Marriage and Death in Tudor and Stuart England* (1997), and Sara Mendelson and Patricia Crawford, *Women in Early Modern England* (1998; all Oxford University Press). Anthony Low celebrated the new intimacy of marriage in poetry as *The Reinvention of Love* (Cambridge University Press, 1993).

Index of Writings

Donne's Poetry

Aire and Angels 286
Anniversarie, The 285–6
Anniversaries 8, 11, 180, 214, 218–23, 225, 267
Apparition, The 207
Autumnall, The 216–17

Blossome, The 212–13
Bracelet, The 164
Break of Day 208
Broken Heart, The 296–7

Calme, The 51
Canonisation, The 7, 163, 251
Change 163
Communitie 203
Confined Love 204–5
Corona, La 167, 224–6
Crosse, The 224
Curse, The 206

Dissolution, The 268
Divine Poems 150, 224–43

Elegies 8, 151, 210
  fourth 147

Elegies *cont.*
  fifth 51
  sixth 104–5
  seventeenth 204
Epithalamious 49–50, 137, 269

Farewell to Love 208
Feaver, A 294–5
Flea, The 137, 195
Funerall Elegie, A 4, 85
Funerall, The 163

Good Friday 1615 87, 90–1, 147, 240
Good-morrow, The 286–7

Holy Sonnets 19, 161, 227–37, 330, 348
Hymne to Christ 240–1, 270
  God my God 241–2
  God the Father 242, 279, 280, 336, 348

I am a little world 19
Indifferent, The 203–4

Lecture upon Shadow, A 289
Litanie, The 237–9
Love's Alchymie 207–8
Deitie 205
Exchange 283
Growth 287
Progress 205–6
Prohibition 206
Warr 52
Lover's Infinitesse 284–5

Message, The 207
Metempsychosis 8–9, 59–62, 152, 195, 202, 219, 221, 225, 340

Nature's lay Ideot 260–1
Nocturnall, A 147, 272–5, 348

Oh, to vex me 20–1

Sapho to Philaenis 208–9
Satyres, 8, 46, 56
first 43, 201
second 44, 69, 9
third 49, 53, 70, 81, 160–2, 200
fourth 54, 69
fifth 53, 56
Show me, deare Christ 150–1, 242–3, 320
Since she whom I lov'd 267–8
Songs and Sonets 8, 151, 165, 211, 281
Sunne Rising, The 180, 295–6

To his Mistress 4, 137, 209–10
To Mr C. B. 40
E. G. 45–6
I. L. 40
S. B. 214
T. W. 45, 75, 217
To Mr Roland Woodward 46
To Mr Tilman 24
Triple Foole, The 206–7
Twicknam Garden 212

Valedection Forbiding Mourning 291–3
of my Name 22, 280–1
of Weeping 294
to his Booke 290–1
Variorum Edition 32, 151

Will, The 167

Donne's Prose

Biathanatos 74–8, 81, 174–5

Character of a Scot 100
Courtier's Library 70

Death's Duell 130–1
Devotions 127, 148, 172–4, 181, 328, 347

Essay of Valour 25
Essayes in Divinity 93–5, 97, 145, 147, 168–9, 251

Ignatius his Conclave 82–4, 181

Paradoxes 42, 202–3, 253
Problems 68–9, 100, 111
Pseudo-Martyr 46, 78–82, 144

General Index

Abott, George 88, 96, 109
Adam 61, 75, 94, 247, 249–50, 335–7
Alford, Henry 18, 301
Allen, William 81–2
Alleyn, Edward 115
'ambition' 159, 169–70
American scholarship 32, 153–4
Ames, William 110
Andreasen, Nancy 199
Andrewes, Lancelot 78, 88, 113–14, 126, 140
Anne, Queen 71, 101, 274, 317, 319
'apostasy' 159–71
Arminians 105–6, 184
artificiality 12–19, 195
atheism 340–2
Atonement 309
Aubrey, John 216, 227, 229
Auden, W. H. 9
Augustine, St 76, 144–5, 182–3, 248, 267, 274, 307, 327, 340, 347

Bacon, Sir Francis 55, 65
Baker, Sir Richard 30
Bald, R. C. 148–9, 152–3, 158, 177
Baptism 123
Barth, Karl 183
Bedford, Countess of 92, 96–7, 180, 212–15, 219, 229, 273, 275, 286
beggars, 173, 175–7
Bell, Iona 257–8, 260
Bellarmine, Roberto 48–9
Bible 109, 112–13, 302–12
Blackwell, George 79
Bloom, Harold 28
Boccaccio 39
Boulstred, Cecilia 233
Britten, Benjamin 9
Brooke, Christopher 39–40, 51, 120, 254
  Rupert 16
  Samuel 217, 254
Brooks, Cleanth 295
Browning, Robert 19
Buckingham *see* Villiers

Cadiz 51
Cain 61

Calvinism 57–8, 105–6, 162, 170, 182–5, 225, 230, 309, 319, 338
Cambridge 36, 102–3, 145
Campbell, Thomas 18
Carew, Thomas 12
Carey, John 158–87, 229–30, 233, 254, 259, 270
Carlisle *see* Doncaster
Carr, Sir Robert 85, 87–92, 95
Catechism 321–2
Cathcart, Dwight 199–200
Catholicism 46, 78–82, 94–5, 123–4, 164–71, 242, 338
Cecils 47, 55, 57, 81
Chamberlain, John 321
Chapman, George 65
Charles I 5, 96, 129, 168, 276, 318–20, 350
Charles II 209, 318
  childbirth 245–6
  childhood 36
Church of England 68–9, 102, 170–1, 242–3
Chute, Sir Walter 261–2
Cockayne, William 30–1
Coleridge, S. T. 3, 299
complexity of character 19, 98–9, 158–89, 196–201, 222–3
conceits 18
Conformity 158–60, 167
Copernicus 11, 84, 138, 180–1
Cornwallis, Sir William 53
Cothell, Robert 209
court life 9, 54–5, 69–70, 118
courtship 62–4, 254–9, 283–9
Cowley, Abraham 18
Cranfield, Lionel 101
Creation 94, 306, 340–1
critics on Donne 12–19, 137–89

Danby, Earl of 228–9
  Thomas 49
Daniel, Samuel 194
Dante 267
Danvers, Sir John 216, 325
David, King 306
Davies, Sir John 45, 67
Davis, Stevie 259
deconstruction 13–14
death 5, 130–4, 222, 233, 241–2, 332–3, 348–50
depressions 72–4, 133, 191–2, 230–1, 264–6, 265–79
Derby, Earl of 155–6, 228
Directions for Preachers 320–2
Docherty, Thomas 138–9, 186–7
Doncaster family 247, 264, 334
Doncaster mission 103–6
Donne, Anne 7–9, 63–6, 108, 142–3, 165, 197–8, 213, 222, 244–98
  Constance 115–16, 130, 266
  Elizabeth 34–7, 47, 80, 167
  Francis 96, 259, 263
  George 254, 276–7, 300
  Henry 35, 48
  John (son) 254, 299–300
  Lucy 213, 264, 275
  Mary 263–4
  Nicholas 263–4
Dorset, Earl of 124, 227–8
Dort, Synod of 105–6, 184–5
Drayton, Michael 19, 304
Drury, Elizabeth 3–4, 85–6, 214, 219–20
  Sir Robert 84–5, 262

Dryden, John 17
du Moulin, Pierre 101
Dwn family 37–8, 141

Ebreo, Leone 288
ecstatic love 197–8, 294–8
Egerton, Lady 283
Sir Thomas 52–4, 56
election 183–6, 231, 339
Eliot, T. S. 13, 16, 33
Elizabeth I 41, 58–9, 66, 218–19, 318
Essex, Earl of 56
(son) 88–90
Eucharist 123
Eve *see* Adam

Fathers of Church 11, 110, 167, 186
feminism 13, 14, 244–6
Ferdinand, Emperor 104
Fish, Stanley 10–11
Fitzherbert, Thomas 78
Flynn, Dennis 155–7, 228
Francis, St 198

Galileo 182
Gardner, Dame Helen 150–5, 161, 196–7, 237, 281–2, 286, 288, 291
Gazet, Angelin 84
Gerrard, George 71
Gibson, Richard 179
God 9–11, 177–9, 182–6, 326–7, 332, 339–40
Goodyer, Sir Henry 74, 92, 97, 193, 214, 237, 251, 256, 259, 263–4
gospels 308
Gosse, Sir Edmund 146–8, 218, 235, 261
Grosart, A. B. 19

Hague, The 105–6, 184–5
Hall, Joseph 110, 220–1, 225
Halpern, Richard 15
Hamilton, Robin 152, 331–2
Harrington, William 48
Hart Hall 35
Healy, Timothy 84
heaven 177–8, 331–2, 350
hell 178, 333–6, 342
Hemingway, Ernest 129
Henri IV 81, 102, 144
Henry, Prince 101, 147, 218
Herbert, Edward 25, 218, 277
George 22–6, 140, 194, 228, 235
Magdalen 22, 193, 215–17, 225, 275, 349
Hester, M. Thomas 200, 244
Heywood, Ellis 47
Jasper 47, 83–4
John 47, 54
Thomas 47
Hilliard, Nicholas 37
homosexuality 14, 208–9
Horace 43
Hoskyns, John 95
Housman, A. E. 16–17
Howard, Frances 87–90
Hume, David 17
Huntingdon, Countess of 193, 214–15, 219

Ignatius Loyola, St 83
Italian influences 36, 149–50, 211, 281–2

James I 26, 59, 66, 69, 78, 82, 89, 92–102, 104–8, 120–1, 295–6, 317–24
James II 320, 322
Jessopp, Augustus 145
Jesuits 82–4
John the Baptist 316–17
Johnson, Samuel 18
Jonson, Ben 12, 25–7, 45, 57, 86, 194, 218–19
Juvenal 8, 53

King, Henry 185, 194, 300–1
Ker, Sir Robert 6–7, 74, 168, 194, 260, 276
Kermode, Sir Frank 107

Lambeth Articles 58–9
Latimer, Lord 257–8, 260
Laud, William 68, 121, 276, 321
Law of Nature 81
law reform 53
Leishman, J. B. 282
Lewis, C. S. 28, 287
Lincoln's Inn 31, 41–3, 48–50, 103, 118–20, 145, 167, 171, 246, 319
Lok, Henry 230
London 31, 118
Low, Anthony 8, 197
Luther, Martin 58, 246

Marckham, Lady 218, 233
Marlowe, Christopher 27
Marotti, Arthur 15, 186–7, 230, 273, 282
marriage in poetry 297–8
  in sermons 245–54
Marriot, John 195
Martz, Louis 167
Mary, B. V. 8, 86, 164, 219, 224–6, 238, 307
Mayne, Jasper 155–6
Meakin, H. L. 244
medical references 20, 173–4, 311
Mermaid tavern 72
metaphysicals 17, 113, 154
Milgate, Walter 59
Milman, Henry 303
Mitcham 71–2, 143, 213, 262
monarchy 81, 316–18, 323–4
More, Anne *see* Donne
  Sir George 64, 89, 254–7
  Sir Robert 262
  Sir Thomas 46–7, 81
Morton, Thomas 39, 43, 70–1, 144
Mousley, Andrew 15

Nicolson, Marjorie 220
Northumberland, Earl of 255, 334–5
Novarr, David 140

Oath of 1605 78–80
Oliver, Isaac 108
  Paul 187–8
Onan 247–8
originality 154
Overbury, Sir Thomas 88–9
Ovid 8, 206, 211

Palatinate 56, 95
Palgrave, Francis 19
parishes, Donne's 125–6
Parliaments 56, 95
Patrides, C. A. 151–2
Paul V 80

Perkins, William 111–12
Persons, Robert 83–4
Petrarch 39, 41, 211–21, 230, 267
Petworth, Ted-Larry 151
Philipot, Thomas 77
Philips, Katharine 208
Pinka, Patricia 297
plague sermon 305
politics in pulpit 316–25
poor 173, 175–7
Pope, Alexander 18
Potter, George 302
prayer 20, 170–1, 188, 326
preaching 9–10, 32–3, 98–9, 108–18, 299–350
predestination *see* Calvinism
Preston, John 112
priesthood 97, 123–4
promiscuity 165–211
Psalms 66, 261
Puritans 108–12, 162, 169, 319

questions about Donne 6–11

Rainsford, Richard 37, 167
Ralegh, Sir Walter 56
reason 76, 110, 307
Religious Imagination 138
Renaissance 154, 211
resurrection of body 328–32
rhetoric 32, 116–18
Rhodes, Neil 173
Roberts, John 15
Rochester *see* Carr

Sabine, Maureen 8, 219
St Dunstan-in-the-West 124–5
St Lucy's Day 131, 167, 272–5
St Paul's Cathedral 31, 110, 120–7, 132–3, 307–8
Salisbury, Countess of 215
scepticism 177–82
Schmidt, Michael 10
sea 310
separations from family 290–4
sermons *see* preaching
Sevenoaks 125
sex and God 3–5, 245–8
Shakespeare, William 28–30, 44, 49, 111
Shawcross, John 151, 289
Sidney, Sir Philip 44, 229, 267, 327–8
Simpson, Evelyn 302
sin 5, 19–21, 119, 315, 336–8
Sinfield, Alan 197
Smith, A. J. 289
Smith L. P. 299–301
Solomon 274, 307
Somerset *see* Carr
soul 328, 331–2
Spanish influence 36–8, 149–50, 168
Spenser, Edmund 44, 50, 65, 267
suffering 342–3, 345–8
suicide 14, 74–8, 163, 174–5
Syminges, John 34, 160

Thavies Inn 41, 48
Theobald, Louis 18
Thirty-nine Articles 58–9
Tillotson, John 113
Trinity 326–7

Villiers, George 89, 96, 121, 168, 277, 321
Virginia 71, 303–5

voyages 51–2
Vulgate Bible 167–8

Walton, Izaak 34–7, 43, 72, 82, 126–7, 139–145, 157, 195, 216, 266, 275, 280, 291, 303, 307
Webber, Joan 6
Whitgift, John 58
Williamson, George 29
Wolley, Sir Francis 261, 283
Wood, Anthony 300
Woodward, Roland 46, 228
Woodward, Thomas 217
work 103
Wotton, Sir Henry 35, 56–7, 66–7, 107, 140, 157, 193, 229, 258, 260, 262–3

Yeats, W. B. 182

Zouch, Thomas 141